Domestic Counter-Terrorism in a Global World

Although both Canada and the United Kingdom had experienced terrorism prior to the attacks of 9/11 and already had in place extensive provisions to deal with terrorism, the events of that day led to the enactment of new and expansive counter-terrorism legislation being enacted in both jurisdictions. This book explores these changes to counter-terrorism laws and policies in the United Kingdom and Canada in order to demonstrate that despite the force of international legal instruments, including the heavily scrutinized UN Security Council Resolution 1373, the evolution of counter-terrorism policies in different jurisdictions is best analysed and understood as a product of local institutional structures and cultures.

The book compares legal and political structures and cultures within Canada and the United Kingdom. It analyses variations in the evolution of post-9/11 counter-terrorism measures in the two jurisdictions and explores the domestic reasons for them. While focus is primarily geared towards security certificates and bail with recognizance/investigative hearings in Canada, and detention without trial, control orders and TPIMs in the United Kingdom, the use of secret evidence in the wider national security context (terrorist listing, civil litigation, criminal prosecutions, etc.) is also discussed. The book reveals how domestic structures and cultures, including the legal system, the relative stability of government, local human rights culture and geopolitical relationships all influence how counter-terrorism measures evolve. In this sense, the book utilizes a methodology that is both comparative and interdisciplinary by engaging in legal, political, historical and cultural analyses.

This book will be particularly useful for target audiences in the fields of comparative law and criminal justice, counter-terrorism law, human rights law and international relations and politics.

Dr Daniel Alati is an Assistant Professor in the Department of Criminology at Ryerson University in Toronto, Canada.

Routledge Research in Terrorism and the Law

Available titles in this series include:

The United States, International Law and the Struggle against Terrorism
Thomas McDonnell

Counter-Terrorism and Beyond
The Culture of Law and Justice After 9/11
Nicola McGarrity, Andrew Lynch and George Williams

Counter-terrorism and the Detention of Suspected Terrorists
Preventative Confinement and International Human Rights Law
Claire Macken

Gender, National Security and Counter-terrorism
Human rights perspectives
Margaret L. Satterthwaite and Jayne Huckerby

Surveillance, Counter-Terrorism and Comparative Constitutionalism
Fergal Davis, Nicola McGarrity and George Williams

Homeland Security, its Law and its State
A Design of Power for the 21st Century
Christos Boukalas

Anti-Terrorism Law and Normalising Northern Ireland
Jessie Blackbourn

The Impact, Legitimacy and Effectiveness of EU Counter-Terrorism
Fiona de Londras and Josephine Doody

Preventive Detention of Terror Suspects
A New Legal Framework
Diane Webber

Domestic Counter-Terrorism in a Global World
Post-9/11 Institutional Structures and Cultures in Canada and the United Kingdom
Daniel Alati

Domestic Counter-Terrorism in a Global World

Post-9/11 Institutional Structures and Cultures in Canada and the United Kingdom

Daniel Alati

Routledge
Taylor & Francis Group
LONDON AND NEW YORK

First published 2018
by Routledge

2 Park Square, Milton Park, Abingdon, Oxfordshire OX14 4RN
52 Vanderbilt Avenue, New York, NY 10017

Routledge is an imprint of the Taylor & Francis Group, an informa business

First issued in paperback 2019

British Library Cataloguing in Publication Data
A catalogue record for this book is available from the British Library

Library of Congress Cataloging in Publication Data
Names: Alati, Daniel, 1986-, author.
Title: Domestic counter-terrorism in a global world : post-9/11 institutional structures and cultures in Canada and the UK / Daniel Alati.
Description: New York : Routledge, 2017. | Series: Routledge research in terrorism and the law | Includes bibliographical references and index.
Identifiers: LCCN 2017016769 | ISBN 9781138684508 (hbk) | ISBN 9781315543772 (ebk)
Subjects: LCSH: Terrorism—Prevention—Law and legislation—Great Britain. | Terrorism—Prevention—Law and legislation—Canada. | Security (Law)—Great Britain. | Security (Law)—Canada.
Classification: LCC K5256 .A93 2017 | DDC 344.4105/3256—dc23
LC record available at https://lccn.loc.gov/2017016769

ISBN: 978-1-138-68450-8 (hbk)
ISBN: 978-0-367-26646-2 (pbk)

Typeset in Galliard
by Keystroke, Neville Lodge, Tettenhall, Wolverhampton

To my mother and father, whose endless love and support is a blessing I will always cherish.

Contents

List of abbreviations xi
Table of cases xiii
Table of statutes xvii
Preface xix
Acknowledgements xxi

1 **Introduction** 1
1.1 Selection of jurisdictions, measures and Resolution 1373 2
1.1.1 Selection of jurisdictions 2
1.1.2 Selection of measures 6
1.1.3 Focus on Resolution 1373 7
1.2 Methodology 9
1.3 Defining legal and political structures and cultures 15
1.3.1 The structure of domestic legal institutions 15
1.3.2 The structure of domestic political institutions 20
1.3.3 The culture of domestic legal institutions 24
1.3.4 The culture of domestic political institutions 27
1.4 Chapter overview 28

2 **Post-9/11 counter-terrorism measures in Canada and the United Kingdom** 36
2.1 The impact of Security Council Resolution 1373 36
2.2 Historical evolution of Canada's post-9/11 measures 41
2.2.1 Pre-9/11 experiences with terrorism 41
2.2.2 Post-9/11: immediate aftermath of the attacks and the *Anti-Terrorism Act* 43
2.2.3 Bail with recognizance provisions undergo parliamentary scrutiny 45
2.2.4 Landmark decision on security certificates: the *Charkaoui* case 46

2.2.5 Investigative hearing and preventive arrest provisions sunset 47
2.2.6 House and Senate Committees release further recommendations 48
2.2.7 The introduction of Bills C-3 and S-3 49
2.2.8 Additional attempts to reinstate Bill S-3 provisions occur 50
2.2.9 Federal Court issues landmark ruling on listing: the *Abdelrazik* case 52
2.2.10 Security certificates face additional legal challenges 53
2.3 More recent significant developments in Canada 54
2.3.1 Security certificates survive Supreme Court scrutiny: the *Harkat* case 54
2.3.2 The October 2014 terrorist attacks and subsequent legislation 56
2.4 Historical evolution of the United Kingdom's post-9/11 measures 58
2.4.1 Pre-9/11 experiences with terrorism 58
2.4.2 Post-9/11 aftermath and the *Anti-Terrorism, Crime and Security Act* 59
2.4.3 Detention without trial begins and undergoes scrutiny 60
2.4.4 *A. v. Secretary of State for the Home Department* and the subsequent *Prevention of Terrorism Act* 2005 62
2.4.5 The 7/7 London bombings and the *Terrorism Act* 2006 64
2.4.6 Control orders and the *Counter-Terrorism Act* 2008 65
2.4.7 *A. v. United Kingdom* and *Secretary of State for the Home Department v. AF* 66
2.4.8 The Supreme Court rules on 1267 listing regulations: the *Ahmed* case 68
2.4.9 The repeal of control orders and the enactment of TPIMs 69
2.5 More recent significant developments in the United Kingdom 70
2.5.1 The *Justice and Security Act* 2013 70
2.5.2 The *Counter-Terrorism and Security Act* 2015 71
2.6 Conclusion 73

3 Canada and the United Kingdom's domestic legal structure 78
3.1 Canada's rights adjudication framework: the Canadian Charter of Rights and Freedoms *79*
3.2 Security certificate case law analyses 82

3.3 United Kingdom's rights adjudication framework: the European Convention on Human Rights *and the* Human Rights Act *90*
3.4 Detention without trial and control order case law analyses 94
3.5 Conclusion 101

4 Canada and the United Kingdom's domestic political structure 105
4.1 Impact of minority government instability in Canada 106
4.2 The role of parliamentary committees within Canada's political structure 110
4.3 Judging the tangible impact of Canadian parliamentary oversight 114
4.4 Impact of the United Kingdom's coalition government 116
4.5 The role of parliamentary committees within the United Kingdom's political structure 119
4.6 Judging the tangible impact of UK parliamentary oversight 125
4.7 Conclusion 126

5 Canada and the United Kingdom's domestic legal culture 129
5.1 Judicial decisions pertaining to the wider use of secret evidence in Canada 131
5.1.1 The *Ahmad* case 131
5.1.2 The *Almalki* cases 133
5.1.3 The *Khadr* cases 135
5.1.4 The *Abdelrazik* case 137
5.1.5 Summary analysis 138
5.2 Judicial decisions pertaining to the wider use of secret evidence in the United Kingdom 140
5.2.1 The *AlRawi* case 141
5.2.2 The *Binyam Mohamed* case 142
5.2.3 The *Ahmed* case 145
5.2.4 The *Tariq* case 146
5.2.5 The *Abu Qatada* cases 148
5.2.6 Summary analysis 150
5.3 Conclusion 151

6 Canada and the United Kingdom's domestic political culture 155
6.1 Societal attitudes towards human rights in Canada 157
6.2 Canada's relationship with the United States 163
6.3 Societal attitudes towards human rights in the United Kingdom 166

6.4 The United Kingdom's 'special relationship' with the United States 171
6.5 Conclusion 173

7 Conclusions 178
7.1 The impact of domestic legal and political structures and cultures on the evolution of counter-terrorism measures 179
7.2 Conclusion: future challenges and lessons to be learned 186

Index 191

List of abbreviations

ATA	Anti-Terrorism Act
ATCSA	Anti-Terrorism, Crime and Security Act
BoRC	Bill of Rights Commission
CAT	Convention Against Torture and Other Cruel, Inhuman or Degrading Treatment or Punishment
CEA	Canada Evidence Act
CIA	Central Intelligence Agency
CMPs	Closed Material Proceedings
CPC	Conservative Party of Canada
CRSIA	Charities Registration (Security Information) Act
CSIS	Canadian Security and Intelligence Service
CTC	Counter-Terrorism Committee
CTSA	Counter-Terrorism and Security Act
DFAIT	Department of Foreign Affairs and International Trade
DPP	Director of Public Prosecutions (UK)
ECHR	European Convention on Human Rights
ECtHR	European Court of Human Rights
EU	European Union
FCA	Federal Court of Appeal
FLQ	Front de Libération du Québec
HRA	Human Rights Act 1998
ICCPR	International Covenant on Civil and Political Rights
IRA	Irish Republican Army
IRPA	Immigration and Refugee Protection Act
JCHR	Joint Select Committee on Human Rights
JSA	Justice and Security Act
Lib	Liberal Party of Canada
MP	Member of Parliament
NDP	National Democratic Party (Canada)
PCMLTFA	Proceeds of Crime (Money Laundering) and Terrorist Financing Act
PII	Public Interest Immunity
RCMP	Royal Canadian Mounted Police

SIAC	Special Immigration Appeals Commission
SIRC	Security Intelligence Review Committee
SNP	Scottish National Party
SoCIS	Security of Canada Information Sharing Act
TEO	Temporary Exclusion Order
TPIMs	Terrorism Prevention and Investigation Measures
TSAS	Terrorism, Security and Society
UK	United Kingdom
UN	United Nations
UNHRC	United Nations Human Rights Committee
US	United States

Table of cases

Canada

Name of case
Abdelrazik v. Canada (Minister of Foreign Affairs) [2010] 1 F.C.R. 267 ..... 52–3, 68, 73, 102, 131, 137–8, 139, 143, 145, 152, 153, 183, 189
Almrei (Re) [2011] 1 F.C.R. 163; 2009 FC 1263 ..... 53–4, 74, 88, 102, 139, 153
Canada v. Almalki [2011] FCA 199 ..... 131, 133–5, 136, 139, 153, 183, 189
Canada v. Almalki [2010] FC 1106 ..... 131, 133–5, 136, 139, 151, 153
Canada v. Schmidt [1987] 1 S.C.R. 500 81
Canada (Attorney General) v. PHS Community Services Society, 2011 SCC 44 ..... 80, 102
Canada (Citizenship and Immigration) v. Harkat [2014] 2 S.C.R. 33 ..... 29, 31
Canada (Justice) v. Khadr [2008] SCC 28 ..... 135–7, 153
Canada (Prime Minister) v. Khadr [2010] 1 S.C.R. 44 ..... 131, 133, 135–7, 139, 152, 153, 183
Canadian Foundation for Children, Youth and the Law v. Canada (Attorney General) [2004] 1 S.C.R. 76 80
Charkaoui v. Canada (Citizenship and Immigration) [2007] 1 S.C.R. 350 ..... 46, 74, 85, 86, 87, 90, 98, 101, 102, 180, 189
Charkaoui v. Canada (Citizenship and Immigration) [2009] 2 S.C.R. 326 ..... 74, 87, 88, 139, 153
Charkaoui (Re) [2010] 4 F.C.R. 448; 2009 FC 1030 88
Chaoulli v. Quebec (Attorney General), 2005 SCC 35 80
Khadr v. Canada (Minister of Justice) [2007] FCA 182 ..... 135–7, 139, 143, 145, 151, 153
Little Sisters Book and Art Emporium v. Canada (Minister of Justice) [2000] 2 S.C.R. 112 ..... 81, 103
R v. Ahmad [2009] O.J. No 6156 ..... 132, 154
R v. Ahmad [2011] 1 S.C.R. 110 ..... 131–3, 138, 151, 154, 183, 190
R v. Heywood [1994] 3 S.C.R. 761 80

R v. Malmo-Levine; R. V. Caine [2003] 3 S.C.R. 571 .... 80, 104
R v. Oakes [1986] 1 S.C.R. 103 .... 81, 85, 104
Re B.C. Motor Vehicle Act [1985] 2 S.C.R. 486 .... 79, 104
Re Charkaoui [2005] F.C.J. 139 87
Re Residential Tenancies Act, 1979 132
Ribic v. Canada (Attorney General) [2005] 1 FCR 33 .... 104, 133
Rodriguez v. British Columbia (Attorney General) [1993] 3 S.C.R. 519 .... 80, 104
Suresh v. Canada (Minister of Citizenship and Immigration) [2002] 1 S.C.R. 3 .... 80–5, 89–90, 95, 101, 104, 179, 181, 190

United Kingdom

Name of case

A and Others v. Secretary of State for the Home Department [2002] EWCA Civ 1502; [2004] QB 335 .... 60, 73, 102
A v. Secretary of State for the Home Department [2004] UKHL 56 .... 62–3, 73, 86, 89–90, 95, 97, 101–2, 180–1, 189
A v. Secretary of State for the Home Department (No 2) [2005] UKHL 71 .... 73, 97, 102
Abu Qatada v. SSHD [2013] EWCA Civ 277 .... 140, 148, 153, 184, 189
HM Treasury v. Ahmed [2010] UKSC 2 .... 140, 153, 183, 190
Al Rawi and Others v. the Security Service and Others [2009] EWHC 2959 (QB) 141, 153
Al Rawi and Others v. the Security Service and Others [2010] EWCA Civ 482 .... 141, 153
Al Rawi and Others v. the Security Service and Others [2011] UKSC 34 .... 71, 140, 141–2, 144, 147, 150–2, 153, 156, 157, 167, 170–4, 183–5, 189
Ghaidan v. Godin Mendoza [2004] UKHL 30 .... 93, 103
Home Office v. Tariq [2011] UKSC 35 .... 71, 136, 140, 146–8, 150, 151, 153, 183, 190
M and Secretary of State for the Home Department, SC/17/2002 61
Mohamed, R (on the Application of) v. Secretary of State for Foreign & Commonwealth Affairs [2010] EWCA Civ 65 .... 71, 118, 136, 140, 142–5, 150, 151, 152, 157, 167, 170, 171, 172, 173, 174, 176, 183, 184, 185, 190
Omar Othman (aka Abu Qatada) v. Secretary of State for the Home Department, SC/15/2005, United Kingdom Special Immigration Appeals Commission, 26 February 2007 140
R (Anufrijeva) v. SSHD [2003] UKHL 36 .... 103, 147
R (Roberts) v. Parole Board [2005] UKHL 45; [2005] 2 AC 738 .... 98, 103
R (Ullah) v. Special Adjudicator [2004] UKHL 26 .... 103, 147
R v. Horncastle [2009] UKSC 14 .... 17, 33, 103, 140

Re E [2008] UKHL 66 .... 91, 104
Secretary of State for the Home Department v. JJ [2007] UKHL 45 .... 65, 76, 98, 104
Secretary of State for the Home Department v. MB [2007] UKHL 46 .... 65, 76, 98, 104, 146, 180, 190
Secretary of State for the Home Department v. E [2007] UKHL 47 .... 65, 76, 98, 104
Secretary of the State for the Home Department v. AF (No 3) [2009] UKHL 28 .... 17, 18, 23, 34
Secretary of the State for the Home Department v. AF (No 3) [2010] 2 AC 2 69 .... 17, 34, 55, 66, 67, 68, 88, 99, 104, 124, 128, 180, 190
Secretary of State for the Home Department v. Rehman [2001] 3 W.L.R. 877 84

European cases (in chronological order)

Name of case

Lawless v. Ireland, App No 332/57 (A/3) [1961] ECHR 2 .... 93, 103
Belgian Logistics (No 2), App No 2126/64 (1968) 1 EHRR 252 .... 93, 102
Greek Case (1969) 12 YB 1 .... 93, 103
Ringeisen v. Austria, App No 2614/65 [1971] ECHR 2 .... 92, 104
Engel v. Netherlands, App No 5370/72 [1976] ECHR 3 .... 91, 102
Handyside v. UK, App No 5493/72 [1976] ECHR 5 .... 16, 32
Ireland v. UK, App No 5310/71 [1978] ECHR 1 .... 91, 93, 103
Konig v. Germany, App No 6232/73 [1978] ECHR 3 .... 92, 103
Sunday Times v. UK, App No 6538/74 [1979] ECHR 1 .... 91, 104
Guzzardi v. Italy, App No 7367/76 [1980] ECHR 5 .... 91, 103
Abdulaziz, Cabales and Balkandali v. UK, App No 9473/81 [1985] ECHR 7 .... 93, 102
Ashingdane v. UK, App No 8225/78 [1985] ECHR 8 .... 91, 102
Leander v. Sweden, App No 9248/81 [1987] ECHR 4 .... 103, 147
Brogan v. UK, App No 11266/84 [1988] ECHR 24 .... 91, 102
Soering v. UK, App No 14038/88 [1989] ECHR 14 .... 91, 104
Fredin v. Sweden (1991) 13 EHHR 784 93
Brannigan and Mcbride v. UK, App No 14553 [1993] ECHR 21 .... 94, 102
Esbester v. United Kingdom, App No 18601/91 [1993] ECHR 64 .... 102, 147
Chahal v. UK, App No 22414/93 [1996] ECHR 54 19
Askoy v. Turkey, App No 21987/93 [1996] ECHR 68 .... 94, 102
National and Provincial Building Society v. UK, App No 21319/93 [1997] ECHR 87 .... 93, 103

Petrovic v. Austria, App No 20458/92 [1998] ECHR 21 .... 93, 103
Heaney and McGuinness v. Ireland (2001) 33 EHRR 12 92
Pretty v. UK, App No 2346/02 [2002] ECHR 423 .... 90, 103
Benjamin and Wilson v. UK, App No 28212/95 [2002] ECHR 636 .... 92, 102
Dodds v. UK, App No 59314/00, 8 April 2003................................... 94, 102
Reid v. UK [2003] ECHR 94 92
Walker v. UK, App No 37212/02, 16 March 2004.............................. 94, 104
Pearson v. UK, App No 8374/03, 27 April 2004 .... 94, 103
Saadi v. Italy, App No 37201/06, 28 February 2008........................... 91, 104
Othman (Abu Qatada) v. UK, App No 8139/09 [2012] ECHR 56 140
Al-Khawaja v. United Kingdom, App No 26766/05 [2009] ECHR 11 .... 17, 31
A v. United Kingdom, App No 3455/05 [2009] ECHR 301...................................... 66, 73, 99, 102, 146, 180, 189
Kennedy v. United Kingdom, App No 26839/05, 18 May 2010.......... 103, 147

Table of statutes

Canada

Name of statute

Anti-Terrorism Act, S.C. 2001, c. 41 .... 2, 31, 39, 73, 102, 107, 178, 189
Anti-Terrorism Act, S.C. 2015, c. 20 .... 29, 31, 56, 73, 102, 181, 189
Canada Evidence Act, R.S.C., 1985, C-5 .... 39, 74, 102, 132, 183, 189
Charities Registration (Security Information) Act, S.C. 2001, c. 41, s. 113 .... 43, 74, 102, 153
Canadian Security Intelligence Service Act, R.S.C., 1985, c. C-23.. 56, 74, 82, 102,
Immigration and Refugee Protection Act, S.C. 2001, c. 27 .... 19, 32, 39, 75, 82, 103
The Canadian Charter of Rights and Freedoms, Part I of the Constitution Act 1982, Being Schedule B to the Canada Act 1982 (UK), 1982, c. 11 .... 3, 42, 76, 79, 104, 131, 156, 179, 190
Proceeds of Crime (Money Laundering) and Terrorist Financing Act, S.C. 2000, c. 17 .... 43, 76, 103, 154
Protection of Canada from Terrorists Act, S.C. 2015, c. 9 .... 29, 33, 56, 76, 103, 109, 181, 190
Security of Canada Information Sharing Act, S.C. 2015, c. 20, s. 2 .... 57, 76, 104
War Measures Act, R.S.C. 1970, c. W-2 .... 42, 77, 188, 190

United Kingdom

Name of statute

Al-Qaida and Taliban (United Nations Measures) Order 2006 (S.I. 2006/2952).. 68, 73, 102, 145, 153
Anti-Terrorism, Crime and Security Act 2001 c. 24 .... 2, 31, 40, 73, 102, 178, 189
Counter-Terrorism Act 2008 c. 28 .... 66, 74, 102
Counter-Terrorism and Security Act 2015 c. 6.......... 29, 31, 71, 102, 166, 181
Counter-Terrorism and Security Act 2015 c. 217 74

Human Rights Act 1998 c. 42 .... 3, 15, 32, 59, 75, 78, 90, 103, 130, 156, 176, 180, 190
Human Rights Act 1998 (Designated Derogation) Order 2001 (S.I. 2001/3644) 60, 75, 103
Justice and Security Act 2013 c. 18 .... 29, 32, 71, 75, 103, 153, 156, 166, 176, 185, 190
Nothern Ireland (Emergency Provisions) Act 1996 c. 22 .... 58, 75, 188, 190
Prevention of Terrorism (Temporary Provisions) Act 1974 s. 1(7)... 58, 76, 103, 188, 190
Prevention of Terrorism (Temporary Provisions) Act 1989 c. 4 .... 58, 76, 103, 188, 190
Prevention of Terrorism Act 2005 c. 2 .... 62, 76, 103
Special Immigration Appeals Commission Act 1997 c. 68 .... 19, 76, 104
Terrorism Act 2000 c. 11... 3, 40, 58, 76, 104, 187
Terrorism Act 2006 c. 11... 64, 76, 104
Terrorism Prevention and Investigation Measures Act 2011 c. 23 .... 70, 76, 104, 181, 190
Terrorism (United Nations Measures) Order 2006 (S.I. 2006/2657).. 68, 76, 104, 145, 154

European Union

Name of statute

European Convention for the Protection of Human Rights and Fundamental Freedoms (European Convention on Human Rights, as Amended).............................3, 40, 74, 78, 90–4, 97, 98, 103, 131, 147, 156, 175, 180
Treaty on European Union (EU), 7 February 1992, 1992 O.J. (c. 191) 1, 31 I.L.M. 77, 104

United Nations

Name of statute

UN General Assembly, *International Convention for the Suppression of the Financing of Terrorism*, 9 December 1999, No. 38349 .... 8, 34, 38, 180, 190
UN Security Council, *Security Council resolution 1267 (1999) [Afghanistan]*, 15 October 1999, S/RES/1267 (1999) 8, 34, 38, 39, 44, 52, 77, 104, 137, 138, 188, 190
UN Security Council, *Security Council resolution 1333 (2000) [Afghanistan]*, 19 December 2000, S/RES/1333(2000)......... 8, 35, 38, 73
UN Security Council, *Security Council resolution 1373 (2001) [on threats to international peace and security caused by terrorist acts]*, 28 September 2001, S/RES/1373 (2001)..............1, 2, 6, 7–8, 28, 30, 35, 36–41, 44, 68, 73, 77, 104, 109, 178, 179, 187, 190

Preface

The foundation for this book was laid during the completion of a Doctorate in Law at the University of Oxford from 2010 to 2014, undertaken under the rigorous and insightful supervision of Professor Lucia Zedner. Subsequent years have provided for unfortunately topical developments in the field of terrorism studies, corresponding with a burgeoning research interest in the fields of comparative law and criminal justice, national security and human rights. The events of 11 September 2001 led to an unprecedented call to action from the international community and states, including Canada and the United Kingdom, responded swiftly and comprehensively. More than 15 years later, societal and academic concern pertaining to terrorism is still very much prevalent, with countries such as Canada and the United Kingdom (and many others around the world) having experienced their own domestic terrorist attacks. This book analyses responses to terrorism in the two jurisdictions and focuses on how and why these responses should be viewed as the product of legal and political structures and cultures in the two jurisdictions. In doing so, it elucidates some problematic trends characteristic of the years since 2001– including the use of measures outside of the ordinary criminal law, the enactment of sprawling legislation without full parliamentary scrutiny and the increased use of secret evidence in a variety of new legal contexts – that should be considered as cautionary lessons for the future.

Acknowledgements

I dedicate this work to my mother and father, Gino and Mary Alati, who brought me into this world and have always supported me. Their unconditional love and dedication to seeing me succeed both as a professional and as a human being is something I have never, nor will I ever, take for granted. To the rest of my family, you are all always in my heart and mind and you are now officially a part of the most important piece of work I have ever engaged in to date.

I would also like to express gratitude to my former colleagues in the Oxford Centre for Criminology (CFC), who were a source of endless inspiration and support during the course of the doctorate. Many have now moved into important and notable roles throughout the world, and I have no doubt that their work will continue to be regarded as important and influential.

Since completing the doctorate, I have had the pleasure of working with colleagues at the City University of Hong Kong and at Ryerson University in Toronto. I would like to thank these colleagues for contributing to a formative time in my professional development. In particular, I would like to thank Professor Lin Feng, Dr Daniel Pascoe, Dr Antonios Kourotakis and Dr Graham Hudson for their valuable insights. I look forward to collaborating with them further in the future.

Last, but certainly not least, I would like to thank Professor Lucia Zedner for her thorough and thoughtful doctoral supervision, and assistance throughout the course of the book proposal writing and review process.

1 Introduction

Although both Canada and the United Kingdom (UK) had experienced terrorism prior to the attacks that occurred in the United States (US) on 11 September 2001, the events of that day 'produced a horrible natural experiment that allows us to compare how international institutions and different countries responded . . . All countries responded in a manner that reflected their own particular histories and legal, political and social cultures'.[1] Many authors have argued that the most significant post-9/11 response from an international institution was the United Nations (UN) Security Council Resolution 1373,[2] which led to the creation of a Counter-Terrorism Committee (CTC) to monitor the implementation of a 90-day deadline for states to report on measures they had implemented in accordance with the Resolution.[3] Despite the fact that both Canada and the UK already had in place various criminal law provisions to deal with terrorism, both countries responded swiftly and comprehensively to Resolution 1373, treating the 90-day reporting requirement as a 'virtual deadline for the enactment of new

1 Kent Roach, *The 9/11 Effect: Comparative Counter-Terrorism* (Cambridge University Press, 2011) [hereinafter "*Roach, 9/11 Effect*"] 15

2 UN Security Council, *Security Council resolution 1373 (2001) [on threats to international peace and security caused by terrorist acts]*, 28 September 2001, S/RES/1373 (2001), at: https://www.unodc.org/pdf/crime/terrorism/res_1373_english.pdf [accessed 20 October 2010] [hereinafter "*Resolution 1373*"]

3 Literature pertaining to the impact of Security Council *Resolution 1373* and the CTC on Canada and the UK's post-9/11 counter-terrorism is further discussed in Chapter 2, including: Tim Daniel, 'International Cooperation in Counteracting Terrorist Financing' in Van Den Herik, L. and Schrijver, N. (eds), *Counter Terrorism Strategies in a Fragmented International Legal Order* (Cambridge University Press, 2013) 240 [hereinafter "*Daniel, International Cooperation*"]; Craig Forcese, *National Security Law: Canadian Practice in International Perspective* (Irwin Law, 2008); Craig Forcese and François Crepeau (eds), *Terrorism, Law and Democracy: 10 Years After 9/11* (Canadian Institute for the Administration of Justice, Montreal, 2012); Cathleen Powell, 'Defining Terrorism: How and Why' in LaViolette, N. and Forcese, C. (eds), *The Human Rights of Antiterrorism* (Irwin Law, 2008) 138; Nicholas Ryder, *The Financial War on Terrorism: A Review of Counter-Terrorist Financing Strategies Since 2001* (Routledge, 2015) [hereinafter "*Ryder, Financial War on Terrorism*"]; Clive Walker, 'Terrorism and Criminal Justice: Past, Present and Future' [2004] *Criminal Law Review* 311

legislation'.[4] Nonetheless, commentators such as Roach have argued that the Canadian Anti-Terrorism Act (*ATA*) and the UK's Anti-Terrorism, Crime and Security Act (*ATCSA*) are legislative responses that reflect the histories and legal, political and social cultures of the countries in which they were enacted. This book acknowledges the force of international legal instruments such as UN Security Council Resolution 1373, but nonetheless argues that the evolution of counter-terrorism policies in different jurisdictions is best analysed and understood as a product of the institutional structures and cultures present in those jurisdictions. Put simply, while Resolution 1373 undoubtedly had an impact on how and when the *ATA* and *ATCSA* were implemented, it is the domestic legal and political structures and cultures in the two jurisdictions that have had the greatest impact on how counter-terrorism measures have since evolved.

In making this argument, this book engages in comparative analyses of legal and political structures and cultures within Canada and the UK, in order to discern how they have affected the evolution of domestic responses to terrorism. This comparative analysis allows for useful findings pertaining to variations in the evolution of counter-terrorism policies in the two jurisdictions and explores the domestic reasons for them. Important differences between the legal and political structures present in Canada and the UK that make the jurisdictions particularly amenable to this kind of analysis are discussed later in this chapter. Similarly, this chapter contains justifications for the selection of jurisdictions, measures and focus on Resolution 1373. The methodology section lays out two contrasting views on the purposes of comparison – universalism and cultural comparativism – in order to explain why this book chooses to engage in analyses typical of cultural comparativism. Section 1.3 below uses academic literature to define and operationalize the important concepts of legal and political structures and cultures. The chapter concludes by providing a brief overview of all subsequent chapters.

1.1 Selection of jurisdictions, measures and Resolution 1373

1.1.1 Selection of jurisdictions

While there are many similarities and differences between Canada and the UK that make the jurisdictions particularly amenable to comparative analyses, there are unique nuances in the structures and cultures of the two countries that make for especially useful comparison. As noted, both countries responded swiftly to UN Security Council Resolution 1373 with sprawling and comprehensive legislation, despite the fact that both countries had provisions pertaining to terrorism on the

4 *Roach, 9/11 Effect,* 35; in Canada, this legislation came in the form of the Anti-Terrorism Act, S.C. 2001, c. 41 (*ATA)* [hereinafter "*ATA*"]. The UK enacted the Anti-Terrorism, Crime and Security Act, 2001, c. 24 (*ATCSA)* [hereinafter "*ATCSA*"]

books.[5] Similarly, both jurisdictions have been criticized in the years following 9/11 for their reliance on immigration law in the fight against terrorism.[6] Both jurisdictions operate under the common law and within Westminster-based parliamentary systems. That said, the key differences between the two jurisdictions can be categorized into four areas: legal structure, including rights adjudication systems in the two jurisdictions; political structure, including government type and mechanisms for parliamentary review; legal culture, including ideas among the judiciary pertaining to the appropriate level of deference in national security cases; and finally, political culture, including societal attitudes towards human rights in each jurisdiction, and relationships with powerful states such as the US. Each of these areas of difference is the focus of subsequent chapters, and each difference contains nuances that are connected to the overall argument of this book.

Comparisons of Canada and the UK's legal structure focus on the operation of the Human Rights Act 1998[7] (*HRA*) in the UK, which gives effect to the European Convention on Human Rights[8] (*ECHR*), and on the Canadian Charter of Rights and Freedoms in Canada.[9] The *Charter* is a constitutionally entrenched Bill of Rights document that gives Canadian courts a formal power to strike down legislation, adjudicated at the highest level by the Supreme Court of Canada. To contrast, the *HRA* allows resort to the European Court of Human Rights (ECtHR) once adjudication in the domestic courts has been exhausted, with UK courts required to 'take into account' ECtHR jurisprudence.[10] While Kavanagh has argued that the powers of the courts under these two systems 'are not dissimilar',[11] others argue that the UK 'form of legislation for human rights is not as strong as the Canadian model'.[12] This difference in legal structure leads to two

5 In particular, the UK had already enacted extensive and recent anti-terrorism legislation prior to 9/11, in the form of the *Terrorism Act* 2000 c. 11

6 Craig Forcese, 'A Distinction with a Legal Difference: The Consequences of Non-Citizenship in the War on Terror' in Edwards, A. and Ferstman, C. (eds), *Human Security and Non-Citizens: Law, Policy and International Affairs* (Cambridge University Press, 2010) [hereinafter "*Forcese, Distinction with a Legal Difference*"]; Kent Roach, 'Sources and Trends in Post-9/11 Anti-Terrorism Laws' in Goold, B. and Lazarus, L. (eds), *Security and Human Rights* (Hart Publishing, 2007)

7 Human Rights Act (1998) c. 42 [hereinafter "*HRA*"]

8 Council of Europe, *European Convention for the Protection of Human Rights and Fundamental Freedoms, as amended by Protocols Nos. 11 and 14*, 4 November 1950 [hereinafter "*ECHR*"]

9 *The Canadian Charter of Rights and Freedoms,* Part I of the Constitution Act 1982, Being Schedule B to the Canada Act 1982 (UK), 1982, c. 11 [hereinafter "*Charter*"]

10 *HRA*, s. 2(1) (a). A full discussion of the academic material pertaining to these similarities and differences of these systems occurs in section 1.3.1 below

11 Aileen Kavanagh, *Constitutional Review under the UK Human Rights Act* (Cambridge University Press, 2009) [hereinafter "*Kavanagh, Constitutional Review*"] 163

12 Helen Fenwick, Gavin Phillipson and Roger Masterman, 'The Human Rights Act in Contemporary Context' in Fenwick, H., Phillipson, G. and Masterman. R. (eds), *Judicial Reasoning under the UK Human Rights Act* (Cambridge University Press, 2007) [hereinafter "*Fenwick et al.*"] 2

questions about its potential impact on the evolution of counter-terrorism measures: 1) How, and to what extent, are domestic legal decisions on counter-terrorism influenced by the structure of the rights adjudication systems in each jurisdiction? and; 2) How, and to what extent, do domestic legal structures allow for international legal instruments to impact domestic legal decisions on counter-terrorism?

Analyses of the political structure of Canada and the UK focus on the government types[13] of the two countries over the last decade, and the systems for parliamentary review and oversight of counter-terrorism measures present in the two jurisdictions. 'Government type' is the term used by Conley to distinguish between minority (or coalition) and majority governments in his analysis of how institutional structures and governing contexts intersect to account for variation in legislative outcomes. Canada and the UK have both had experience of minority (or coalition) governments in the years since 9/11, albeit at different times, and there is much academic debate about how legislation may evolve differently under minority (or coalition) or majority governments.[14] This leads to the following question for analysis: Has the existence of minority (or coalition) governments had an impact on the evolution of domestic counter-terrorism measures in the two jurisdictions? Moreover, a significant difference in the UK and Canada's political structure is the comparative abundance of parliamentary oversight and review of counter-terrorism provisions in the UK and the glaring lack of these review mechanisms in Canada.[15] This leads to the following question for analysis: How, and to what extent, have systems for parliamentary review and oversight of counter-terrorism measures had an impact on the evolution of domestic counter-terrorism measures in the two jurisdictions? Both of these questions contribute to analyses of how, and to what extent, differences in domestic political structure have an impact on the evolution of counter-terrorism measures in the two jurisdictions.

Analyses of the differences in legal culture between the two countries will focus on what judicial decisions in national security cases tell us about the judiciary's role in these cases. This includes analyses of what judges in each country believe

13 Richard Conley, 'Legislative Activity in the Canadian House of Commons: Does Majority or Minority Government Matter?' (2011) 41 *American Review of Canadian Studies* 422 [hereinafter "*Conley*"]

14 An extensive literature on this topic is discussed in section 1.3.2 below

15 As noted by: Clive Walker, 'Keeping Control of Terrorists without Losing Control of Constitutionalism' (2007) 59 *Stanford Law Review* 1395 [hereinafter "*Walker, Keeping Control*"]; Craig Forcese and Kent Roach, *False Security: The Radicalization of Canadian Anti-Terrorism* (Irwin Law, 2015); Craig Forcese, 'Fixing the Deficiencies of Parliament Review of Anti-Terrorism Law: Lessons from the United Kingdom and Australia' (2008) 14:4 *IRPP Choices* 2 [hereinafter "*Forcese, Deficiencies*"]; Kent Roach, 'A Comparative Assessment of Canadian Counter-Terrorism Laws and Practises' in Forcese, C. and Crepeau, F. (eds), *Terrorism, Law and Democracy: 10 Years After 9/11* (Canadian Institute for the Administration of Justice, Montreal, 2012)

to be the appropriate levels of deference to the executive, and analyses of whether judicial decisions on national security provide evidence of a human rights culture in the two jurisdictions. Fenwick et al. have argued that Canadian judges have given the *Charter* quite a warm reception and suggest that judges in the UK have been reluctant to adopt an expansive approach to interpreting rights under the *HRA* because of a lack of popular support among the public and political branches.[16] Others disagree and argue that national security is no longer viewed as a non-justiciable issue in the UK,[17] and suggest that judicial scrutiny of national security 'appears never to have been more intense than it is now'.[18] Here again comparative analyses prove useful because judicial decisions on counter-terrorism in the two countries may exhibit different levels of judicial deference, and may be differentially indicative of the existence of human rights cultures, with different impacts on the evolution of counter-terrorism measures. As a result, two important questions arise: 1) How, and to what extent, do the judiciaries of Canada and the UK express deference to the executive in national security cases? 2) To what extent can judicial decisions in national security cases be argued to be indicative of a human rights culture in the two jurisdictions?

Analyses of the differences in political culture between Canada and the UK will focus on differing societal attitudes towards human rights in the two countries, as well as differences in the relationship of the two countries with the US. Criticism of the *HRA* in the UK has been rampant, prompting a UK Bill of Rights Commission to argue that there is a lack of public ownership of the *HRA*, with the current rights framework 'widely regarded by the public as foreign or European'.[19] To contrast, it has been argued that there is a 'patriotic attachment' to the *Charter* among the public and politicians in Canada, who view it as a home-grown, specifically Canadian achievement.[20] This gives rise to the following question: Is there a difference in societal attitudes towards human rights in the two jurisdictions and, coupled with the analysis of legal culture in Chapter 5, can it be argued that a human rights culture exists in the two jurisdictions? Moreover, both Canada and the UK each have a significant relationship with the US. Roach has argued that this relationship has had an impact on the evolution of domestic counter-terrorism measures in both jurisdictions, by specifically focusing on a number of key recent events: the passage of the Justice and Security Act in the UK; the passage of Bill S-7 in Canada; the Omar Khadr repatriation affair in

16 *Fenwick et al.*, 5

17 Aileen Kavanagh, 'Judging the Judges under the Human Rights Act: Deference, Disillusionment and the War on Terror' [2009] *PL* 287 [hereinafter "*Kavanagh, Judging*"] 304

18 Adam Tomkins, 'National Security and the Role of the Court: A Changed Landscape?' (2010) 126 *LQR* 543, 545

19 UK Bill of Rights Commission, *A UK Bill of Rights? The Choice before Us* (December 2012, Vol 1), para. 35

20 *Fenwick et al.*, 3

Canada; and the UK's (eventually successful) attempts to deport Abu Qatada.[21] This leads to the research question: What impact has the relationship with the US had on the evolution of domestic counter-terrorism measures in the two jurisdictions?

1.1.2 Selection of measures

Any comparativist must make difficult choices about which measures or institutions to compare. This book primarily focuses on security certificates, and bail with recognizance and investigative hearings in the Canadian context. In its UK analysis, it focuses on detention without trial, control orders and Terrorism Prevention and Investigation Measures (TPIMs). The content, legislative origins and evolution of these measures are extensively detailed in Chapter 2 of this book. Nonetheless, it is necessary to justify the selection of these measures here. First and foremost, the implementation/use of these measures came about principally as a result of the legislative responses of Canada and the UK to United Nations Security Council Resolution 1373 in the aftermath of 9/11. While security certificates were used as an immigration law removal measure prior to 9/11,[22] Roach argues both Canada and the UK's post-9/11 counter-terrorism efforts relied on immigration law after 9/11, noting that this trend is connected to the Security Council's requirement that countries ensure that refugee status not be abused by terrorists. This reliance on immigration law has been criticized because it often permits 'the government in question to act without the full panoply of rights protections and oversight required for citizens'.[23] The investigative hearings and bail with recognizance provisions in Canada, which were brought in under the *ATA*, have been included to further reveal this reliance, as they are criminal code provisions that have never been used and were allowed to expire in 2007, before being re-enacted on 24 April 2013 amidst court challenges to security certificates.

Despite this primary focus, some attention will also be given to post-9/11 measures aimed at countering terrorist financing through asset freezing and

21 Kent Roach, 'Substitute Justice? Challenges to American Counter-Terrorism Activities in Non-American Courts' (2013) 82 *Mississippi Law Journal* 907; Kent Roach, 'Uneasy Neighbours: Comparative American and Canadian Counter-Terrorism' (2012) 38 *William Mitchell Law Review* 1701; Kent Roach, 'Counter-Terrorism in and outside Canada and in and outside the Anti-Terrorism Act' (2012) 6 *Review of Constitutional Studies* 243; Kent Roach, 'Secret Evidence and Its Alternatives' in Masferrer, A. (ed), *Post- 9/11 and the State of Permanent Legal Emergency: Security and Human Rights in Countering Terrorism* (Springer, 2011) 179

22 'Although first legislated in the late 1970s, security certificates were seldom used and rarely publicized. Since 2000, all men named in security certificates . . . have been Muslim men originally from the Middle East or North African, accused of connection to Muslim extremism and Al Qaeda', see Audrey Macklin, 'Stuck at the Border: Ten Years After 9/11' in Forcese, C. and Crepeau, F. (eds), *Terrorism, Law and Democracy: 10 Years after 9/11* (Canadian Institute for the Administration of Justice, Montreal, 2012) 274

23 *Forcese, Distinction with a Legal Difference*, 422

listing, which many authors argue is also a result of a requirement in Security Council Resolution 1373, that which compels states to take measures to tackle terrorist financing.[24] The unifying theme of measures to be analysed is that they are a direct result of compulsions from Resolution 1373, their use was extremely prevalent in the aftermath of 9/11, and they all utilize (problematically, for reasons discussed below) secret evidence. Moreover, the measures selected have been chosen because they carry significant human rights implications which have made them the subject of numerous judicial decisions over the course of the last decade.[25] It has been argued that these human rights implications stem from a relative silence in the language of Resolution 1373 on the need to protect due process and human rights.[26] According to Dyzenhaus, the most notable of these implications is the impact upon the right to a fair trial that occurs because of the reliance of the measures on secret evidence; evidence that cannot be disclosed in open court or subject to the same rigour of criminal proceedings.[27] Finally, the measures have also been subject to scrutiny in both countries' political institutions as they have evolved.[28] The fact that the measures have been subject to scrutiny in both the legal and political institutions in each respective jurisdiction makes them particularly amenable to the analyses this book engages in, because this scrutiny has led to various materials for analysis in the forms of judicial decisions, legislation, parliamentary committee reports and public bill committee debates.

1.1.3 Focus on Resolution 1373

As is noted at the start of the Chapter 3, 'Although the UN had selectively engaged terrorism issues before 9/11, the role of the Security Council in leading global counter-terrorism efforts after 9/11 was unprecedented'.[29] Resolution 1373 provided the impetus for legislation in both jurisdictions that was passed in less than 90 days, despite the fact that provisions pertaining to terrorism existed in both countries, with many of the remnants of that legislation still remaining in statute more than a decade later. The passing of Security Council Resolution

24 For example, both Kent Roach and Tim Daniel have noted a link (discussed further below) between the focus on terrorism financing in *Resolution 1373* and the sparse ratification of the 1999 International Convention for the Suppression of the Financing of Terrorism prior to 9/11, see *Roach, 9/11 Effect,* 34 and *Daniel, International Cooperation,* 248. Furthermore, Nicholas Ryder has called *Resolution 1373* 'the cornerstone of the financial war on terrorism', see *Ryder, Financial War on Terrorism,* 58

25 These decisions are first noted in Chapters 2.2 and 2.34, and are then extensively discussed in Chapter 3

26 Arguments to this effect are extensively detailed in Chapter 2.1

27 David Dyzenhaus, *The Constitution of Law: Legality in a Time of Emergency* (Cambridge University Press, 2006) [hereinafter "*Dyzenhaus, Legality*"] 205

28 The parliamentary committee reports and public bill committee debates pertaining to these measures are laid out in Chapter 2 and further analysed in Chapter 4

29 *Roach, 9/11 Effect,* 35. Furthermore, see Roach's argument that *Resolution 1373* was the Security Council's most influential response to 9/11, 34.

1373, and the establishment of a Counter-Terrorism Committee to monitor its implementation, has been referred to as a 'much debated quasi-legislative function as it had never been exercised before'.[30] Although Chapter 2 further discusses the significance of Resolution 1373, a question could be raised as to why other UN Conventions and Security Council resolutions on terrorism that pre-dated 9/11 are not the subject of focus here. After all, the years immediately preceding 9/11 had seen the passage of significant international instruments, including Security Council Resolutions 1267[31] and 1333,[32] as well as the 1999 International Convention on the Suppression of the Financing of Terrorism,[33] all of which are relevant to analyses pertaining to counter-terrorist financing measures in this book. Nonetheless, it has been forcefully argued that it was Resolution 1373 that led to international recognition of the issues these international instruments sought to address. For example, Daniel has noted that before 9/11 and Resolution 1373 only Sri Lanka, Botswana, Uzbekistan and the UK had ratified the 1999 International Convention on the Suppression of Terrorism.[34] Between 9/11 and 19 February 2002, 90 countries had signed up to this Convention, and 13 more had ratified, in large part due to Resolution 1373.[35] As such, while these other international instruments will be considered in some parts of this book (particularly Security Council Resolution 1267, insofar as it is relevant to certain measures to tackle terrorist financing), it becomes clear that it is justifiable to focus on Resolution 1373 as the driving force behind post-9/11 measures in the two jurisdictions. Lastly, it should be noted that other areas of law, namely European Union (EU) law, could have been considered in this book. A wealth of literature exists pertaining to the impact of the EU on counter-terrorism.[36] There has also been extensive debate pertaining to the UK's 2014 decision to opt-out of EU

30 Larissa Van Den Herik and Nico Schrijver, 'The Fragmented International Legal Response to Terrorism' in Van Den Herik, L. and Schrijver, N. (eds), *Counter Terrorism Strategies in a Fragmented International Legal Order* (Cambridge University Press, 2013) 9–10

31 UN Security Council, *Security Council resolution 1267 (1999) [Afghanistan]*, 15 October 1999, S/RES/1267 (1999), available at: http://www.un.org/ga/search/view_doc.asp?symbol=S/RES/1267(1999) [accessed 20 January 2012]

32 UN Security Council, *Security Council resolution 1333 (2000) [Afghanistan]*, 19 December 2000, S/RES/1333(2000), available at: http://www.un.org/ga/search/view_doc.asp?symbol=S/RES/1333%282000%29 [accessed 3 April 2017]

33 UN General Assembly, *International Convention for the Suppression of the Financing of Terrorism*, 9 December 1999, No. 38349, available at: http://www.un.org/law/cod/finterr.htm [accessed 20 January 2012]

34 *Daniel, International Cooperation*, 248

35 Ibid. The link between *Resolution 1373* and the ratification of the 1999 Convention is also noted by Kent Roach. See *Roach, 9/11 Effect*, 34

36 Christina Eckes, *EU Counter-Terrorist Policies and Fundamental Rights: The Case of Individual Sanctions* (Oxford University Press, 2009); Steve Peers, *EU Justice and Home Affairs* (3rd edn, Oxford University Press, 2010); Oldrich Bures, *EU Counterterrorism Policy* (Ashgate, 2011); Cian Murphy, *EU Counter-Terrorism Law* (Hart, 2013)

policing and criminal law measures adopted before the Treaty of Lisbon.[37] Nonetheless, the decision to leave out consideration of EU law was made principally because no such equivalent arrangement exists for Canada.

1.2 Methodology

While it might be thought that much comparative academic work, including comparative criminal justice research, is simply about uncovering similarities and differences, Nelken argues that 'Showing similarities or difference in itself is not enough. We must have theoretical justifications for showing why our findings are interesting (because unexpected)'.[38] The purpose of this methodology section is to illuminate and evaluate two distinct visions of comparative law and criminology that are intrinsically connected to competing claims about the purpose of comparison: the universalist view of comparative law as a functional science,[39] and the cultural comparativist view that seeks to go beyond rule-comparison by considering the social, political and cultural dynamics that shape laws differently in different jurisdictions.[40] As the analyses in this book focus on how domestic legal, political and cultural dynamics have shaped the evolution of counter-terrorism laws differently in Canada and the UK, it subscribes to the purpose of comparison argued for by the cultural comparativists. This section will elucidate the key points of argument between universalist comparative legal scholars and cultural comparativists. It will also reflect on the difficulties and complexities associated with the comparative exercise. As Legrand notes, 'The more reflective and self-critical the process of understanding another law becomes, the more differential the comparativists' account proves to be'.[41] A number of scholars make claims about the practical difficulties faced by the comparative researcher, including: statements about how long the researcher should live in the place whose law they are trying to understand;[42] how the comparativist may or may not be able to disassociate themselves from their training in the national law of their

37 Home Office, *Table of Measures*, 2013, House of Lords European Union Committee, *5th Report of Session 2013–14: Follow-Up Report on EU Police and Criminal Justice Measures: The UK's 2014 Opt-Out Decision* (2013–14 HL Paper 69)

38 David Nelken, *Comparative Criminal Justice: Making Sense of Difference* (Sage Publications, 2010) 31

39 Represented in the works of authors such as Anselm von Feuerhach, Konrad Zweigert and Hein Kötz and James Gordley, discussed below

40 Represented in the works of authors such as Liora Lazarus, Pierre Legrand and David Nelken, referred to as 'Cultural comparativists', discussed below

41 Pierre Legrand, 'Comparative Legal Studies and the Matter of Authenticity' (2006) 1 *Journal of Comparative Legal Studies* [hereinafter "*Legrand, Matter of Authenticity*"] 365–368

42 Liora Lazarus, *Contrasting Prisoner's Rights: A Comparative Examination of Germany and England* (Oxford University Press, 2004) [hereinafter "*Lazarus, Prisoners*"] 14–15

own country; and[43] finally, how the comparativist acknowledges and analyses political biases of the experts and sources he or she consults.[44]

The field of comparative legal studies lacks a discipline-wide consensus about the goals and methods of comparison,[45] and there is a stark division between those with a universalist view of comparative law as a functional science, and those who view social, political and cultural analyses as intrinsically connected to the comparative endeavour. The universalist sees law 'as an autonomous system ultimately similar in form and content across all cultures',[46] a form of 'universal legal science'[47] where there is no room for cultural analysis and 'local substance'.[48] The central methodological principle of this universalist view of comparative law is functionalism, most often and forcefully posited by Zweigert and Kötz.[49] They argue that the questions of any comparative study must be posed in purely functional terms and, as such, 'The solutions we find in the different jurisdictions must be cut loose from their conceptual context and stripped of their national doctrinal overtones so that they may be seen purely in the light of their function'.[50] According to the universalist, regard to cultural contexts and analyses are theoretically incoherent and lacking in rigour,[51] because they lack a certain scientificity and cannot be empirically quantified. Judicial decisions are not representative of a country's culture,[52] and the social, political and cultural traditions of a country have little to contribute to the comparative endeavour.

43 Pierre Legrand, 'How to Compare Now' (1996) 16 *Journal of Legal Studies* 232 [hereinafter "*Legrand, How to Compare Now*"] 241

44 David Nelken, *Comparative Criminal Justice and Globalization* (Ashgate, 2011) [hereinafter "*Nelken, Comparative Criminal Justice*"] 91

45 'Comparative law has provided a seemingly unending pastime for comparativists and others to discuss its true meaning, historical development, dangers, virtues, scope, functions, aims and purposes, uses and misuses, and method': Esin Örücü, 'Untie Venit, Quo Tendit Comparative Law?' in Harding, A. and Örücü, E. (eds), *Comparative Law in the 21st Century* (Kluwer, 2002) 236

46 *Lazarus, Prisoners*, 7

47 The idea of a universal legal science was developed by Anselm von Feuerhach in his essay 'Idee und Notwendigkeit einer Universaljurisprudenz', cited in W. Hug, 'The History of Comparative Law' [1931/32] XLV *Harvard L Rev* 1027

48 B. Puchalska-Tych and M. Salter, 'Comparing Legal Cultures of Eastern Europe: The Need for a Dialectical Analysis' (1996) 16 *Legal Studies* 157, 175

49 Konrad Zweigert and Hein Kötz, *An Introduction to Comparative Law* (Weir T tr, 3rd rev edn, Oxford University Press, 1998) [hereinafter "*Zweigert and Kötz, Comparative Law*"]

50 Ibid, 44

51 Roger Cotterell, 'The Concept of Legal Culture' in Nelken, D. (ed), *Comparing Legal Cultures* (Dartmouth, 1997) 13–14

52 'When we describe judicial decisions as applications of German or French or American law, we mean little more than that the court making the decision had jurisdiction, because the case arose in these countries. There is nothing distinctively German, French or American about the decisions themselves': James Gordley, 'Comparative Legal Research: Its Function in the Development of Harmonized Law' (1995) 43 *American Journal of Comparative Law* 555, 563

Cultural comparativists, such as Liora Lazarus, Pierre Legrand and David Nelken, take issue with this universalist view, arguing that when comparativists focus merely on the legal rules in question, 'They forget about the historical, social, economic, political, cultural, and psychological context which has made that rule or proposition what it is'.[53] Their comparative projects seek to identify the social, political and cultural contexts that have shaped the method and manner of conceiving of the legal rights they analyse.[54] This book will analyse these contexts in order to better understand why similarities and differences exist between the evolution of Canada and the UK's counter-terrorism policies. These are the most crucial analyses for Legrand because 'The question is not whether difference across laws exists: *it does*. The issue is rather what to make of it and the answer often lies in the conscious or unconscious decision to pay no attention to culture.'[55] Some comparativists in this camp, such as John Merryman, acknowledge that there are instances in which rule-comparison is directly useful, but argue that 'scholarship is supposed to have larger concerns'[56] and, as such, it is crucial to understand the 'context or institutional setting in which rules operate'.[57] According to cultural comparativists, complex legal problems such as terrorism and their legal treatment do not occur in a vacuum, and 'only if one is willing to ignore the embeddedness of the law may one say that a problem and its treatment by the law can be considered irrespective of space or time'.[58]

Cultural comparativists who take issue with the universalist view often acknowledge the complexities associated with conducting cultural analyses. Lazarus notes that 'Whilst the power of culture as an explanatory tool lies in the potential breadth of its descriptive reach, it is also in this its weakness lies'.[59] Despite acknowledgements to this effect, these cultural comparativists argue that focusing on a law's local environment doesn't entail a strict refusal of the proposition that law displays certain universal features, such as rights and duties, obligations, rules and norms.[60] Conversely, the universalist view does not seem to make the same kind of accommodation or acknowledgement of the value of social, cultural and political analyses, seeing them as an impediment to the comparative endeavour of proving a 'unitary sense of justice'.[61] If, as Nelken argues, countries that make up the local sites in comparative research projects are not just 'objects of study', but are composed of criminal justice actors and ordinary citizens whose

53 *Legrand, How to Compare Now*, 234
54 *Lazarus, Prisoners*, 3
55 *Legrand, Matter of Authenticity*, 445 (emphasis in original)
56 Pierre Legrand, 'John Merryman and Comparative Legal Studies: A Dialogue' (1999) 27 *American Journal of Comparative Law* 50
57 J. Bell, 'Comparing Public Law' in Harding, A. and Örücü, E. (eds), *Comparative Law in the 21st Century* (Kluwer, 2002) 1
58 Ibid, 367
59 *Lazarus, Prisoners*, 12
60 Ibid, 10
61 *Zweigert and Kötz, Comparative Law*, 3

understanding of what is being done elsewhere is crucial to grasp,[62] then the universalist's analyses could be missing out on a crucial part of the story. Purely doctrinal comparative legal studies that focus on the black letter of the law in different jurisdictions can miss out on key differences in the legal and political cultures and structures of states. If these differences can be shown to impact the evolution of legislation, then the universalist view inevitably misses a crucial part of the larger picture.

Lazarus, Nelken and Legrand make a number of additional claims about the difficulties faced by the comparative researcher, all of which are applicable to this book. Nelken argues that 'Actually living in a place for a long period is the best – perhaps the only reliable – way to get a sense of what is salient'.[63] Lazarus has noted that living for many years in both of the countries that were the subject of her comparative analysis allowed her opportunities to observe and reflect on the language, sensibilities, habits, beliefs and opinions of the people in both jurisdictions.[64] In the context of this book, these claims hold weight. It might be easy for one to argue that taking up research on a country like the UK, which shares a common law legal tradition with Canada and a number of other similarities crucial to the comparative exercise, most specifically language, could be easily done from abroad. However, being immersed in the political and legal culture of the UK has made it easier to identify what is salient there. There is surely something to be said for immersion, the day-to-day process whereby one has the opportunity to meet and listen to local experts in the field in which they work, listen to local news and see the local reaction to that news and learn and work from within the bureaucracy and confines of the relevant local educational or professional institutions. Moreover, it is not unfair to argue that the benefits of this immersion would be further increased when doing research on a country with a markedly different culture, legal system and language.

Similarly, Legrand makes an argument about the importance of the comparativist maintaining a 'healthy distance from her own national community or at the minimum from certain locales of power within it'.[65] Although he is not referring to geographical distance, as Nelken was, Legrand is arguing that the comparativist must learn not to think like a national lawyer, which will probably require them to unlearn much of what they have been taught, in order to engage in comparative work about the law through the 'meta-language of comparison which requires her always to operate beyond the language of any national law'.[66] Trying to disassociate from the roots of one's national legal and political traditions is indeed quite difficult. Writing and comparing as if one is not a product of one's historical

62 *Nelken, Comparative Criminal Justice*, 4
63 *Nelken, Comparative Criminal Justice*, 96
64 *Lazarus, Prisoners*, 14–15
65 *Legrand, How to Compare Now*, 241
66 Ibid

and educational upbringing is a difficult process, as Lazarus has noted.[67] Nonetheless, Legrand is right to observe the utility of approaching another jurisdiction's law without letting one's own ideas of how it is done at home colour the picture. Doing so allows one to analyse and uncover differences and similarities that are interesting on their own merits.

Nelken notes that another one of the complexities faced by the foreign researcher pertains to whether the study of foreign cultures is actually more about the home country than the setting being studied.[68] He argues that:

> An insider-outsider who spends a long time in a foreign country is likely to become less interested in examining it for the lessons it supposedly has to teach those back home (except when writing for an audience in their country of origin) and as much, or more, in trying to understand it in relation to its own history and current challenges. They may also, by choice or otherwise, embrace a general world view closer to the new place where they are located.[69]

Nelken makes a valid point about the interests of the researcher, which can change as the researcher grows more immersed in the country he or she is in and becomes more familiar with its system of law and political landscape. It becomes easier to understand a country in relation to its own history and current challenges when one sees that history and those challenges every day and, conversely, as one becomes progressively less connected to one's country of origin. Nelken's point about embracing a general world view closer to the new place where the insider-outsider is located may have greater salience in the context of a researcher who is going to a country that has a significantly different culture from that of their own.

Another complexity or personal hurdle that Legrand discusses is the anxiety that can be present for a legal comparativist in embracing an interdisciplinary programme of research.[70] This anxiety may be particularly exacerbated for those legal comparativists who have been trained, or are doing research in, educational institutions and legal departments that largely encourage traditional doctrinal legal research. For such researchers, looking outside the wording of a statute for lessons that can be learned from other disciplines such as criminology, sociology, socio-legal studies, political science and international relations may not come naturally. Researchers who have previous experience with interdisciplinary research may be more comfortable with utilizing the various analytical lenses afforded by disciplines other than traditional doctrinal legal studies. Moreover, the use of these interdisciplinary analytical lenses may be institutionally supported to varying degrees, depending on the flexibility, variety and availability of methodological training offered by the researcher's institution.

67 *Lazarus, Prisoners*, 16–17
68 *Nelken, Comparative Criminal Justice*, 99
69 Ibid
70 *Legrand, Comparative Legal Studies*, 448

A further complexity that comparativists must face, noted by Nelken, pertains to their ability to see through political bias in a foreign setting. He argues that:

> Most researchers are reluctant to recognize the implications of the fact that, in all cultures, descriptions and criticisms of social and legal ideas and practices carry, and are intended to carry, political implications. When we think of experts in our own culture we will often, without much difficulty, be able to associate them with standing for given political policy positions. But it is no less essential, if more difficult, to be aware of this factor when we rely on informants abroad.[71]

Nelken is right to note that it is often more natural and therefore less difficult to be able to spot political bias in experts or politicians within one's own country. This is something that comes with years of being raised, educated and immersed in the political and legal norms of one's home country. It would appear relatively easy to pick up on the political biases of another country that has a similar parliamentary system and similar parties with similar platforms (i.e. liberals, conservatives, etc.) but there are nuances behind these labels that take time to familiarize oneself with, particularly with regard to understanding what each party's position has historically been in one's particular field.

Yet another complexity faced by the comparativist that is discussed by Lazarus, Nelken and Legrand is the decision about how to do cross-cultural research, since there is no real definitive guidance on doing this kind of research and because 'terms like culture and legal culture are highly controversial' and 'it is often objected that explaining behavior by reference to culture tends to assume that it is determining, bounded and unchanging'.[72] Legrand notes that opponents to cultural analysis often point to 'the failure to establish an empirical link between "culture" and "result" but this does not mean that no such connection exists. Not everything is observable and not everything is observed'.[73] Lazarus echoes this statement, arguing that the very fluidity of the concept of culture is what enables the researcher to identify the local nuances of the social context of the law.[74] There is no particular roadmap for the use of the term culture, only the myriad of viewpoints of cultural comparativists that have been bold enough to engage in the process before. Perhaps this is why Legrand and Nelken place such emphasis on self-reflection in the comparative exercise, and this process of self-reflection proves to be useful to this book. Comparative work, by its very nature, brings up more questions than answers and more differences than research which is focused on a single country, and it is useful to think critically about the value that can be assigned to cultural revelations that the research discloses.

71 *Nelken, Comparative Criminal Justice*, 91
72 *Nelken, Comparative Criminal Justice*, 50
73 *Legrand, Comparative Legal Studies*, 456
74 *Lazarus, Prisoners*, 13

While certain cultural variables such as 'societal attitudes towards human rights' are not particularly measurable variables that can be said to have a scientificity about them, they are still crucial parts of the story when trying to understand any piece of legislation.

1.3 Defining legal and political structures and cultures

1.3.1 The structure of domestic legal institutions

The structure of a state's legal system, including its formal rights adjudication system, can influence how decision-makers within those institutions operate. Discussion of formal rights adjudication systems here will focus on the operation of the *HRA*[75] and the ECHR in the UK and on the *Charter* in Canada. There will be a greater focus on the *ECHR* and the *HRA* as the Canadian legal system, unlike that of the UK, has no equivalent court of last resort outside of its domestic jurisdiction (this role is played by the Supreme Court of Canada). Moreover, the structure of both countries' immigration law systems will be laid out, as they also form an integral part of the anti-terrorism framework in both Canada and the UK.

The UK's rights adjudication system has unique aspects that make it particularly amenable to analysis that investigates how structural aspects of a state's domestic legal institutions influence the actions of decision-makers within those institutions. Before turning to these, it should be noted that comparison of Canada and the UK's rights adjudication systems is frequent in the literature. For instance, while Kavanagh argues that 'The powers of the courts under the *HRA* are not dissimilar to those possessed by constitutional courts in jurisdictions with an entrenched Bill of Rights';[76] others disagree, arguing instead that:

> This form of legislation for human rights is not as strong as the Canadian model, which gives courts the power to strike down primary legislation but allows the legislature to enact measures for a limited period 'notwithstanding' its contravention of provisions in the Charter of Fundamental Rights and Freedoms.[77]

75 Human Rights Act 1998, c. 42 [hereinafter "*HRA*"]

76 *Kavanagh, Constitutional Review*, 163

77 John Wadham, *Blackstone's Guide to the Human Rights Act 1998* (5th edn, Oxford University Press, 2009) [hereinafter "*Wadham, Blackstones*"] para. 1.28. The 'notwithstanding clause' attracts significant attention in this literature, and warrants further discussion when it is compared with the power to issue a declaration of incompatibility. For further information on the clause, including the argument that s. 1 of the Canadian Charter, which houses the clause, has no such equivalent in the ECHR, see Andrew Ashworth, 'Security, Terrorism and the Value of Human Rights' in Goold, B. and Lazarus, L. (eds), *Security and Human Rights* (Hart Publishing, 2007) 211

Moreover, it is argued that the historical pedigree of the two rights adjudications systems has been very different. Fenwick et al. note that:

> Judicial receptivity to the ECHR under the Human Rights Act was less consistent than was the case in Canada: broadly speaking, the Canadian judges gave the Charter quite a warm reception, given the widespread popular support for its adoption, whereas, among British judges, some resistance to the Convention was evident.[78]

Furthermore, they argue that in Canada, there is a patriotic attachment to the *Charter* among the judiciary, policy-makers and public, who view it as a home-grown, specifically *Canadian* achievement.[79]

This is in stark contrast to the system in the UK, where human rights are often seen as externally imposed. As a result, there are aspects of the rights adjudication process in the UK that have no parallel with that in Canada. The strongest example of this is the margin of appreciation, through which the ECtHR decides what level of deference, if any, it should pay to domestic courts because of its practical distance from domestic legal, political and cultural realities. The margin of appreciation doctrine was first developed by the ECtHR in *Handyside v. UK*,[80] in which the Court argued that national authorities are in principle in a better position than the international judge to decide on certain issues because of their direct and continuous contact with the vital forces of their countries, but also qualified this by saying that states were not given an unlimited margin of appreciation.[81] Since then, the extent to which, and manner in which, the doctrine has been utilized has varied widely. That being said, various factors can be elucidated that affect the extent of deference Strasbourg will show the state: 1) the nature of the right, particularly when it is characterized as fundamental; 2) the nature of the justification offered by the state, such as national security or public morality; and 3) whether a positive obligation is being imposed.

The margin of appreciation takes into account the idea that national authorities will be best placed to make certain decisions because of the 'geographical, cultural, philosophical, historical and intellectual distance between the judges in Strasbourg and local institutions'.[82] However, it must be noted that domestic authorities and the Strasbourg Court can, and sometimes do, choose to disagree. This often occurs in relation to section 2 of the *HRA*, which requires domestic courts to 'take into account' Strasbourg jurisprudence.[83] Kavanagh notes that while domestic courts are entitled to distinguish Strasbourg jurisprudence as

78 *Fenwick et al.*, 2
79 Ibid, 3. This claim is further analysed in Chapters 5 and 6
80 *Handyside v. UK*, App No 5493/72 [1976] ECHR 5
81 Ibid, paras. 48–9
82 *Wadham, Blackstones*, para. 41.25
83 *HRA*, s. 2(1) (a)

inappropriate because of domestic context factors, they have interpreted section 2 as creating a strong presumption in favour of following this jurisprudence, which can only be rebutted in special circumstances.[84] That being said, there are instances in which the Supreme Court will disagree with the ECtHR and choose not to take its decision into account. In *R v. Horncastle*,[85] a UK Supreme Court ruling on the admissibility of hearsay evidence with similar facts to the Strasbourg Court's decision in *Al-Khawaja*,[86] the Supreme Court chose not to take into account the ECtHR jurisprudence, stating that it had the ability to do so on rare occasions.[87] Moreover, in dismissing the appeal, Lord Phillips reasoned that the Strasbourg Court had failed to appreciate the strengths of the common law tradition with regard to criminal evidence.[88]

Grasping this process is important as this interaction between the UK courts and the ECtHR is something that does not occur within the Canadian rights adjudication system. The Canadian Supreme Court would never engage in the same kind of reasoning process that the House of Lords did in *Handyside*, *Horncastle* or in the *SSHD v. AF (No 3)*[89] case. Kavanagh notes that the Court's dicta in *SSHD v. AF (No 3)* that it had 'no option but to accept' a ECtHR decision pertaining to the human rights validity of control orders speaks to the rarity with which UK courts will not take into account decisions of the ECtHR, despite the fact that the government explicitly wanted the courts to have the flexibility to do so if a decision was unsuitable for application in the UK context when they developed the *HRA*.[90] While *Horncastle* is a notable example of this flexibility, it is a very rare one. Importantly, the fact remains that the Supreme Court of Canada would not have to engage in a similar type of reasoning process. As the highest final court of last resort in Canada, it operates under different institutional confines than the UK Supreme Court, which must take into account decisions of the ECtHR. This difference in structure is a crucial difference in the legal systems of the two countries that will be illuminative for analyses in subsequent chapters pertaining to how these structures influence decision-makers working within them.

84 Aileen Kavanagh, 'Special Advocates, Control Orders and the Right to a Fair Trial' (2010) 73 *MLR* 824 [hereinafter "*Kavanagh, Special Advocates*"] 845

85 [2009] UKSC 14 [hereinafter "*Horncastle*"]

86 *Al-Khawaja v. United Kingdom*, App No 26766/05 [2009] ECHR 11

87 These rare occasions being 'where this court has concerns as to whether a decision of the Strasbourg Court sufficiently appreciates or accommodates particular aspects of our domestic process': *Horncastle*, paras. 10–11

88 Ibid, para. 14

89 *Secretary of State for the Home Department v. AF (No 3)* [2009] UKHL 28 [hereinafter "*SSHD v. AF No 3*"]. This case (and the related ECtHR judgment) is a landmark ruling pertaining to the human rights validity of control order provisions and, as such, is subject to extensive analyses in Chapters 2 and 3

90 *Kavanagh, Special Advocates*, 844

Another interesting aspect of the UK rights adjudication system is the interplay between statutory interpretation and the issuing of declarations of incompatibility, which falls under sections 3 and 4 of the *HRA*, respectively. Section 3 states that, so far as it is possible to do so, primary legislation must be read and given effect in a way which is compatible with the Convention rights.[91] Again, there is a useful contrast present here between Canadian and UK systems because Canadian judges have a formal 'strike down' power that can render rights-infringing legislation to be of no force and effect, whereas this element is absent in the UK system.[92] There are mixed views on the section 3 and 4 provisions and the case for formal strike down power. Kavanagh argues that they characterize institutional limitations that the UK courts work under, which allows them to only engage in partial rather than comprehensive legal reform.[93] By contrast, a report of the UK Joint Committee on Human Rights argues against the courts having a strike down power, arguing that it would be against the UK's tradition of parliamentary democracy.[94] This kind of discussion would be absent in Canada. With regard to the aforementioned *SSHD v. AF (No 3)* case, Kavanagh argues that the government supported a section 3 interpretation because, to the general public, it would seem like a clean bill of health in human rights terms as opposed to a declaration of incompatibility under section 4, which is hard to present as anything other than a failure to protect human rights.[95] The choice of the courts between sections 3 and 4 complicates decision-making in a way not faced by Canadian Courts. Although courts in Canada are careful when they engage in statutory interpretation, they never have to worry, as the UK courts do, that the choice of a declaration of incompatibility could result in the government taking months or years to respond.[96] The interplay between sections 3 and 4 of the *HRA* usefully illustrates the structural constraints under which UK courts work that are not present within the Canadian rights adjudication framework.

Another key aspect of the structure of domestic legal institutions in the two jurisdictions is the legal frameworks provided under immigration law. In Canada, the legal framework for the security certificate regime is found in sections 77–85 of the *Immigration and Refugee Protection Act (IRPA*). Section 77 (1) allows the Minister of Citizenship and Immigration to sign a certificate stating that a permanent resident or foreign national should not be admitted on various grounds. Once this occurs, all other proceedings against that person, including refugee status applications, are halted until the judge decides if the certificate is

91 *HRA*, s. 3(1)

92 UK judges can issue a declaration of incompatibility under s. 4 of the HRA, but it is up to Parliament to respond to this declaration with amendments to the legislation

93 *Kavanagh, Judging*, 304

94 Joint Committee on Human Rights. *A Bill of Rights for the UK?* (HC 150–1, 2008)

95 *Kavanagh, Special Advocates*, 849

96 *Wadham, Blackstones*, para. 4.93

'reasonable'.[97] The Minister is obliged to file with the Court the information on which the certificate is based, in order to enable the person named in the certificate to be reasonably informed of the case made against them, subject to redactions that might be made due to national security concerns. In Canada, the Federal Court is exclusively responsible for deciding what information would be 'injurious to national security'[98] and whether to disclose it, but it can send the case to the Federal Court of Appeal 'if the judge certifies that a serious question of general importance is involved'.[99] One of the most contentious aspects of the security certificate regime is that the Federal Court judge hears the evidence in the absence of the named person,[100] which goes against fundamental legal principles such as the right to a fair trial and the rule of law. To mitigate this problem, the judge can appoint a special advocate to protect the interests of the named person when information or other evidence is heard *in camera*.[101] Unfortunately, these special advocates are not allowed to communicate with the named person once they have seen closed material.[102] As such, serious questions have been raised about whether the special advocate truly acts as a procedural safeguard that can protect the named person's *Charter* rights to a fair trial.

In the UK, the Special Immigration Appeals Commission (SIAC) engages in a similar function to that of the Federal Court of Canada under the *IRPA*. SIAC was created when the ECtHR rejected the UK Government's argument that national security grounds are inherently incapable of being tested in a court of law, and held that the previous advisory committee did not constitute a court under the meaning of Article 5(4) of the ECHR in which one could challenge the legality of their detention.[103] Subsequently established by the Special Immigration Appeals Commission Act 1997,[104] SIAC has the authority to scrutinize the Secretary of State's public interest claims against disclosure of information on the law and the facts.[105] SIAC is constituted of members with judicial, immigration and national security experience[106] and, like the Federal Court of Canada, can pass cases on to the Court of Appeal on 'any question of law'.[107] If proceedings are held in closed session for national security reasons, a special advocate is provided to protect the interests of the appellant in a hearing before SIAC,[108] performing similar functions to those of special advocates in Canada, such as cross-examination

97 Immigration and Refugee Protection Act S.C. 2001, c. 27 [hereinafter "*IRPA*"], s. 77(3)
98 Ibid, s. 77(2)
99 Ibid, s. 79
100 Ibid, s. 83(1) (c)
101 Ibid, s. 85.1(1)
102 Ibid, s. 85.5
103 *Chahal v. UK*, App No 22414/93 [1996] ECHR 54
104 C. 68 [hereinafter "*SIAC Act*"]
105 Ibid, s. 2
106 *SIAC Act*, schedule 1, s. 5
107 Ibid, s. 7(1)
108 Ibid, s. 6

of witnesses and the making of submissions at any hearings from which the appellant parties are excluded. As is the case in the Canadian system, the special advocate in the UK system cannot communicate with the appellant once they have seen the closed material.

Both SIAC and the Federal Court under the *IRPA* face a difficult and unenviable task. Both are asked to balance national security considerations with fundamental legal principles such as the right to a fair trial and the rule of law. The provision of the special advocate within both of these regimes is a novel attempt to achieve this balance, but there are still significant issues with both systems, most especially the fact that in both systems the special advocate cannot communicate with the appellant and his or her counsel after having access to the closed material. According to Dyzenhaus, this is the most notable defect of the process.[109] The fact that these measures are in the immigration law context and outside of the normal criminal process is equally disconcerting, because the impression is given that the detainee has some procedural rights but these rights lack true substance in practice – what Dyzenhaus calls a 'legal grey hole'.[110]

1.3.2 The structure of domestic political institutions

> David Feldman argues that human rights can only be fully realized when they are taken as seriously by the executive and the legislature as they are by the judiciary, and notes that systematic engagement with human rights in a democratic political process can come about only when it is seen as a goal of all institutions, executive, legislative and judicial, working towards a common goal when exercising their different but complementary functions.[111]

This book conceptualizes the structure of domestic political institutions to encapsulate the actual political system in place in a state, including bodies that may function with important roles within this system, namely those responsible for parliamentary review. It also includes Conley's aforementioned concept of 'government types' in order to distinguish between minority (or coalition) and majority governments.[112] These structures can influence how political decisions are made because, as Kavanagh notes, their decision-makers act within, and according to, their institutional structures.[113] This argument is further

109 *Dyzenhaus, Legality*, 205

110 Ibid, 50

111 David Feldman, 'The Impact of Human Rights on the UK Legislative Process' (2004) 25 *Stat LR* 91 [hereinafter "*Feldman, Impact of Human Rights*"] 92

112 *Conley*

113 Aileen Kavanagh, 'Constitutional Review, the Courts, and Democratic Scepticism' (2009) 62 *CLP* 102, 127

echoed in the works of Knill and Lehmkuhl[114] and Cortell and Davis,[115] discussed further below.

Canada and the UK share certain common structural political features. Of these, Kavanagh notes that the fact that the legislature is popularly elected and democratically accountable is one of the most significant.[116] That being said, some are sceptical of just how representative the political branches in Canada and the UK are of its people. Fenwick et al. note that the 'overall result of an election commonly is that a party with a majority in the House of Commons won fewer than half of the votes cast in the election'.[117] These scepticisms are exacerbated in political systems based on minority or coalition governments which, until 2011, Canada had been experiencing since 2006, and which had been a feature of the UK political system from 2010 to 15. Conley argues that under minority or coalition government types, governments operate under a 'manifest uncertainty and fear of imminent defeat that threatens their stability and capacity to govern effectively'.[118] Lacey has also written on how the dynamics of bargaining under conditions of coalition government affect the environment for criminal justice policy-making, in the context of the prisoners' dilemma.[119] Regardless of one's political affiliation, one must acknowledge that in a majority government type it is less onerous to pass legislation and, as such, the government is less constrained structurally by instability when it tries to introduce domestic measures to combat global problems.[120]

The importance of parliamentary review committees in both Canada and the UK is a much discussed topic in the field of terrorism studies and in related academic fields.[121] Knill and Lehmkuhl argue that parliamentary committees act as crucial 'veto points' that 'prevent national governments from initiating and pushing through reform against political and societal resistance'.[122] Parliament and government departments are increasingly aware of UK human rights

114 Christopher Knill and Dirk Lehmkuhl, 'Private Actors and the State: Internationalization and Changing Patterns of Governance' (2002) 5 *Governance* 41 [hereinafter "*Knill and Lehmkuhl*"]

115 Andrew Cortell and James Davis, Jr., 'How Do International Institutions Matter? The Domestic Impact of International Rules and Norms' (1996) 40 *International Studies Quarterly* 451 [hereinafter "*Cortell and Davis*"]

116 *Kavanagh, Constitutional Review*, 192

117 *Fenwick et al.*, 7

118 *Conley*, 7

119 Nicola Lacey. 'Political Systems and Criminal Justice: The Prisoners' Dilemma After the Coalition' [2012] *CLP* 1

120 This argument is the focus of analyses in Chapter 4

121 At a theoretical level, both Walker and Zedner argue that independent legislative scrutiny and external executive oversight are crucial components of any system of security measures. See *Walker, Keeping Control;* Lucia Zedner, 'Securing Liberty in the Face of Terror: Reflections from Criminal Justice' (2005) 32 *Journal of Law and Society* 507 [hereinafter "*Zedner, Securing Liberty*"] 531

122 *Knill and Lehmkuhl*, 47

obligations because of the work of select committees, 'affecting both the content of legislation and the way in which scrutiny of government is conducted'.[123] While there are several committees in the UK that may deal occasionally with questions of rights compatibility, including the Joint Committee on Statutory Instruments, the Commons Home Affairs Committee and the Lords Delegated Powers and Regulatory Reform Committee, it is clear that the Joint Select Committee on Human Rights (JCHR) plays the most significant role in critically assessing legislation.[124] The JCHR was established with effect from January 2001, with David Feldman appointed as its first legal advisor.[125] Its formal remit is to consider: 1) matters relating to human rights in the UK (but excluding consideration of individual cases); 2) proposals for remedial orders, draft remedial orders and remedial orders made under the Human Rights Act 1998; and 3) in respect of draft remedial and remedial orders, whether the special attention of the House should be drawn to them on any of the grounds specified in HC Standing Order No. 151.[126] In practice what this means is that the JCHR scrutinizes bills for compatibility with human rights, releases regular reports pertaining to human rights issues and urges the government to make fuller statements of the reasoning behind section 19 rights-compatibility statements.[127]

Academic commentary on the actual ability of the JCHR to influence legislation has been mixed. Kavanagh argues that it has been of 'immense importance in strengthening parliamentary review of legislative proposals for compliance with Convention rights'.[128] Wadham points out that the JCHR has had a particular influence on Parliament in relation to specific pieces of human rights sensitive legislation such as the Anti-Terrorism, Crime and Security Act 2001 and the Terrorist Act 2006.[129] That being said, Tomkins argues that while the 'JCHR is a remarkably energetic committee, which undertakes a formidable workload',[130] he also notes that the present control order regime survives 'in a manner in which

123 David Feldman, 'The Internationalization of Public Law and Its Impact on the United Kingdom' in Jowell, J. and Oliver, D. (eds), *The Changing Constitution* (6th edn, Oxford University Press, 2007) 124

124 David Feldman, 'Institutional Roles and Meanings of "Compatibility" under the Human Rights Act 1998' in Fenwick, H., Phillipson, G. and Masterman, R. (eds), *Judicial Reasoning under the UK Human Rights Act* (Cambridge University Press, 2007) 102

125 Colin Turpin and Adam Tomkins, *British Government and the Constitution* (6th edn, Cambridge University Press, 2007) 273

126 United Kingdom Parliament Website, 'Joint Select Committee on Human Rights', available at: http://www.parliament.uk/business/committees/committees-a-z/joint-select/human-rights-committee [accessed 28 August 2011]

127 Dawn Oliver, *Constitutional Reform in the UK* (Oxford University Press, 2003) 118

128 *Kavanagh, Constitutional Review*, 420

129 *Wadham, Blackstones,* para. 1.50

130 Adam Tomkins, 'Parliament, Human Rights and Counter-Terrorism' in Tomkins, A., Ewing, K.D. and Campbell, T. (eds), *The Legal Protection of Human Rights: Skeptical Essays* (Oxford University Press, 2011) 23

only two of the JCHR's nine recommendations have been put into practise'.[131] Moreover, it is fair to argue that these two recommendations – that amendments to the Prevention of Terrorism Act 2005 should confer a duty on the Secretary of State to give as full an explanation as possible of his or her reasons for making a control order and require him or her to provide the controlee with at least a summary of the information against them – were more likely implemented as a result of the decisions in *A v. UK* and *SSHD v. AF (No 3)*. As such, despite the important role and admirable aspirations of the JCHR, one must exercise caution when evaluating its tangible impact.[132]

Similar caution may be appropriate in the Canadian context. In Canada, Senate and House of Commons Committees as well as public inquiries into counter-terrorism mechanisms are occasionally authorized by Parliament, but are not as frequent as those released in the UK. Forcese has more critically argued that 'To date, however, parliamentary review of national security has been largely perfunctory'.[133] For instance, two special committees completed comprehensive reviews of Canada's entire anti-terrorism legislative framework in 2007,[134] both of which made a number of recommendations pertaining to security certificates and urged the government to consider a specific renunciation of torture in its counter-terrorism legislation. Unfortunately, the government chose not to implement many of the Committee recommendations and decided instead to tailor its amendments to the *Charkaoui* decision, in an extremely minimalist way.[135] Similarly, Forcese argues that the debates on preventive detention and investigative hearings in February 2007 were 'disappointing and superficial' and advocates for a stable system of parliamentary review that 'could prove to be especially valuable in periods of crisis or their aftermath, or in periods of intense partisanship (such as minority governments)'.[136] Cortell and Davis argue that international rules and norms can affect national policy choices by operating through the domestic political process, but that 'the structure of domestic political institutions plays an important role in determining whether and how an appeal to an international norm will influence policy choice'.[137] There is no shortage of recent instances

131 Ibid, 38
132 Analyses of the JCHR and Independent Reviewer's impact on specific counter-terrorism legislation take place in Chapter 4
133 *Forcese, Deficiencies*, 2
134 Special Senate Committee on the Anti-Terrorism Act, *Fundamental Justice in Extraordinary Times: Main Report of the Special Senate Committee on the Anti-Terrorism Act* (Special Senate Committee on the Anti-Terrorism Act, February 2007); Standing Committee on Public Safety and National Security, *Rights, Limits, Security: A Comprehensive Review of the Anti-Terrorism Act and Related Issues* (Standing Committee on Public Safety and National Security, March 2007)
135 The work of the committees, the Supreme Court's decision in the *Charkaoui* case and subsequent government amendments are all discussed extensively in Chapter 2.2
136 *Forcese, Deficiencies*, 19
137 *Cortell and Davis*, 471

wherein the Canadian Conservative Government has ignored carefully thought out reports of parliamentary committees or inquiry bodies.[138]

These instances suggest that one should exercise caution when assigning weight to the influence of parliamentary committees and inquiries in Canada, despite the invaluable role they can and should exercise. This problem is exacerbated by the sporadic nature of review in Canada. For the better part of a decade, Roach and Forcese have repeatedly argued for increased independent review of national security strategies, often by making comparison to the independent reviews of security strategies carried out in the UK by Lord Carlile and the Privy Councillors.[139] Roach further argues that 'A committee of Parliamentarians with access to classified information follows best international practice, but it will be revolutionary in Canadian politics'.[140] While he notes that a bill (c-81) was introduced in November 2005 to create such a committee,[141] this bill died on the Order Paper on 30 November 2005 when Parliament was dissolved, speaking to the potential impact of political instability discussed above. Consequently, independent review of national security activities in Canada has not been as extensive or regular as that which has occurred in the UK. While increased scrutiny of the government's anti-terrorism policies would indeed be a welcome development, this increased role would nonetheless have to be evaluated carefully in order to assess its tangible impact on legislative outcomes.[142]

1.3.3 The culture of domestic legal institutions

As discussed in the above methodology section, a vast literature in the field of comparative law exists pertaining to the complexities of the concepts of culture and legal culture. While it is easy to argue that culture, and associated concepts such as legal culture, are not specifically measurable social variables, it is perhaps more useful to celebrate the capacity of the concept to encompass diverse variables

138 Significant public inquiries investigating the Air India bombing and the torture of Canadian citizens suggested a number of amendments to Canada's system for public interest immunity and non-disclosure which the government has signalled no intention of responding to through legislation: Commission of Inquiry into the Investigation of the Bombing of Air India Flight 182, *Air India Flight 182: A Canadian Tragedy* (Ottawa, 2010); The Honourable Frank Iacobucci QC LLD, *Internal Inquiry into the Actions of Canadian Officials in Relation to Abdullah Almalki, Ahmad Abou-Elmaati and Muayyed Nureddin* (Ottawa, 2008)

139 Craig Forcese and Kent Roach, *False Security: The Radicalization of Canadian Anti-Terrorism* (Irwin Law, 2016); Kent Roach, 'Must We Trade Rights for Security? The Choice between Smart, Harsh, or Proportionate Security Strategies in Canada and Britain' (2006) 27 *Cardozo Law Review* 2151 [hereinafter "*Roach, The Choice*"] 2171; *Forcese, Deficiencies,* 18

140 *Roach, The Choice*, 2170

141 Ibid

142 The mechanisms for parliamentary review of counter-terrorism activities in Canada, or lack thereof, are analysed in Chapter 4

and understand 'immeasurable aspects of cultural ideas and meanings'.[143] Similarly, the concept of a culture of rights can have a variety of conceptualizations. Eric Feldman usefully distinguishes between rights, rhetoric about rights and rights rhetoric,[144] illustrating that rhetoric about rights pertains to how societal beliefs are illuminated when actors within that society talk about rights. Lazarus contributes to this discussion by arguing that rhetoric about rights takes a different tone in different legal cultures because the histories and traditions of the countries being analysed have 'produced different conceptions about the right and the role of fundamental rights'.[145] This book analyses how the histories and traditions of Canada and the UK affect this tone and invariably influence the actions of decision-makers in domestic institutions. Moreover, Feldman's concept of rights rhetoric also requires one to be cognizant of how rights are used to conceptualize debates about social policy. As such, this book investigates how rights are used in the discourses contained in various social policy arenas, including the courts and Parliament.

Another important consideration pertaining to the culture of domestic legal institutions is the concept of judicial deference. Many judicial decisions in the realm of national security, and academic commentary pertaining to these decisions, discuss the appropriate role of the judiciary in national security cases and make claims about appropriate levels of judicial deference. Claims pertaining to the appropriate level of deference often relate to arguments about institutional legitimacy and competence or expertise. The institutional legitimacy claim, the idea that judges should defer because they are unelected and, thus, dispossessed of the same accountability and legitimacy as elected Members of Parliament (MPs) is well discussed.[146] There is a strong debate as to the weight that this argument carries, with Kavanagh offering perhaps the most enlightened viewpoint: 'We can say that the democratic legitimacy of the elected branches of government is indeed one of the reasons why the courts owe the decisions of the elected branches deference, but that deference is only minimal'.[147] The weight of the institutional legitimacy claim cannot be ignored, but this does not mean the courts have to

143 David Nelken, 'Puzzling Out Legal Culture: A Comment on Blankenburg' and Lawrence Friedman, 'The Concept of Legal Culture: A Reply' in Nelken, D. (ed), *Comparing Legal Cultures* (Aldershot, 1997) 33, 69, 74

144 Eric Feldman, 'Patients' Rights, Citizens' Movements and Japanese Legal Culture' in Nelken, D. (ed), *Comparing Legal Cultures* (Dartmouth, 1997)

145 *Lazarus, Prisoners*, 16

146 *Kavanagh, Judging*, 304; Sandra Fredman, 'From Deference to Democracy: The Role of Equality under the Human Rights Act 1998' (2006) 122 *LQR* 53 [hereinafter "*Fredman, Deference*"]; Jeff A. King, 'Institutional Approaches to Judicial Restraint' (2008) 28 *Oxford Journal of Legal Studies* [hereinafter "*King, Institutional Approaches*"] 409

147 *Kavanagh, Constitutional Review*, 192

engage in substantial deference, which Kavanagh claims 'has to be earned by the elected branches'.[148]

The institutional competence claim, the idea that judges should defer because they don't have the same competence or expertise as the government, especially in cases involving national security where there is secret information they do not see, is also widely discussed.[149] Ramraj argues that:

> Even allowing that the executive has a special expertise in assessing the magnitude of the risk of terrorism because of its privileged access to intelligence information, it still has no special expertise in measuring the risk of terrorism against state incursions on fundamental, but intangible public values, such as liberty.[150]

This is a persuasive argument that is evident in the literature, that is, that although the courts do not have competence to assess national security claims because of a lack of evidence, they are the best placed, and indeed it is their fundamental function, to make legal judgments on incursions into rights. The result is what Kavanagh calls an acute dilemma raised in the national security context: on the one hand, judges are constitutionally mandated to ensure that legislative and executive decisions comply with the rule of law and Convention rights, but on the other, they have to acknowledge the expertise and legitimacy of the elected branches.[151]

Novel ideas are presented as a solution to this dilemma. Hunt argues that British courts should adopt a due deference approach, 'premised on the assumption that power in our Constitution is shared amongst the various actors rather than to be parcelled out according to some inflexible and outdated idea of the separation of powers and co-existing supremacies'.[152] His approach centres on the explicit articulation and evaluation of reasons for deferring. Moreover, these reasons need to be theorized in terms of what justifies judicial intervention, requiring a reconfiguration of public law in terms of what Mureinik and Dyzenhaus have called a 'culture of justification'.[153] According to Dyzenhaus:

> In a culture of justification, Parliament should be required to earn judicial deference from the courts on human rights questions by demonstrating the

148 Ibid, 182. Kavanagh's distinction between minimal and substantial deference is found to be particularly relevant in Chapter 5's analyses

149 *Fredman, Deference*; *King, Institutional Approaches*; *Kavanagh, Judging*

150 Victor V. Ramraj, 'Terrorism, Risk Perception and Judicial Review' in Ramraj, V.V., Roach, K. and Hor, M.Y.M. (eds), *Global Anti-Terrorism Law and Policy* (Cambridge University Press, 2005) [hereinafter "*Ramraj, Terrorism*"] 120

151 *Kavanagh, Judging*, 301

152 Murray Hunt, 'Sovereignty's Blight: Why Contemporary Public Law Needs the Concept of "Due Deference"' in Bamforth, N. and Leyland, P. (eds), *Public Law in a Multi-Layered Constitution* (Hart Publishing, 2003) [hereinafter "*Hunt, Sovereignty*"] 370

153 Ibid, 347–51

quality of its reasoned judgments on compatibility, not entitled to expect it by virtue of its sovereign position in the constitution.[154]

Like Hunt, Dyzenhaus argues that the judiciary recognizes that 'other actors in the legal order have a legitimate role in interpreting the law but at the same time stands ready to review these actors' decisions to ensure that the decisions are properly justified'.[155] Chapter 5 will analyse if such a culture exists in Canada or the UK.

1.3.4 The culture of domestic political institutions

Opinions vary on how well Canadian or UK society is truly committed to a 'culture of rights'.[156] Zedner argues that whether such a culture has emerged is unclear, as promotion of rights varies according to 'surrounding attitudes, political climate, and political receptivity'.[157] While Dyzenhaus argues that the *HRA* in the UK gave concrete institutional expression to a culture that was already developing[158] others argue that 'At the highest level of government there is a continuing and deeply worrying failure to respect the culture of human rights that underpins the Human Rights Act'.[159] As aforementioned by Feldman, the establishment of a human rights culture requires the interaction of legal and political institutions.[160] There are many authors who discuss whether or not a culture of rights exists in the UK and whether or not the *HRA* has helped this to occur. Ewing and Tham can be said to provide the strongest critique of the *HRA*. They argue that there are sharp differences in opinion about the place of the *HRA* in the contemporary constitution, stating that 'The surprising vigour of parliamentary sovereignty not only provides evidence for the deep roots and unshakeable strength of the principle, but also raises questions about the most effective way of protecting human rights under the British constitution'.[161] Ewing and Tham's viewpoints illustrate the remnants of what many authors refer to as the 'Diceyan' constitutional viewpoint. This view, that Parliament is omnipotent and its supremacy is unchallengeable, has been significantly eroded in recent years.[162] Kavanagh argues that the *HRA*, albeit slowly, is contributing to a change in the way we characterize

154 *Dyzenhaus, Legality*, 153
155 Ibid, 141
156 Chapters 5 and 6 analyse whether or not a rights culture can be said to exist in the two countries
157 *Zedner, Securing Liberty*, 519
158 *Dyzenhaus, Legality*, 145
159 Lord Lester and Kate Beattie, 'Human Rights and the British Constitution' in Jowell, J. and Oliver, D. (eds), *The Changing Constitution* (6th edn, Oxford University Press, 2007) [hereinafter "*Lester and Beattie*"] 81
160 *Feldman, Impact of Human Rights*, 114–15
161 K.D. Ewing and Joo-Cheong Tham, 'The Continuing Futility of the Human Rights Act' [2008] 688 *PL* 670
162 Jonathan Lewis, 'The European Ceiling on Human Rights' [2007] *PL* 720

the appropriate relationship between Parliament and the courts and has led to the reassessment of the theoretical foundations of UK constitutional law.[163] Hunt argues that 'in today's conditions, both the courts and the political branches share a commitment *both* to representative democracy *and* to certain rights' and argues that the time has come to move away from conceptualizing public law in terms of competing sovereignties and formalistic concepts like the separation of powers.[164] Viewpoints such as Ewing and Tham's, based on an outdated concept of Diceyan constitutionalism are still present[165] and hamper attempts to conceptualize the relationship between domestic branches as a dialogue or cooperation.

The opinions of the public, the media and interested civil society groups can all have an impact on domestic institutions and decision-makers.[166] For example, Kavanagh has credited the work that the civil society organization JUSTICE has done in the UK in calling into question secret evidence.[167] However, public opinion can also have its negative impacts. Fenwick et al. suggest that a lack of popular support for the *HRA* may lead judges away from adopting an expansive approach to interpreting rights out of fear that it may be radically modified or repealed,[168] while Lester and Beattie have noted assaults on the Act by the tabloid press.[169] Ramraj notes that often a response to public fear is to 'respond legislatively to popular opinion, enacting strict anti-terrorism measures', which he sees as problematic because 'social forces amplify and distort our judgments about risk, particularly in emotionally charged situations'.[170] Indeed, emotionally charged situations such as emergencies and the climate of fear that attend them can also be seized upon by decision-makers in domestic political institutions. This book will detail and describe several legislative responses to terrorism in which proper parliamentary consideration of legislation and its impact has been foregone in the aftermath of significant terrorist attacks or events.

1.4 Chapter overview

The next chapter begins with a discussion of the impact of Resolution 1373 more specifically on Canada and the UK's post-9/11 counter-terrorism legislation.

163 *Kavanagh, Constitutional Review*, 415

164 *Hunt, Sovereignty*, 340. Wadham also argues that speaking of encroachment or politicization is also not as useful as the developing notion of dialogue, which he believes is the most helpful model to have in mind when evaluating the interaction between the branches under the *HRA*. See *Wadham, Blackstones*, para. 1.34

165 Campbell also argues that courts have taken a divergent role from what was previously understood as their proper role and has called them ill-equipped to do so: David Campbell, 'The Threat of Terror and the Plausibility of Positivism' [2009] *PL* 501

166 This is the subject of analyses in Chapter 6

167 *Kavanagh, Special Advocates*, 842

168 *Fenwick et al.*, 5

169 *Lester and Beattie,* 81

170 *Ramraj, Terrorism*, 107

Focus then turns to analysis of the historical evolution of Canada's post-9/11 measures, including a short description of measures that existed before 9/11 and a detailed analysis of the passage of key pieces of legislation, and significant developments in the form of scrutiny reports and judicial decisions. This historical background will prove useful for subsequent analyses in Chapters 3–6, which provide for a much more thorough and in-depth analysis of these developments. Moreover, more recent significant developments in Canada are discussed, including a recent ruling on the constitutionality of the security certificate regime,[171] the October 2014 terrorist attacks, and the legislation that was subsequently passed as a result of these attacks.[172] Focus then turns to analogous consideration of the UK, starting with its pre-9/11 experiences with terrorism and proceeding through the same analysis of its post-9/11 counter-terrorism legislation evolution. Several key events, cases and legislation are discussed, again with an eye towards subsequent analyses in Chapters 3–6. The chapter concludes by considering two recent significant developments in the UK, the enactment of the Justice and Security Act[173] and the Counter-Terrorism and Security Act.[174]

Chapter 3 (Legal structure) provides for a detailed analysis of the rights adjudication frameworks in each jurisdiction. The *Charter* is extensively discussed, as is the statutory basis for security certificates, in order to ground the reader in the necessary legal framework required to comprehend the subsequent case law analyses pertaining to the security certificate regime. In the second half of the chapter, analogous analyses occur for the UK, starting with an explanation of its rights adjudication framework under the *ECHR* and the *HRA*. The statutory basis for detention without trial/control order provisions is also laid out in order to prepare the reader for the subsequent case law analyses pertaining to those provisions.

Chapter 4 (Political structure) begins with a discussion of the potential impact of minority government instability in Canada, in particular looking at how this form of government has precluded proper study and review of, as well as amendments to, the post-9/11 legislation. Focus then turns to an area of Canada's political structure that is argued to be significantly lacking, its mechanisms for parliamentary and independent review and oversight of counter-terrorism activities. Reasons for, and the implications of, this lack of a crucial domestic scrutiny mechanism are provided. In the analogous UK analysis, the potential impact of the UK's coalition government on the control order and TPIMs legislation is analysed. The subsequent section notes a significant difference in the

171 *Canada (Citizenship and Immigration) v. Harkat* [2014] 2 S.C.R. 33

172 Anti-Terrorism Act, S.C. 2015, c. 20 [hereinafter "*ATA 2015*"]; Protection of Canada from Terrorists Act, S.C. 2015, c. 9 [hereinafter "*PCTA*"]

173 2013 c. 18 [hereinafter "*JSA*"]

174 2015 c. 6 [hereinafter "*CTSA*"]

wealth of mechanisms present in the UK for review and oversight of counter-terrorism activities, and analyses whether this aspect of the UK's political structure has had a tangible impact on legislative outcomes.

Chapter 5 (Legal culture) engages in extensive analyses of judicial decisions in the wider national security realm, outside of those decisions canvassed in Chapter 3. The use of secret evidence in other legal contexts, such as civil litigation, criminal prosecutions and terrorist listing is analysed and scrutinized, with key case law principles elucidated. Analyses focus on whether it can be said that the judiciary in either jurisdiction exhibits what might be called a 'rights culture', wherein decisions of the executive branch are rightly scrutinized and deference is earned by the elected branches rather than dispersed out as a result of some rigid conceptualization of the separation of powers. Consideration is also given to how, and to what extent, the courts in both jurisdictions have been influenced by outside sources, i.e. international instruments and judgments from other jurisdictions. These analyses aid the subsequent analyses in Chapter 6, which investigates whether a culture of rights can be said to exist throughout the jurisdictions more broadly. They also allow for consideration of how the existence of this rights culture (or lack thereof) has influenced the evolution of post-9/11 counter-terrorism measures.

Chapter 6 (Political culture) discusses societal attitudes towards human rights in both jurisdictions, noting a considerable difference in public levels of support for the *Charter* and the *HRA*. Reasons for, and implications of, this difference are analysed, towards a larger aim of arriving at a conclusion about whether or not a culture of rights exists in the two jurisdictions more broadly and what this means for the evolution of post-9/11 counter-terrorism measures. Moreover, the impact of the relationship with the US is analysed both with regard to Canada and the UK. While the close symbolic, geographic and economic ties between the US and Canada may seem evident, there have been recent events that have placed tensions on this relationship. The same can be said for the US/UK relationship, particularly with regard to the release of sensitive security intelligence information in UK courts. The impact of these events and tensions on the evolution of post-9/11 counter-terrorism measures in both jurisdictions is analysed.

Chapter 7 (Conclusions) ties together all of the analyses in previous chapters and uses them to reiterate the main argument of this book: that despite the force of international legal instruments such as UN Security Council Resolution 1373, the evolution of post-9/11 counter-terrorism policies in the two jurisdictions is best analysed and understood as a product of the institutional structures and cultures present in those jurisdictions. Put simply, while Resolution 1373 undoubtedly had an impact on how and when the *ATA* and *ATCSA* were implemented, it is the domestic legal and political structures and cultures in the two jurisdictions that have had the greatest impact on how counter-terrorism measures have since evolved. Once this point has been forcefully reiterated, the chapter connects the book's findings with a short discussion of its contribution to the field of comparative criminal justice and the cultural comparativist methodological tradition it situates itself in. The final conclusion then argues that some of the more recent counter-terrorism legislation in the two jurisdictions repeats the mistakes of the past and has not learned from lessons that should be kept in mind for the future, namely that: 1) counter-terrorism measures that are enacted in the direct aftermath of terrorist attacks and are subject to limited pre-legislative scrutiny will always prove to be problematic; 2) counter-terrorism mechanisms that operate outside of the normal criminal justice process, particularly immigration law measures and other mechanisms that utilize secret evidence, will continue to provide both logistical and philosophical challenges to the protection of fundamental due process and human rights, imposing a huge burden on the courts and those subjected to these measures; and 3) political instability or uncertainty should not preclude the appropriate and comprehensive consideration of legislation once it has been enacted.

Bibliography

Al-Khawaja v. United Kingdom, App No 26766/05 [2009] ECHR 11
Anti-Terrorism Act, S.C. 2001, c. 41
Anti-Terrorism Act, S.C. 2015, c. 20
Anti-Terrorism, Crime and Security Act 2001, c. 24
Ashworth, A. 'Security, Terrorism and the Value of Human Rights' in Goold, B. and Lazarus, L. (eds), *Security and Human Rights* (Hart Publishing, 2007)
Bell, J. 'Comparing Public Law' in Harding, A. and Örücü, E. (eds), *Comparative Law in the 21st Century* (Kluwer, 2002)
Bures, O. *EU Counterterrorism Policy* (Ashgate, 2011)
Campbell, D. 'The Threat of Terror and the Plausibility of Positivism' [2009] *PL* 501
Canada (Citizenship and Immigration) v. Harkat [2014] 2 S.C.R. 33
Canadian Charter of Rights and Freedoms, s.15, Part I of the *Constitution Act,* 1982
Commission of Inquiry into the Investigation of the Bombing of Air India Flight 182, *Air India Flight 182: A Canadian Tragedy* (Public Works and Government Services Canada, 2010)
Conley, R. 'Legislative Activity in the Canadian House of Commons: Does Majority or Minority Government Matter?' (2011) 41 *American Review of Canadian Studies* 422
Cortell, A. and Davis, J., Jr. 'How Do International Institutions Matter? The Domestic Impact of International Rules and Norms' (1996) 40 *International Studies Quarterly* 451
Cotterell, R. 'The Concept of Legal Culture' in Nelken, D. (ed), *Comparing Legal Cultures* (Dartmouth, 1997)
Counter-Terrorism and Security Act 2015, c. 6
Daniel, T. 'International Cooperation in Counteracting Terrorist Financing' in Van Den Herik, L. and Schrijver, N. (eds), *Counter-Terrorism Strategies in a Fragmented International Legal Order* (Cambridge University Press, 2013)
Dyzenhaus, D. *The Constitution of Law: Legality in a Time of Emergency* (Cambridge University Press, 2006)
Eckes, C. *EU Counter-Terrorist Policies and Fundamental Rights: The Case of Individual Sanctions* (Oxford University Press, 2009)
Ewing, K.D. and Tham, J.-C. 'The Continuing Futility of the Human Rights Act' [2008] *PL* 688

Feldman, D. 'The Impact of Human Rights on the UK Legislative Process' (2004) 25 *Stat LR* 91

—. 'Institutional Roles and Meanings of "Compatibility" under the Human Rights Act 1998' in Fenwick, H., Phillipson, G. and Masterman, R. (eds), *Judicial Reasoning under the UK Human Rights Act* (Cambridge University Press, 2007)

—. 'The Internationalization of Public Law and Its Impact on the United Kingdom' in Jowell, J. and Oliver, D. (eds), *The Changing Constitution* (6th edn, Oxford University Press, 2007)

Feldman, E. 'Patients' Rights, Citizens' Movements and Japanese Legal Culture' in Nelken, D. (ed), *Comparing Legal Cultures* (Darmouth, 1997)

Fenwick, H., Phillipson, G. and Masterman, R. 'The Human Rights Act in Contemporary Context' in Fenwick, H., Phillipson, G. and Masterman, R. (eds), *Judicial Reasoning under the UK Human Rights Act* (Cambridge University Press, 2007)

Feuerhach, A.V. 'Idee und Notwendigkeit Einer Universaljurisprudenz' [1931/32] *Harvard Law Review* 1027

Forcese, C. 'Fixing the Deficiencies of Parliament Review of Anti-Terrorism Law: Lessons from the United Kingdom and Australia' (2008) 14:4 *IRPP Choices* 2

—. *National Security Law: Canadian Practice in International Perspective* (Irwin Law, 2008)

—. 'A Distinction with a Legal Difference: The Consequences of Non-Citizenship in the War on Terror' in Edwards, A. and Ferstman, C. (eds), *Human Security and Non-Citizens: Law, Policy and International Affairs* (Cambridge University Press, 2010)

Forcese, C. and Crepeau, F. (eds), *Terrorism, Law and Democracy: 10 Years After 9/11* (Canadian Institute for the Administration of Justice, Montreal, 2012)

Forcese, C. and Roach, K. *False Security: The Radicalization of Canadian Anti-Terrorism* (Irwin Law, 2015)

Fredman, S. 'From Deference to Democracy: The Role of Equality under the Human Rights Act 1998' (2006) 122 *LQR* 53

Friedman, L. 'The Concept of Legal Culture: A Reply' in Nelken, D. (ed), *Comparing Legal Cultures* (Aldershot, 1997) 33

Gordley, J. 'Comparative Legal Research: Its Function in the Development of Harmonized Law' (1995) 43 *American Journal of Comparative Law* 555

Handyside v. UK, App No 5493/72 [1976] ECHR 5

Home Office. *Table of Measures*, 2013, House of Lords European Union Committee, *5th Report of Session 2013–14: Follow-Up Report on EU Police and Criminal Justice Measures: The UK's 2014 Opt-Out Decision* (2013–14 HL Paper 69)

Hug, W. 'The History of Comparative Law' [1931/32] XLV *Harvard L Rev* 1027

Human Rights Act (1998), c. 42

Hunt, M. 'Sovereignty's Blight: Why Contemporary Public Law Needs the Concept of "Due Deference"' in Bamforth, N. and Leyland, P. (eds), *Public Law in a Multi-Layered Constitution* (Hart Publishing, 2003)

Immigration and Refugee Protection Act S.C. 2001, c. 27

Joint Committee on Human Rights, *A Bill of Rights for the UK?* (HC 150–1, 2008)

Justice and Security Act 2013, c. 18

Kavanagh, A. 'Constitutional Review, the Courts, and Democratic Scepticism' (2009) 62 *CLP* 102

___. *Constitutional Review under the U.K. Human Rights Act* (Cambridge University Press, 2009)
—. 'Judging the Judges under the Human Rights Act: Deference, Disillusionment and the War on Terror' [2009] *PL* 287
—. 'Special Advocates, Control Orders and the Right to a Fair Trial' (2010) 73 *MLR* 824
King, J.A. 'Institutional Approaches to Judicial Restraint' (2008) 28 *Oxford Journal of Legal Studies* 409
Knill, C. and Lehmkuhl, D. 'Private Actors and the State: Internationalization and Changing Patterns of Governance' (2002) 5 *Governance* 41
Lacey, N. 'Political Systems and Criminal Justice: The Prisoners' Dilemma after the Coalition' [2012] *CLP* 1
Laviolette, N. and Forcese, C. (eds), *The Human Rights of Antiterrorism* (Irwin Law, 2008)
Lazarus, L. *Contrasting Prisoner's Rights: A Comparative Examination of Germany and England* (Oxford University Press, 2004)
Legrand, P. 'How to Compare Now' (1996) 16 *Journal of Legal Studies* 232
—. 'John Merryman and Comparative Legal Studies: A Dialogue' (1999) 27 *American Journal of Comparative Law* 50
—. 'Comparative Legal Studies and the Matter of Authenticity' (2006) 1 *Journal of Comparative Legal Studies* 365
Lester, L. and Beattie, K. 'Human Rights and the British Constitution' in Jowell, J. and Oliver, D. (eds), *The Changing Constitution* (6th edn, Oxford University Press, 2007)
Lewis, J. 'The European Ceiling on Human Rights' [2007] *PL* 720
Murphy, C. *EU Counter-Terrorism Law* (Hart, 2013)
Nelken, D. 'Puzzling out Legal Culture: A Comment on Blankenburg' in Nelken, D. (ed), *Comparing Legal Cultures* (Darmouth, 1997)
—. *Comparative Criminal Justice: Making Sense of Difference* (Sage Publications, 2010)
—. *Comparative Criminal Justice and Globalization* (Ashgate, 2011)
Oliver, D. *Constitutional Reform in the UK* (Oxford University Press, 2003)
Örücü, E. 'Untie Venit, Quo Tendit Comparative Law?' in Harding, A. and Örücü, E. (eds), *Comparative Law in the 21st Century* (Kluwer, 2002)
Peers, S. *EU Justice and Home Affairs* (3rd edn, Oxford University Press, 2010)
Powell, C. 'Defining Terrorism: How and Why' in LaViolette, N. and Forcese, C. (eds), *The Human Rights of Antiterrorism* (Irwin Law, 2008) 138
Protection of Canada from Terrorists Act, S.C. 2015, c. 9
Puchalska-Tych, B. and Salter, M. 'Comparing Legal Cultures of Eastern Europe: The Need for a Dialectical Analysis' (1996) 16 *Legal Studies* 157
R v. Horncastle [2009] UKSC 14
Ramraj, V.V. 'Terrorism, Risk Perception and Judicial Review' in Ramraj, V.V., Roach, K. and Hor, M.Y.M. (eds), *Global Anti-Terrorism Law and Policy* (Cambridge University Press, 2005)
Roach, K. 'Must We Trade Rights for Security? The Choice between Smart, Harsh, or Proportionate Security Strategies in Canada and Britain' (2006) 27 *Cardozo Law Review* 2151
—. 'Sources and Trends in Post-9/11 Anti-Terrorism Laws' in Goold, B. and Lazarus, L. (eds), *Security and Human Rights* (Hart Publishing, 2007) 227

—. 'Secret Evidence and Its Alternatives' in Masferrer, A. (ed), *Post-9/11 and the State of Permanent Legal Emergency: Security and Human Rights in Countering Terrorism* (Springer, 2011) 179

—. *The 9/11 Effect: Comparative Counter-Terrorism* (Cambridge University Press, 2011)

—. 'A Comparative Assessment of Canadian Counter-Terrorism Laws and Practices' in Forcese, C. and Crepeau, F. (eds), *Terrorism, Law and Democracy: 10 Years After 9/11* (Canadian Institute for the Administration of Justice, Montreal, 2012) 65

—. 'Counter-Terrorism in and outside Canada and in and outside the Anti-Terrorism Act' (2012) 6 *Review of Constitutional Studies* 243

—. 'Uneasy Neighbours: Comparative American and Canadian Counter-Terrorism' (2012) 38 *William Mitchell Law Review* 1701

—. 'Substitute Justice? Challenges to American Counter-Terrorism Activities in Non-American Courts' (2013) 82 *Mississippi Law Journal* 907

Ryder, N. *The Financial War on Terrorism: A Review of Counter-Terrorist Financing Strategies Since 2001* (Routledge, 2015)

Secretary of State for the Home Department v. AF (No 3) [2009] UKHL 28

Special Senate Committee on the Anti-Terrorism Act, *Fundamental Justice in Extraordinary Times: Main Report of the Special Senate Committee on the Anti-Terrorism Act* (Public Works and Government Services Canada, February 2007)

Standing Committee on Public Safety and National Security, *Review of the Findings and Recommendations Arising from the Iacobucci and O'Connor Inquiries* (Public Works and Government Services Canada, June 2009)

Subcommittee on the Review of the Anti Terrorism Act, *Rights, Limits, Security: A Comprehensive Review of the Anti-Terrorism Act and Related Issues* (Public Works and Government Services Canada, 2007)

The Honourable Frank Iacobucci QC LLD, *Internal Inquiry into the Actions of Canadian Officials in Relation to Abdullah Almalki, Ahmad Abou-Elmaati and Muayyed Nureddin* (Public Works and Government Services Canada, 2008)

Tomkins, A. 'National Security and the Role of the Court: A Changed Landscape?' (2010) 126 *LQR* 543

___. 'Parliament, Human Rights and Counter-Terrorism' in Tomkins, A., Ewing, K.D. and Campbell, T. (eds), *The Legal Protection of Human Rights: Skeptical Essays* (Oxford University Press, 2011)

Turpin, C. and Tomkins, A. *British Government and the Constitution* (6th edn, Cambridge University Press, 2007)

UK Bill of Rights Commission, *A UK Bill of Rights? The Choice before Us* (December 2012, Vol 1)

UN General Assembly, *International Convention for the Suppression of the Financing of Terrorism*, 9 December 1999, No. 38349, available at: http://www.un.org/law/cod/finterr.htm [accessed 20 January 2012]

United Kingdom Parliament Website, 'Joint Select Committee on Human Rights' available at: http://www.parliament.uk/business/committees/committees-a-z/joint-select/human-rights-committee [accessed 28 August 2011]

UN Security Council, *Security Council resolution 1267 (1999) [Afghanistan]*, 15 October 1999, S/RES/1267 (1999), available at: http://www.un.org/ga/search/view_doc.asp?symbol=S/RES/1267(1999) [accessed 20 January 2012]

UN Security Council, *Security Council resolution 1333 (2000) [Afghanistan]*, 19 December 2000, S/RES/1333(2000), available at: http://www.un.org/ga/search/view_doc.asp?symbol=S/RES/1333%282000%29 [accessed 3 April 2017]

UN Security Council, *Security Council resolution 1373 (2001) [on threats to international peace and security caused by terrorist acts]*, 28 September 2001, S/RES/1373 (2001)

Van Den Herik, L. and Schrijver, N. 'The Fragmented International Legal Response to Terrorism' in Van Den Herik, L. and Schrijver, N. (eds), *Counter-Terrorism Strategies in a Fragmented International Legal Order* (Cambridge University Press, 2013)

Wadham, J. (ed) *Blackstone's Guide to the Human Rights Act 1998* (5th edn, Oxford University Press, 2009)

Walker, C. 'Terrorism and Criminal Justice: Past, Present and Future' [2004] *Criminal Law Review* 311

—. 'Keeping Control of Terrorists without Losing Control of Constitutionalism' (2007) 59 *Stanford Law Review* 1395

___. *Blackstone's Guide to the Anti-Terrorism Legislation* (2nd edn, Oxford University Press, 2009)

Zedner, L. 'Securing Liberty in the Face of Terror: Reflections from Criminal Justice' (2005) 32 *Journal of Law and Society* 507

—. 'Pre-Crime and Post-Criminology?' (2007) 11 *Theoretical Criminology* 261

—. 'Preventive Justice or Pre-Punishment?' (2007) 60 *CLP* 174

___. 'Seeking Security by Eroding Rights, the Side-Stepping of Due Process' in Goold, B. and Lazarus, L. (eds), *Security and Human Rights* (Hart Publishing, 2007)

Zweigert, K. and Kötz, H. *An Introduction to Comparative Law* (Weir, T. tr, 3rd rev edn, Oxford University Press, 1998)

2 Post-9/11 counter-terrorism measures in Canada and the United Kingdom

It has been argued that '9/11 produced a horrible natural experiment that allows us to compare how international institutions and different countries responded . . . All countries responded in a manner that reflected their own particular histories and legal, political and social cultures'.[1] This chapter begins by discussing perspectives on the impact of UN Security Council Resolution 1373,[2] with a particular eye towards its impact on Canada and the UK. It then proceeds to give a brief history of the evolution of Canada and the UK's post-9/11 counter-terrorism measures, most specifically security certificates, bail with recognizance and investigative hearings in Canada, detention without trial, control orders and TPIMs in the UK, and measures to counter-terrorist financing in both jurisdictions. By noting the key judicial decisions, parliamentary committee reports, legislative amendments and public bill committee debates, this historical analysis paves the way for analysis in subsequent chapters pertaining to how this evolution has occurred in accordance with domestic structures and cultures. Both sections on each respective jurisdiction conclude with a discussion of more recent significant developments. In particular, both jurisdictions have had changes to their government types in recent years and, as such, a discussion of general election results is necessary. Perhaps more significantly, both jurisdictions have passed sprawling and problematic legislation in recent years. This recent legislation and its problematic aspects will be laid out with an eye towards analyses in subsequent chapters.

2.1 The impact of Security Council Resolution 1373

Much of the literature pertaining to post-9/11 counter-terrorism legislation discusses the impact of the UN Security Council on the domestic responses to the

1 Kent Roach, *The 9/11 Effect: Comparative Counter-Terrorism* (Cambridge University Press, 2011) [hereinafter "*Roach, 9/11 Effect*"] 15

2 UN Security Council, *Security Council resolution 1373 (2001) [on threats to international peace and security caused by terrorist acts]*, 28 September 2001, S/RES/1373 (2001) available at: https://www.unodc.org/pdf/crime/terrorism/res_1373_english.pdf [accessed 20 October 2010] [hereinafter "*Resolution 1373*"]

attacks on 11 September 2001. As Forcese notes, 'By virtue of Chapter VII of the UN Charter, the UN Security Council is easily the most potent of the world's international organizations'.[3] Powell laments the fact that the Security Council can, and has, exercised 'untrammelled power in a manner which would be unthinkable in a domestic constitutional system subject to the rule of law'.[4] Roach further argues that 'Although the UN had selectively engaged terrorism issues before 9/11, the role of the Security Council in leading global counter-terrorism efforts after 9/11 was unprecedented'.[5] Academic attention and concern has focused on a number of post-9/11 Security Council resolutions, but it has been argued that *Resolution 1373* has been the most forceful and problematic, both in terms of the speed with which it passed and was responded to by states, and also in terms of its silence regarding the respect of human rights obligations.[6] *Resolution 1373* called upon states to act in a number of ways, including: to take measures to prevent and criminalize the financing of terrorist acts;[7] to deny safe haven to terrorists and prevent them from using states' territories for terrorist purposes;[8] to assist other states in their investigations or criminal proceedings against states;[9] to prevent the movement of terrorists through effective border controls and to ensure that they do not abuse refugee status;[10] and, finally, to report within 90 days on the steps they had taken to the Counter-Terrorism Committee established by the Resolution.[11]

Roach explains that it took all of five minutes for the Resolution to be unanimously approved by all 15 members of the Security Council, leading to the creation of a Counter Terrorism Committee (CTC) to monitor the implementation of the legally binding instrument which enforced a 90-day deadline for states to report on measures they had implemented.[12] With regard to terrorist financing,

3 Craig Forcese, *National Security Law: Canadian Practice in International Perspective* (Irwin Law, 2008) [hereainafter "*Forcese, National Security Law*"] 59
4 Cathleen Powell, 'Defining Terrorism: How and Why,' in LaViolette, N. and Forcese, C. (eds), *The Human Rights of Antiterrorism* (Irwin Law, 2008) 138
5 *Roach, 9/11 Effect*, 35
6 *Resolution 1373*, s. 3(f) is the only section in the Resolution that mentions human rights: 'Take appropriate measures in conformity with the relevant provisions of national and international law, including international standards of human rights, before granting refugee status, for the purpose of ensuring that the asylum-seeker has not planned, facilitated or participated in the commission of terrorist acts'. The speed with which the Resolution was passed and its human rights implications are discussed further below
7 Ibid, ss. 1(a)–(d)
8 Ibid, ss. 2(d)–(e)
9 Ibid, ss. 2(f), 3(a)–(c)
10 Ibid, ss. 2(g) and 3(g), respectively
11 Ibid, s. 6
12 Kent Roach, 'Sources and Trends in Post-9/11 Anti-Terrorism Laws' in Goold, B. and Lazarus, L. (eds), *Security and Human Rights* (Hart Publishing, 2007) [hereinafter "*Roach, Sources and Trends*"] 230–1. As discussed below, Roach argues that both Canada and the UK treated this reporting requirement as a virtual deadline

several authors have noted that *Resolution 1373* strongly reinforced pre-9/11 international instruments aimed at tackling terrorist financing.[13] Ryder has called *Resolution 1373* 'the cornerstone of the financial war on terrorism'.[14] Daniel has reinforced this argument by pointing to the number of states that signed up to, and ratified, the *1999 Convention* as a result of the compulsion created by *Resolution 1373* and the Counter-Terrorism Committee.[15] He notes that only four states had ratified the *1999 Convention* prior to 9/11 and *Resolution 1373*, while 90 countries signed up to the Convention and an additional 13 ratified subsequent to *Resolution 1373* in the period between 9/11 and 19 February 2002.[16] Arguing that *Resolution 1373* was the Security Council 'heavily reinvesting in attempts to stop terrorism through criminalizing terrorism financing',[17] Roach also makes the same connection between the force of *Resolution 1373* and the post-9/11 signing and ratification of the *1999 Convention.*[18]

Furthermore, a number of authors have commented on *Resolution 1373*'s relative silence on the issue of protecting due process and human rights. As noted above, *Resolution 1373* contained a singular provision that made mention of the protection of due process and human rights. Forcese argues that a lack of a concrete definition of terrorism in the Resolution has led to various concerns about the human rights impact of domestic legislation implemented to accord with obligations under the Resolution:

> The impact of the Security Council's post-9/11counterterrorism activities on human rights has attracted particular attention. As noted, Resolution 1373 mandated significant state actions to suppress terrorism, but failed to define the concept. In the wake of this failure, human rights groups noted that some states cited their UN anti-terrorism obligations to justify abusive policies and practices.[19]

13 In particular, Security Council Resolutions 1267 and 1333, and the 1999 UN Convention for the Suppression of the Financing of Terrorism: UN Security Council, *Security Council resolution 1267 (1999) [Afghanistan]*, 15 October 1999, S/RES/1267 (1999) [hereinafter "*Resolution 1267*"]; UN Security Council, *Security Council resolution 1333 (2000) [Afghanistan]*, 19 December 2000, S/RES/1333(2000) [hereinafter "*Resolution 1333*"]; UN General Assembly, *International Convention for the Suppression of the Financing of Terrorism,* 9 December 1999, No. 38349 [hereinafter "*1999 Convention*"]

14 Nicholas Ryder, *The Financial War on Terrorism: A Review of Counter-Terrorist Financing Strategies Since 2001* (Routledge, 2015) [hereinafter "*Ryder, Financial War on Terrorism*"] 58

15 Tim Daniel, 'International Cooperation in Counteracting Terrorist Financing' in Van Den Herik, L. and Schrijver, N. (eds), *Counter-Terrorism Strategies in a Fragmented International Legal Order* (Cambridge University Press, 2013) 240 [hereinafter "*Daniel, International Cooperation*"] 248

16 Ibid

17 *Roach, 9/11 Effect,* 1

18 Ibid, 34

19 *Forcese, National Security Law,* 250

Walker also argues that in the UK the resolution has been used to justify derogation from fundamental human rights.[20] Moreover, Roach notes that 'The Security Council and its CTC did not concern itself with human rights in the first few years after 9/11'.[21] Further human rights concerns arise specific to the terrorist financing context, as enforcement of several laws to combat this aspect of terrorist activity depend on listings made up by the UN Security Council Committee created by *Resolution 1267*.[22] Roach notes that these lists (as well as corresponding domestic lists) can inherently lead to the violation of fair trial norms, to the extent that their compilation is based on secret evidence or intelligence which is not made available for challenge by those who are listed.[23] As such, the impact of *Resolution 1373* has not just been felt with regard to the volume of legislation it has prompted, but also with regard to the substance of this legislation (notably, a lack of concern with due process and human rights that parallels the relative silence on these issues within the Resolution).

Like many other countries, Canada and the UK responded swiftly and comprehensively to *Resolution 1373*, treating the 90-day reporting requirement as a 'virtual deadline for the enactment of new legislation'.[24] Forcese notes that Canada already had in place various criminal law provisions to deal with terrorism, but argues that the Canadian Government nevertheless proceeded 'rapidly to create a significant new anti-terrorism criminal law architecture'.[25] The specific content of Bill C-36, Canada's 2001 *Anti-Terrorism Act* (*ATA*)[26] is discussed further below, but it is nonetheless important to note that the Canadian Government specifically characterized the *ATA* as responsive to *Resolution 1373* in its reporting to the CTC.[27] Forcese argues that the *ATA*, which made consequential amendments to a number of other pieces of Canadian legislation, including the *Canada Evidence Act* (*CEA*)[28] and the *Immigration and Refugee Protection Act* (*IRPA*),[29] is unique in that it is the only 'Canadian statutory provision enacted specifically to comply with Security Council instructions,

20 Clive Walker, 'Terrorism and Criminal Justice: Past, Present and Future' [2004] *Criminal Law Review* 311

21 Kent Roach, 'A Comparative Assessment of Canadian Counter-Terrorism Laws and Practices' in Forcese, C. and Crepeau, F. (eds), *Terrorism, Law and Democracy: 10 Years after 9/11* (Canadian Institute for the Administration of Justice, Montreal, 2012) [hereinafter "*Roach, Comparative Assessment*"] 69

22 Commonly referred to as the '1267 Committee'. For a further discussion of the establishment of this committee, see *Daniel, International Cooperation*, 258. Also, see the Committee's website, available at: https://www.un.org/sc/suborg/en/sanctions/1267

23 *Roach, 9/11 Effect*, 39

24 Ibid, 35

25 *Forcese, National Security Law*, 256

26 S.C. 2001, c. 41 [hereinafter "*ATA*"]

27 *Forcese, National Security Law*, 262

28 R.S.C., 1985, C-5 [hereinafter "*CEA*"]

29 S.C. 2001, c. 27 [hereinafter "*IRPA*"]

a fact that reflects the unusual scope of Resolution 1373'.[30] Furthermore, Macklin has argued that 'The *ATA* signalled Canada's solidarity and compliance' with *Resolution 1373*.[31]

Like Canada, the UK responded to *Resolution 1373* and the 90-day reporting requirement, despite having a wealth of counter-terrorism legislation on the statue books. As Bonner notes, 'When the United Kingdom government responded with new legislation, it was marching in the "war on terrorism" to the beat of drums other than the purely national'.[32] Roach further emphasizes the wealth of counter-terrorism laws that existed in UK law prior to 9/11, including a very modern and broad law in the form of the *Terrorism Act* 2000,[33] to place the UK's legislative response subsequent to 9/11 and *Resolution 1373* in context.[34] That legislative response came in the form of the *Anti-Terrorism, Crime and Security Act* 2001 (*ATCSA*),[35] described by Roach as a 'massive' set of legislation that was passed in an extraordinarily short period of time.[36] The *ATCSA*, which is further discussed below, required derogation from the European Convention on Human Rights under Article 15 of that convention. This was to allow for indeterminate detention of non-nationals suspected of terrorism who could not be deported because of concerns that they would be tortured in their country of origin. Roach argues that this aspect of the *ATCSA* was a direct response to *Resolution 1373*'s requirement for countries to ensure that refugee status would not be abused by terrorists.[37] It has been argued that this requirement has led several countries, including Canada and the UK, to rely on limited tools of immigration law as a response to international terrorism.[38] Forcese has criticized the use of immigration law because this often permits 'the government in question to act without the full panoply of right protections and oversight required for citizens'.[39] Furthermore, Roach notes that:

30 *Forcese, National Security Law*, 263

31 Audrey Macklin, 'Stuck at the Border: Ten Years After 9/11' in Forcese, C. and Crepeau, F. (eds), *Terrorism, Law and Democracy: 10 Years after 9/11* (Canadian Institute for the Administration of Justice, Montreal, 2012) [hereinafter "*Macklin, Stuck at the Border*"] 263

32 David Bonner, *Executive Measures, Terrorism and National Security* (Ashgate, 2007) [hereinafter "*Bonner, Executive Measures*"] 208

33 C. 11

34 *Roach, 9/11 Effect*, 277

35 C. 24 [hereinafter "*ATCSA*"]

36 *Roach, 9/11 Effect*, 277: The legislation was introduced into Parliament in November of 2001 and became law less than a month later. It was subject to only 16 hours of debate in the House of Commons, and only eight days of debate in the House of Lords.

37 *Roach, 9/11 Effect*, 255

38 Kent Roach, 'Sources and Trends in Post-9/11 Anti-Terrorism Laws' in Goold, B. and Lazarus, L. (eds), *Security and Human Rights* (Hart Publishing, 2007) [hereinafter "*Roach, Sources and Trends*"] 2.39

39 Craig Forcese, 'A Distinction with a Legal Difference: The Consequences of Non-Citizenship in the War on Terror' in Edwards, A. and Ferstman, C. (eds), *Human Security and Non-Citizens: Law, Policy and International Affairs* (Cambridge University Press, 2010) 422.

> Security certificates were part of a post-9/11 global erosion in confidence in the criminal law as a means of responding to terrorism . . . These alternatives to the criminal law respect rights including rights to an impartial jury less than the criminal law.[40]

This reliance on immigration law and measures outside of the ordinary criminal law is another example of how *Resolution 1373* has impacted not just the volume but also the substance of post-9/11 counter-terrorism legislation.

Resolution 1373 had a substantial impact on the post-9/11 legislation adopted by Canada and the UK. Although both countries had experience of terrorism and legislation that pre-dated 9/11, both felt the need to enact sweeping legislation to comply with the Resolution and the CTC's 90-day reporting requirement that many states, including Canada and the UK, treated as a deadline for the passage of legislation. Canada and the UK's post-9/11 legislative responses have since evolved, as they have been subjected to judicial and political scrutiny, in a manner that reflects the legal and political structures and cultures of both countries. Before this book turns its focus to analysing the impact of these structures and cultures in subsequent chapters, it is necessary to provide a brief history of the evolution of these post-9/11 legislative responses over the course of more than a decade.

2.2 Historical evolution of Canada's post-9/11 measures

2.2.1 Pre-9/11 experiences with terrorism

Although it certainly cannot be said that Canada had the same extensive experience with terrorism prior to 9/11 that had occurred in the UK, it would be a mistake to assume that Canadian history was devoid of experiences of terrorism during this time (or even prior to the October 2014 terrorist attacks in Ottawa). Using a database compiled by the Canadian Network for Research on Terrorism, Security and Society (TSAS),[41] Forcese and Roach note that there have been 1,405 terrorist or extremist incidents and 469 deaths in Canada during the period stemming from 1960 to 2014, with the latter figure including what was the largest mass murder in Canadian history, the Air India Flight 182 bombing that led to 329 deaths.[42] The Air India Flight 182 bombing represents the most significant loss of Canadian

Forcese gives an extensive and detailed account of how 'fair trial guarantees have been relaxed in national security-related immigration proceedings relative to what would be required of governments of criminal proceedings'

40 *Roach, Comparative Assessment,* 85

41 For more information about the extensive work facilitated by this network, see http://www.tsas.ca/ [accessed 3 April 2017]

42 Craig Forcese and Kent Roach, *False Security: The Radicalization of Canadian Anti-Terrorism* (Irwin Law, 2015) [hereinafter "*Forcese and Roach, False Security*"] 22

life to occur as the result of terrorist activity, but it does not stand alone in its significance in the hierarchy of Canada's pre-9/11 experiences with terrorism. The 'October Crisis', which refers to a period of separatist terrorism in Canada that required the controversial invocation of the *War Measures Act*[43] in Canada has been described as a 'legendary event in Canadian history'.[44] Forcese and Roach note that prior to 9/11, the most common act committed by 'separatist' organizations (including, most famously, the Front de Libération du Québec, or FLQ) was the bombing of English-language symbols and federal institutions in Quebec, which resulted in 5 deaths and 144 injuries.[45] The most famous of these activities was the kidnapping by the FLQ of a British trade commissioner (James Cross) and a Quebec Government minister (Pierre Laporte). Laporte was subsequently murdered by the kidnappers, while negotiations eventually led to Cross's release.[46]

The significance of these two pre-9/11 experiences with terrorism in Canada cannot be understated, particularly because of what Forcese and Roach argue are over-reactions and under-reactions that occurred in response to them, which have some parallels with modern-day counter-terrorism measures in Canada.[47] Clement extensively details the human rights abuses that were authorized across Canada as a result of the invocation of the *War Measures Act*, noting that within hours police had conducted over 3,000 searches and detained 497people, with many detained for up to 21 days without access to legal counsel.[48] Furthermore, it has been argued that the October Crisis had important after-effects on what are now important aspects of Canada's legal structure and anti-terrorism framework, including the *Canadian Charter of Rights and Freedoms*,[49] the Royal Canadian Mounted Police (RCMP) and the Canadian Security and Intelligence Service (CSIS).[50] Relatedly, the Air India Flight 182 bombing has been an extensively studied event in Canadian history and is the subject of a significant public inquiry.[51]

43 R.S.C. 1970, c. W-2

44 Dominique Clement, 'The October Crisis of 1970: Human Rights Abuses Under the War Measures Act' (2008) 42 *Journal of Canadian Studies* 160 [hereinafter "*Clement, October Crisis*"] 161

45 *Forcese and Roach, False Security*, 26

46 *Clement, October Crisis*, 175

47 *Forcese and Roach, False Security*, 25–54: Forcese and Roach provide a detailed account of the over-reaction to the October Crisis, with particular emphasis on the invocation of the *War Measures Act* and its parallels to more modern-day counter-terrorism legislation. Similarly, they describe the reaction to the Air India Flight 182 bombing as an under-reaction, pointing to limitations in intelligence oversight structures that still exist in Canada today

48 *Clement, October Crisis*, 167

49 *The Canadian Charter of Rights and Freedoms*, Part I of the Constitution Act 1982, Being Schedule B to the Canada Act 1982 (UK), 1982, c. 11 [hereinafter "*Charter*"]

50 *Roach and Forcese, False Security*, 38–44

51 Commission of Inquiry into the Investigation of the bombing of Air India Flight 182, *Air India Flight 182: A Canadian Tragedy* (Public Works and Government Services Canada, 2010) available at: http://publications.gc.ca/site/eng/371132/publication.html [accessed

Despite the exhaustive work engaged in by this Commission, Forcese and Roach lament that a considerable amount of reform related to lessons that should have been learned from the Air India Flight 182 bombing remains unfinished today, particularly with regard to the collection and distribution of intelligence with the aim of preventing similar attacks in the future.[52]

2.2.2 Post-9/11: immediate aftermath of the attacks and the Anti-Terrorism Act

The Canadian House of Commons Subcommittee on the Review of the Anti-Terrorism Act has characterized the mood of the immediate aftermath of 9/11 by stating that:

> In the immediate aftermath of the worldwide shock of these extraordinary events, legislative and other steps were taken by the international community and by many countries. These initiatives were taken at a time when the full impact and consequences of these terrorist attacks were not clear.[53]

It was in this context that Bill C-36, also known as Canada's *Anti-Terrorism Act* (or *ATA*) was introduced. Within less than three months, the Act had been passed, changing aspects of Canada's Criminal Code, including controversial new provisions allowing for investigative hearings and bail with recognizance, as well as amending aspects of the *Proceeds of Crime (Money Laundering) and Terrorism Financing Act (PCMLTFA)*[54] and creating the *Charities Registration (Security Information) Act (CRSIA)*.[55] Concerns were voiced that the investigative hearing and bail with recognizance powers could lead to a variety of abuses, including racial profiling and undue restrictions on personal liberty.[56] As a result, the provisions were equipped with a sunset clause that would see them expire unless extended by a motion of Parliament. The sunset clause, found in section

2 October 2010]. An important part of the Commission's work was its commissioning of 15 research papers completed by leading Canadian academics, which were published in four volumes in the Final Report's Research Studies Section: *Canada, Commission of Inquiry into the Investigation of the Bombing of Air India Flight 182*, Research Studies, vols 1–4 (Canadian Government Publishing, 2010)

52 *Roach and Forcese, False Security*, 54

53 Subcommittee on the Review of the Anti-Terrorism Act, *Review of the Anti-Terrorism Act Investigative Hearings and Recognizance with Conditions: Interim Report of the Standing Committee on Public Safety and National Security* (Standing Committee on Public Safety and National Security, October 2006) [hereinafter "*House Interim Report*"] 1

54 The *ATA* amended this act and changed its name to the *Proceeds of Crime (Money Laundering) and Terrorist Financing Act*, S.C. 2000, c. 17 [hereinafter "*PCMLTFA*"]

55 S.C. 2001, c. 41, s. 113 [hereinafter "*CRSIA*"]

56 Ronald Daniels, Patrick Macklem and Kent Roach (eds), *The Security of Freedom: Essays on Canada's Anti-Terrorism Bill* (University of Toronto Press, 2001)

83.32 of the Criminal Code, applied to no other part of the Act, despite the recommendation of a Special Senate Committee which suggested that 'The entire Act be sunsetted, in other words be subject to expiry on a future date and renewed or re-enacted if it was determined to be justified'.[57] However, this recommendation was never acted upon and the rest of the Act, including the changes to various measures aimed at countering terrorist financing, passed without a sunset clause.

Canadian academics have voiced concern regarding the new powers created by the *ATA*. In *The Security of Freedom: Essays on Canada's Anti-Terrorism Bill*, a direct response to, and commentary on, the *ATA*, Martin Friedland noted:

> A person can be arrested if the peace officer 'suspects on reasonable grounds that the detention of the person in custody is necessary in order to prevent the commission of an indictable offence, where the act or omission constituting the offence also constitutes a terrorist activity' . . . This is arrest on a reasonable suspicion, not on a reasonable belief. Is this acceptable?[58]

Mariana Valverde expressed a similar concern, stating that 'We are seeing not only worrying moves in the governance of security but also moves that amount to "governing through security"'.[59] Moreover, concerns have been raised pertaining to changes made by the *ATA* to Canada's framework for countering terrorism financing. Roach has noted that the newly created *CRSIA* can lead to a charity being stripped of their charitable status on the basis of secret evidence that may not be disclosed to the applicant.[60] Anand has noted that the changes to the Criminal Code, *PCMLTFA* and the *CRSIA* can be seen as a significant regulatory expansion that accords with the requirements of *Resolution 1267* and the *1999 Convention* that were re-enforced by *Resolution 1373*, albeit with significant questions about effectiveness.[61] The concern surrounding these measures and discussions of their problematic aspects continued for many years after 9/11.

57 Special Senate Committee on the Anti-Terrorism Act, *Fundamental Justice in Extraordinary Times: Main Report of the Special Senate Committee on the Anti-Terrorism Act* (Special Senate Committee on the Anti-Terrorism Act, February 2007) [hereinafter "*Senate Main Report*"] 114

58 Martin Friedland, 'Police Powers in Bill C-36' in Daniels, R., Macklem, P. and Roach, K. (eds), *The Security of Freedom: Essays on Canada's Anti-Terrorism Bill* (University of Toronto Press, 2001) 279

59 Marianna Valverde, 'Governing Security, Governing through Security' in Daniels, R., Macklem, P. and Roach, K. (eds), *The Security of Freedom: Essays on Canada's Anti-Terrorism Bill* (University of Toronto Press, 2001) 89

60 Kent Roach, 'The Air India Report and the Regulation of Charities and Terrorism Financing' (2011) 61 *University of Toronto Law Journal* 45

61 Anita Anand, 'Combating Terrorist Financing: Is Canada's Legal Regime Effective?' (2011) 61 *University of Toronto Law Journal* 59

2.2.3 Bail with recognizance provisions undergo parliamentary scrutiny

On 4 December 2004, a House of Commons motion authorized a Standing Committee on Justice, Human Rights, Public Safety and Emergency Preparedness to review the *ATA*. Out of this motion, the Subcommittee on Public Safety and National Security was born, beginning its review in February 2005. On 13 December 2004, the Senate adopted a similar motion to review the *ATA* and a Special Senate Committee was formed shortly after to undertake a separate review. These committees began holding hearings during the corresponding 38th sitting of Parliament and, in November 2005, proposed a specific National Security Committee of Parliamentarians (Bill C-81),[62] heeding a call by many to have an expert group of parliamentarians that could review national security activities, provisions and issues. Unfortunately, on 30 November 2005, Parliament was dissolved. As a result, Bill C-81 died on the Order Paper before becoming legislation and the work of the Committees was subsequently put on hold. With the 39th sitting of Parliament came the revival of the work of both the Senate and House Committees. By 23 October 2006 the House Subcommittee had released an interim version of its report, dealing exclusively with the sunset provisions.[63] It suggested that both investigative hearing and recognizance with conditions provisions be extended until 31 December 2011 (Recommendations one and two), stating that 'Canada has had only five years' experience with these two measures. This has not been a long enough period of time to fully assess their necessity and effectiveness'[64] The *House Interim Report* also recommended that any further extension of the provisions be 'subject to a prior comprehensive parliamentary review of the provisions and the operations of these measures'.[65]

The *Special Senate Committee Main Report*, released in the context of an ongoing challenge to the constitutionality of Canada's security certificate regime, clearly exhibited a strong commitment towards the study of Canada's entire anti-terrorism package. The report still contained a chapter dedicated specifically to the investigative hearing and bail with recognizance provisions, but also contained lengthy discussions about other problematic aspects of Canada's anti-terrorism response, including issues with detention and deportation under security certificates and chapters pertaining to counter-terrorist financing.[66] With regard

62 Bill C-81, An Act to Establish the National Security Committee of Parliamentarians, November 24, 2005 [hereinafter "*Bill C-81*"]

63 *House Interim Report*: There is no mention in the report of any of the changes made to the laws governing measures to counter terrorist financing, perhaps evidencing a lack of concern with the potential implications of these changes at the time.

64 *House Interim Report*, 5.

65 Ibid, 11

66 *Senate Main Report*: See pp. 100–14 pertaining to security certificates, and pp. 43–58 pertaining to various measures aimed at tackling terrorist financing, including listing and revocation of charitable status

to the investigative hearing and bail with recognizance provisions, the Senate Special Committee came to a similar conclusion to that of its House predecessor, arguing that a measure that had gone unused could still be useful in the future.[67] As such, the Committee suggested that the provisions should be extended another three years, and argued that they should be 're-evaluated by the established parliamentary committee or committees, before expiry, to determine what further extension is warranted'.[68] Moreover, the Committee urged the government to amend the security certificate regime so that it would include a specific renunciation of torture and measures to ensure that deportation to torture did not occur. The Committee repeatedly emphasized that Canada's security certificate regime needed to include an express prohibition against deportation to torture 'in order to confirm that torture is never justifiable, as well as to uphold its international obligations'.[69] The Report also noted a number of due process concerns associated with measures aimed at countering terrorist financing, particularly the use of secret evidence in the listing and revocation of charitable status processes.[70]

2.2.4 Landmark decision on security certificates: the Charkaoui *case*[71]

Only a day after the Special Senate Committee had released its report, the Supreme Court of Canada released a landmark decision pertaining to the security certificate regime on 23 February 2007. In Canada, the *IRPA* allows the Minister of Citizenship and Immigration and the Minister of Public Safety and Emergency Preparedness to issue a certificate declaring that a foreign national or permanent resident is inadmissible to Canada on grounds of security, leading to the detention of the person named in the certificate. Both the detention and the certificate are reviewable in Federal Court.[72] Certificates of inadmissibility were issued by the Ministers against the appellants C, H and A on the basis of allegations that they constituted a threat to the security of Canada by reason of involvement in terrorist activities.[73] The Supreme Court had several issues to consider in this case, including: what the proper balance between security and rights was and, more specifically, whether a person's right to face their accuser and the case against them could be violated in the name of protecting information that the government deemed essential to protect national security; whether the security certificate scheme produced a situation where a person was likely to be deported to a country where

67 Ibid, 70–1
68 Ibid, 72
69 Ibid, 110
70 Ibid, 47–9
71 *Charkaoui v. Canada (Citizenship and Immigration)* [2007] 1 S.C.R. 350 [hereinafter "*Charkaoui*"]
72 Ibid, s. 78. The confirmation of a security certificate operates as a removal order (s. 80)
73 *Charkaoui*, paras. 5–6

they would likely suffer torture and, finally, whether there were issues with the procedures for, and lengths of, detention endured by people initially named in a security certificate.

In writing their conclusion, the Supreme Court argued that the *IRPA* suffered from two defects that were inconsistent with principles under the *Charter*. The first was that section 78(*g*) allowed for the use of evidence that is never disclosed to the named person without providing adequate measures to compensate for this non-disclosure, noting that other countries, such as the UK, had provided such measures in the form of a special advocate. This was a violation of the *Charter* that could not be justified. As such, the Court declared this procedure to be of no force or effect.[74] Despite striking down the law, the Court gave Parliament one year from the date of judgment to amend the law in order to bring it into accordance with the *Charter*. The second defect was found in section 84(2) of the *IRPA*, which denied a prompt hearing for foreign nationals by imposing a 120-day waiting period for review.[75] The Supreme Court concluded that the appropriate remedy for this defect was to strike down section 84(2) and to read foreign nationals into section 83. This decision materially changed the provisions of the security certificate regime and placed the onus on Parliament to make further amendments.

2.2.5 Investigative hearing and preventive arrest provisions sunset

Only a week after the *Charkaoui* decision was levied, the investigative hearing and bail with recognizance provisions of the *ATA* were set to expire unless they were extended by both Houses of Parliament. The Conservative minority government of the day tabled a motion to extend the measures without amendment for three years. In stark contrast to the ease with which the provisions originally became legislation, the government's motion was defeated in the House by a vote of 159 to 124. It is interesting to compare the sunsetting of the *ATA* provisions with the regular renewal of the indefinite detention measures in the UK. In the Canadian case, the provisions (unused, controversial and perhaps not worth the political risk in a coalition government) were not renewed, despite the relative ease with which they were passed by a majority government in the immediate post-9/11 climate. In the UK, the detention without trial and subsequent control order measures passed through several annual reviews and survived expiry in what was arguably a markedly different political climate. In the years following the sunsetting of the Canadian provisions, it became clear that the discussion regarding them and the battle to have them reinstated was far from over.

74 *Charkaoui*, paras. 77–8
75 *Charkaoui*, paras. 78–9

2.2.6 House and Senate Committees release further recommendations

On 27 March 2007, the House Subcommittee on the *ATA* released its final report.[76] It was relatively silent on the topic of the preventive arrest and bail with recognizance provisions, simply restating that the provisions should be extended for five years so as to allow additional time for them to be studied. The report instead focused on the more relevant issue of the day, the security certificate regime, arguing that more needed to be done to further ensure the rights and freedoms of those subject to it.[77] It discussed at length how the government should meet the court imposed deadline with a solution that would balance the need for sensitive information to be protected whilst respecting constitutionally entrenched rights, noting that Canada's Security Intelligence Review Committee (SIRC) had been using a panel of security-cleared lawyers for years.[78] The suggestion for something resembling a special advocate system had been in discussion since *Charkaoui*, where it was noted that a similar system existed in the UK. As was the case with the *House Interim Report*, Joe Comartin and Serge Menard once again wrote a dissenting opinion, re-iterating their opinion that terrorism cannot be fought with additional special legislation.[79] They also had strong words in relation to the security certificate regime, calling it an unacceptable violation of Canada's international commitments.[80]

Only a day after the *House Final Report* was released, the Special Senate Committee released a supplementary report[81] specifically focused on the Supreme Court's ruling in the *Charkaoui* case. It urged the government to take comprehensive action, arguing against the approach of simply amending the *IRPA* just enough so that it would fall into line with the Supreme Court's decision. It suggested that the government appoint a special advocate in all proceedings where the need to protect confidential information encroached on an individual's ability to make full answer and defence to the charges against them.[82] It reminded the government that it had gone further than the Court in its main report and recommended detention review for permanent residents and foreign nationals within 30 days of detention and every 90 days thereafter, as opposed to just every six months.[83] To emphasize this point, the report stated: 'We hope that the government will recognize that the Supreme Court has set out minimum

76 Subcommittee on the Review of the Anti Terrorism Act, *Rights, Limits, Security: A Comprehensive Review of the Anti-Terrorism Act and Related Issues* (Standing Committee on Public Safety and National Security, 2007) [hereinafter "*House Final Report*"]

77 *House Final Report*, 71

78 Ibid, 78

79 Ibid, 116

80 Ibid, 134

81 Special Senate Committee on the Anti-Terrorism Act, *Fourth Report* (Special Senate Committee on the Anti-Terrorism Act, 28 March 2007) [hereinafter "*Senate Fourth Report*"]

82 *Senate Fourth Report*, 1–2

83 Ibid, 2

constitutional protections and that nothing prevents Parliament from adopting other amendments to ensure due process when individuals have been deprived of their liberty'.[84]

2.2.7 The introduction of Bills C-3 and S-3

Bill C-3 (An Act to amend the Immigration and Refugee Protection Act, Certificate and Special Advocate, and to make a Consequential Amendment to Another Act) was introduced in the House of Commons on 22 October 2007. Bill S-3 (An Act to Amend the Criminal Code, Investigative Hearings and Recognizance with Conditions) was subsequently introduced in the Senate on the following day. The wording used in the legislative summaries of both of these bills is interesting for a number of reasons. According to the description and analysis section of Bill C-3's legislative summary:

> Bill C-3 substantially changes the security certificate procedure. It provides for the appointment of a special advocate as well as for a limited right of appeal. It provides for equal treatment of permanent residents and foreign nationals in making detention decisions, and requires periodic reviews of such detentions.[85]

To contrast, Bill S-3's legislative summary stated that it would reinstate provisions that expired in February 2007 which were 'substantially similar to the original provisions'.[86] It is interesting to note the difference in wording between the legislative summaries of these two proposed amendments. Bill C-3, which refers to security certificate provisions that had failed to withstand constitutional scrutiny, included what were referred to as substantial changes to the security certificate procedure. To contrast, Bill S-3 dealing with the bail with recognizance and preventive arrest provisions that had not faced such constitutional scrutiny, introduced provisions that were substantially similar to their original form.

The commentary section in Bill C-3's legislative summary states that 'Bill C-3 appears to address the charter violations identified by the Supreme Court that served as the catalyst for legislative changes'.[87] To contrast, Bill S-3's provisions had no such catalyst for legislative change, leading to the end result of legislation that 're-enacts sections 83.28 of 83.3 of the *Criminal Code* with only minor

84 Ibid

85 Library of Parliament, *Bill C-3: An Act to Amend the Immigration and Refugee Protection Act (Certificate and Special Advocate): Legislative Summary* (Parliamentary Information and Research Service, LS-567-E, 2008) [hereinafter "*Bill C-3 Legislative Summary*"] 13

86 Library of Parliament, *Bill S-3: An Act to Amend the Criminal Code (Investigative Hearing and Recognizance with Conditions): Legislative Summary* (Parliamentary Information and Research Service, LS-574-E, 2008) [hereinafter "*Bill S-3 Legislative Summary*"] 1

87 *Bill C-3 Legislative Summary*, 18

changes to the wording and intent of the earlier provisions derived from the *Anti-Terrorism Act*.[88] Another difference between the two bills pertains to their geneses through both Houses of Parliament. Bill C-3's legislative summary lists a number of concerns that were raised when the bill was tabled and notes that 'The *Charkaoui* case turned on the court's conclusion that the government had better options in the design of its security certificate system. That conclusion is not fully reflected in the bill presented by the government on Monday'.[89]

After passing swiftly through the House of Commons, Bill C-3 reached the Senate with very limited time for consideration and amendment. A Special Senate Committee sat for ten hours during a single day of public hearings on 11 February 2008, with several witnesses calling for the Bill to be amended or scrapped altogether.[90] Rather than considering amendments to the Bill in haste, the Committee decided to report the Bill without amendment and it subsequently passed through the Senate the next day. It received Royal Assent only two days later, exactly nine days before the expiry of the one-year, court-imposed deadline. To contrast, Bill S-3 was not rushed through the legislative process despite the fact that it attracted similar criticism. Instead, Bill S-3 went through its First Reading on 23 October 2007, and then took several months to reach the committee meeting and report stage. On 5 March 2008, two consequential amendments were made to the Bill by the Special Senate Committee, one of which addressed the need for regular review of anti-terrorism activities that is a recurring theme in this book's analysis of Canada's anti-terrorism framework.[91] Following amendment, Bill S-3 passed through the Senate on 6 March 2008. Just a day later, it was introduced into the House of Commons and was set to work its way through to Royal Assent. However, as was the case with Bill C-81 in November of 2005, Bill S-3 died on the Order Paper on 7 September 2008 when the 39th Parliament was dissolved.

2.2.8 Additional attempts to reinstate Bill S-3 provisions occur

Although the dissolution of the 39th Parliament brought the death of Bill S-3, it was not the end of the discussion pertaining to renewing the provisions. On 12 March 2009, Bill C-19 was introduced into the House of Commons. The Bill attracted fiery debates on the days it was discussed in the House. Rob Moore, Parliamentary Secretary to the Minister of Justice and Conservative Party member, argued that the provisions only sunsetted because they were voted on before full reports on them were made available.[92] Many of the members reiterated the need

88 *Bill S-3 Legislative Summary,* 38
89 *Bill C-3 Legislative Summary,* 18
90 Ibid, commentary section
91 Ibid, 6. Subsequent chapters discuss at length Canada's glaring lack of parliamentary mechanisms to review and oversee counter-terrorism measures
92 Canadian House of Commons Debates, 8 June 2009, 1800

to better utilize criminal prosecution, arguing that the Criminal Code could effectively fight terrorism and that this was proved by the fact that the provisions had never been used. These views were most frequently raised by members of the Bloc Québécois and the National Democratic Party (NDP). Conservative members frequently cited the fact that the provisions had been upheld as constitutional[93] and touted the important changes that were made to the Bill when it went through the Senate Special Committee as Bill S-3. Several Liberal members echoed this sentiment and said much had changed in the provisions since they chose not to support them before they were to sunset.[94] Despite recommendations for it to go forward to committee and the very real possibility of it becoming law given Conservative and Liberal support exhibited in the Hansard, Bill C-19 suffered a similar demise to that of Bill S-3 as a result of the controversial 2009 proroguing of Parliament. The 2009 proroguing of Parliament did not spell an end to the genesis of the preventive arrest and bail with recognizance provisions. Bill C-17, identical in title, content and legislative summary to its predecessor, was reintroduced in Parliament on 23 April 2010. The Bill made its way through First and Second Reading and, on 2 March 2011 was amended at the Committee Stage to include a shortening of its sunset clause from five to two years, as well as the requirement that both the House of Commons and the Senate would participate in mandatory parliamentary review before the law could be further renewed.[95]

Despite these relative improvements, Bill C-17 suffered the fate of its predecessors when the House of Commons passed a non-confidence vote on 25 March 2011, and Parliament was subsequently dissolved the next day. The subsequent federal election on 2 May 2011 saw Prime Minister Stephen Harper and his Conservative Party win a majority government. Bolstered by their resounding victory, the Conservatives reintroduced the Bill C-17 provisions as Bill S-7 on 15 February 2012. Bill S-7's legislative summary states that 'It is important to note that part of Bill S-7 contains the provisions found in the former Bill C-17, as it was originally introduced in the House of Commons on 23 April 2010'.[96] As such, while the requirement for mandatory parliamentary review remained, the length of the sunset clause in the Bill was restored to five

93 *Vancouver Sun (Re)*, [2004] 2 S.C.R. 332, 2004 SCC 43: The investigative hearing provision was upheld in the context of the Air India trial. Although the hearing was never actually held, the Supreme Court confirmed the constitutionality of the provision, focusing on the fact that information obtained during the hearing could not be used against the person giving the information, thus protecting the right against self-incrimination

94 Canadian House of Commons Debates, 9 June 2009, 1555–600

95 Library of Parliament, *Legislative Summary of Bill C-17: An Act to Amend the Criminal Code (Investigative Hearing and Recognizance with Conditions)* (Parliamentary Information and Research Service, 40-3-C17, March 2011)

96 Library of Parliament, *Legislative Summary of Bill S-7: An Act to Amend the Criminal Code, the Canada Evidence Act and the Security of Information Act* (Parliamentary Information and Research Service, 41-1-S7-e, June 2012) [hereinafter "*Bill S-7 Legislative Summary*"] 2

years.[97] Unhindered by the previous constraints imposed by a minority government, the Bill passed through the Senate on 31 May 2012 and received First Reading in the House of Commons on 5 June 2012. Bill S-7 passed through the House of Commons Standing Committee on Public Safety and National Security to Third Reading stage in April 2013, despite the fact that 'although the re-enacted provisions take into account one recommendation made by the House of Commons Subcommittee . . . they do not address other recommendations made by the subcommittee'.[98] This fact, coupled with the fact that debates on Bill S-7 at Third Reading stage were moved to three consecutive days in April (22–4) that coincided with the aftermath of the Boston marathon bombings and the announcement of a foiled VIA rail train attack in Toronto, did not go unnoticed by critics of the Bill and will be extensively discussed in subsequent chapters.[99] After six years' worth of attempts to reinstate the sunsetted investigative hearing and bail with recognizance provisions, the Conservative Government succeeded when Bill S-7 received Royal Assent on 25 April 2013.

2.2.9 Federal Court issues landmark ruling on listing: the Abdelrazik *case*[100]

The *Abdelrazik* case can be rightfully considered as a domestic pushback to the listing process established by *Resolution 1267*. Abousfian Abdelrazik is a Canadian of Sudanese origin who was listed by the UN Security Council's 1267 Committee in 2006. His case came to the Federal Court after a long and protracted legal battle over the denial to allow him to return to Canada after a period of interrogation and detention in Sudan.[101] The Federal Court found that his right to enter Canada had been breached and that the Canadian Government should take steps to facilitate his immediate return to Canada, in a decision that clearly elucidates issues with the 1267 listing process and the tension between Canada's international and national obligations.[102] In doing so, the judge in the case likened the 1267 Committee Regime to 'a situation for a listed person not unlike that of Josef K. in Kafka's *The Trial*, who awakens one morning and, for reasons never revealed to him or the reader, is arrested and prosecuted for an unspecified crime'.[103] He also noted that listing by the 1267 Committee carries severe sanctions, including subjecting the listing person to a global asset freeze and

97 *Bill S-7 Legislative Summary*, 3

98 Ibid, 12

99 Chapters 4 and 6 detail and analyse the process whereby Bill S-7 became law and preventive arrest and bail with recognizance most recently once again became part of Canada's counter-terrorism framework

100 *Abdelrazik v. Canada (Minister of Foreign Affairs)* [2010] 1 F.C.R. 267 [hereinafter "*Abdelrazik*"]

101 Ibid, paras. 1–3

102 Ibid, para. 2

103 Ibid, para. 58

a global travel ban,[104] and characterized the process as a 'denial of basic legal remedies' that was 'untenable under the principles of international human rights'.[105] The decision overall is a damning evaluation of the 1267 listing process as it is currently composed, and raises significant questions about the legitimacy of the process and the role of domestic courts in interpreting international obligations in the face of human rights concerns.

2.2.10 Security certificates face additional legal challenges

After the passage of Bill C-3, the government issued five new security certificates under the new legislation, most notably against Adil Charkaoui, Hassan Almrei and Mohammad Harkat.[106] Since late 2009, the Federal Court has reached differing rulings in these men's cases, which further complicated the status of the security certificate regime in Canada.[107] In a landmark ruling on 14 October 2009,[108] Justice Tremblay-Lamer brought an end to a six-year legal battle when she declared Adil Charkaoui's certificate void, largely because the government withdrew evidence that it did not want released for national security reasons. Tremblay-Lamer also ensured there would be no appeal or future certification of Charkaoui by denying a government argument that there was a higher legal question outside of the case that could be raised at appeal.[109] The case was a significant setback for the security certificate regime and a long-awaited vindication for Charkaoui, who launched a civil suit against the government for $24.5 million on 22 February 2010.[110] Similarly, Hassan Almrei also saw a battle with the security certificate regime that lasted more than eight years come to an end on 14 December 2009. Justice Richard Mosley issued a landmark 185-page judgment that dismissed the certificate against Almrei.[111] Mosley decided that it was reasonable to believe that Almrei posed a risk to the security of Canada in the aftermath of 9/11, but argued that much had changed since that time.[112] Not only did Mosley find that Almrei was no longer a security threat, he also expressed

104 Ibid, para. 26

105 Ibid, para. 51

106 The extensive case law pertaining to these men, and others subject to security certificates in Canada over the last decade, is the subject of analysis in Chapter 3

107 For an in-depth analysis of these three cases, see Lorne Waldman, 'An Evaluation of the Special Advocates Program in Canada' in Forcese, C. and Crepeau, F. (eds), *Terrorism, Law and Democracy: 10 Years after 9/11* (Canadian Institute for the Administration of Justice, Montreal, 2012)

108 *Charkaoui (Re)* [2009] FC 1030

109 Ibid, paras. 111–12

110 Sidhartha Banerjee, 'Suspect Launches Suit after Terror Case Ordeal' (*The Toronto Star*) available at: https://www.thestar.com/news/canada/2010/03/13/suspect_launches_suit_after_terrorcase_ordeal.html [accessed 27 March 2010]. Charkaoui's requests for an official apology have been turned down by the government and his civil suit is ongoing

111 *(Re) Almrei* [2009] FC 1263

112 Ibid, para. 6

scathing views of the way the ministers and intelligence services proceeded during the course of the case, concluding by finding them in 'breach of their duty of candour to the Court'.[113] Similar to the final *Charkaoui* case, the Ministers proposed a number of questions that could lead to a possible appeal, but Mosley declined to rule on these, noting that it would be unfair to subject Almrei to a long appeal process after he had succeeded on the factual merits of the case against him,[114] and suggested instead that the parties take some time to consider whether to submit or withdraw an appeal. No such appeal has since been launched and Hassan Almrei began the process of suing the government for $16 million in damages in September 2012.[115] The decisions in the Federal Court cases pertaining to Charkaoui and Almrei raised serious doubts as to the future feasibility of the security certificate regime. However, on 9 December 2010 in a judgment in Mohammed Harkat's case,[116] Justice Simon Noel found that the evidence to support Harkat's certificate was reliable and that 'although the danger associated with Mr. Harkat has diminished over time, he still poses a danger to Canada'.[117] Harkat was found to be disingenuous in his testimony to the court, and Noel argued that the evidence he heard lead him to believe that 'Mr. Harkat has engaged in terrorism, that he is a danger to the security of Canada and that he is a member of the Bin Laden Network through his past work for the Khattab group'.[118] Harkat subsequently petitioned the Supreme Court of Canada in order to challenge the overall constitutionality of the security certificate scheme.

2.3 More recent significant developments in Canada

2.3.1 Security certificates survive Supreme Court scrutiny: the Harkat *case*[119]

In *Harkat,* the Supreme Court of Canada was once again tasked with assessing the constitutionality of the security certificate process, this time in the aftermath of its *Charkaoui* decision and the legislative amendments that resulted from that decision. Ultimately, the Supreme Court decided that the security certificate scheme was constitutional, arguing that Parliament had responded to *Charkaoui* in a manner that conferred upon judges a discretion and flexibility to fashion a fair

113 Ibid, para. 503
114 Ibid, para. 511
115 Canadian Press, 'Hassan Almrei Wants Speedy Lawsuit Judgment' (*CBC News Canada*) available at: http://www.cbc.ca/news/canada/toronto/hassan-almrei-wants-speedy-lawsuit-judgment-1.1227881 [accessed 10 September 2012]
116 *(Re) Harkat* [2010] FC 1243
117 Ibid, para. 13
118 Ibid, para. 548
119 *Canada (Citizenship and Immigration) v. Harkat* [2014] 2 S.C.R. 33 [hereinafter "*Harkat*"]

process in each particular case before them.[120] Referencing the UK Supreme Court's decision in *Secretary of State for the Home Department v. AF (No 3)* [2009] UKHL 28, the Court found that this fair process would generally occur when the named person was provided with sufficient information about the allegations against them, i.e. more than purely general assertions.[121] The Court also noted that the level of disclosure required in any case would be case-specific, and that ultimately the judge in the case 'is the arbiter of whether this standard has been met'.[122] Another important aspect of the Court's judgment pertained to restrictions on the ability of the special advocate to communicate with the named person once they have seen closed material, which has long been regarded as a difficult aspect of the process. Ultimately, the Supreme Court was satisfied that restrictions on communication are not absolute (a judge can allow them, subject to any conditions, via s. 85.4(2) of the *IRPA*) and found that the availability of this judicial authorization meant that special advocates were able to perform their role in a constitutionally sufficient manner.[123] In its concluding remarks on the constitutionality of the *IRPA* scheme, the Court acknowledged that 'these provisions remain an imperfect substitute for full disclosure in an open court' but also pointed to the ability of judges to grant remedies (including a stay of proceedings under s. 24(1) if necessary) based on their assessment of the overall fairness of the proceedings.[124]

With regard to the Court's reasoning on s. 85.4(2) and judicial authorization of communication with the special advocate, Hudson has noted that there is an inherent practical difficulty that arises as a result of special advocates receiving such permission only after submitting a formal request during interlocutory hearings attended by the Ministers, which may require the special advocate to divulge prior communications and litigation strategies that could prejudice the named person.[125] While the Supreme Court in *Harkat* itself recognized that the *IRPA* was an imperfect process that allowed for the possibility of an unfair process, this would not always be the case (and, in fact, was not found to be the case for Mr Harkat).[126] As such, it appears as though the Supreme Court's decision in *Harkat* has effectively 'resulted in the constitutionalization of the certificate regime'.[127] Nonetheless, Forcese and Roach have described the decision in *Harkat* as 'not a true win on the law for the government' and have suggested that the government has chosen to not again use security certificates in terrorism matters, outside of

120 *Harkat,* para. 4
121 Ibid, para. 56
122 Ibid, para. 57
123 Ibid, paras. 69–70
124 Ibid, para. 77
125 Graham Hudson, 'As Good as It Gets? Security, Asylum and the Rule of Law after the Certificate Trilogy' (2015) 52 *Osgoode Hall Law Journal* 905, 921 [hereinafter "*Hudson*"]
126 *Harkat,* para. 106
127 *Hudson,* 928

the original five cases.[128] After almost 15 years of protracted litigation, it appears as though security certificates may no longer be a prominent feature of the Canadian anti-terrorism framework. That said, it would be wrong to assume that issues associated with the use of secret evidence will be any less relevant going forward, particularly in light of the more recent developments and legislation to which focus now turns.

2.3.2 The October 2014 terrorist attacks and subsequent legislation

Months after the decision in *Harkat,* Canada suffered what might be considered to be the most significant domestic terrorist attack in its history on 22 October 2014 when Michael Zehaf-Bibeau shot and killed an unarmed soldier at a War Memorial in Ottawa before proceeding to enter the Canadian Parliament buildings with a loaded weapon. Although Bibeau was eventually killed by Sergeant-at-Arms Kevin Vickers and RCMP officers, that was not before he had wounded an unarmed parliamentary guard and come remarkably close to where the prime minister, the leader of the opposition, and nearly 230 MPs were in caucus meetings. All of this occurred only two days after another man, Martin Rouleau, had driven his car into two Canadian forces personnel. The events shocked the Canadian public and drew immediate condemnation from political leaders, leading directly to the introduction of new and omnibus terrorism legislation in the form of Bills C-44[129] and C-51.[130] Although the former had been tabled prior to the attacks, the latter can be seen as a direct response, and both benefited greatly from the political capital afforded to the Conservative Government by the attacks.[131] For various reasons discussed below, the wide-ranging and sprawling legislation immediately raised concern amongst academics, parliamentarians and human rights groups.[132]

The *PCTA* makes a number of significant amendments to the law governing the activities of CSIS.[133] One of the most problematic amendments to the *Canadian Security Intelligence Service Act* 1985 as a result of the legislation is that which gives CSIS the power to engage in extraterritorial surveillance (i.e. conduct investigations outside of Canada), and the extension of a 'blanket'

128 *Forcese and Roach, False Security,* 208–10

129 Which would become the Protection of Canada from Terrorists Act, S.C. 2015, c. 9 [hereinafter "*PCTA*"]

130 Which would become the Anti-Terrorism Act, S.C. 2015, c. 20 [hereinafter "*ATA 2015*"]

131 See the following press release from the day Bill C-44 was tabled that reminds Canadians that the threat of terrorism continues to be apparent both at home and abroad: Press Release, Government of Canada, 'The Government of Canada Introduces Protection of Canada from Terrorists Act' (27 October 2014), available at: http://news.gc.ca/web/article-en.do?nid=897129 [accessed 3 April 2017]

132 John Barber, 'Canada's New Anti-Terror Legislation Prompts Civil Liberties Fears' (30 January 2015) *Guardian,* available at: http://www.theguardian.com/world/2015/jan/30/canadas-anti-terror-legislation-civil-liberties-fears [accessed 2 February 2015]

133 Canadian Security Intelligence Service Act, R.S.C. 1985, c. C-23 [hereinafter "*CSIS Act*"]

human source privilege to sources. As a result of the legislation, the Federal Court will now have to decide (based on secret evidence) whether to authorize warrants that allow CSIS operatives to engage in spying activities overseas, potentially violating the sovereignty of other nations.[134] Perhaps even more problematic is the extension of a blanket human source privilege.[135] Forcese and Roach have argued that this aspect of the legislation ignores guidance provided by both the Air India Commission and the Supreme Court, and may very well contribute to the further complication and/or minimization of criminal prosecutions for terrorist activity.[136] Furthermore, the problematic nature of expanded powers for CSIS is exacerbated in Canada due to its lack of meaningful review or oversight of intelligence activities.[137]

The *ATA 2015* might be fairly argued to be the more problematic of the two pieces of legislation, particularly given its wide-reaching and expansive nature. Particularly disconcerting are the number of new measures created by the *ATA 2015*, including: 1) the enactment of the Security of Canada Information Sharing Act (*SoCIS*),[138] which will allow Canadian Government institutions to disclose a wide range of information to agencies such as the CSIS or the RCMP; 2) amendments to the *Criminal Code* providing for offences of advocating or promoting the commission of terrorism offences 'in general'; 3) amendments to the *CSIS Act* giving CSIS additional powers within and outside Canada, including 'police-like' disruption powers traditionally outside of their remit; and 4) amendments to the *IRPA* that would further allow Ministers to claim non-disclosure of security-sensitive information.[139] While an in-depth consideration of how Canada's post-October 2014 legislation fails to take into account lessons learned from nearly 15 years of experience with the original *ATA* enacted in 2001 will occur in this book's conclusion, it is worth noting here that this legislation clearly continues a trend of passing expansive legislation in the aftermath of significant terrorist events without full and proper consideration of its long-lasting implications. As of 19 October 2015, Canada has a Liberal government, led by Justin Trudeau, who has promised to make consequential amendments to the worst aspects of the *ATA 2015*.[140] If the analyses of Canada's post-9/11 measures

134 For an in-depth discussion of the judicialization of extra-territorial spying, see Craig Forcese, 'The Judicialization of Extraterritorial Spying: Gaps and Gap-Fillers in the World of CSIS Foreign Operations' (2014) 61 *CLQ* 440

135 See Kent Roach, 'The Problems with the New CSIS Human Source Privilege in Bill C-44' (2014) 61 *CLQ* 451

136 *Forcese and Roach, False Security*, 301–3

137 This is the subject of extensive discussion in Chapter 4

138 S.C. 2015, c. 20, s. 2 [hereinafter "*SoCIS*"]

139 To see the expansive list of laws that the *ATA 2015* amends or creates, see http://laws-lois.justice.gc.ca/eng/AnnualStatutes/2015_20

140 See the Liberal Government's Bill C-51 platform, available at: https://www.liberal.ca/realchange/bill-c-51

in subsequent chapters of this book are anything to go by, this may prove to be a long and arduous process.

2.4 Historical evolution of the United Kingdom's post-9/11 measures

2.4.1 Pre-9/11 experiences with terrorism

As was the case in Canada, the UK was certainly not immune to terrorism prior to 9/11. In fact, and in contrast, the UK had extensive experience with terrorism well before the 9/11 attacks, most notably from a 'sovereigntist' group of its own, the Irish Republican Army (IRA). There are many parallels between the pre and post-9/11 strategies employed by the UK to counter terrorism, including the use of proscription, the use of secret evidence and the use of powers outside of the ordinary criminal justice system, including the use of immigration law.[141] For example, it has been noted that the 1974 Prevention of Terrorism (Temporary Provisions) Act[142] utilized proscription, immigration law and secret evidence as a means to displace terrorism.[143] In a parallel to the *ATCSA* discussed below, the 1974 Prevention of Terrorism Act was subjected to a mere 17 hours of parliamentary debate following the infamous Birmingham pub bombings.[144] Many of these same powers were also found within the Prevention of Terrorism (Temporary Provisions) Act 1989[145] and the 1996 Northern Ireland (Emergency Provisions) Act,[146] but Ryder notes that an extensive 1998 Home Office review of these powers characterized them as underutilized and ineffective, leading to the eventual passage of another significant piece of pre-9/11 legislation.[147]

On 20 July 2000, the *Terrorism Act* 2000[148] was introduced, with the majority of the Act coming into force on 19 February 2001 and replacing the aforementioned 1989 and 1996 legislation. The Act itself is divided into eight parts and includes, among other things, a new definition of terrorism and an attempt to subject a wider range of measures to judicial or quasi-judicial oversight.[149] According the Walker, the legislation was offered the opportunity to provide for a considered, comprehensive and principled code, rather than the hastily drafted and fragmented emergency laws that had characterized previous legislation.[150] As Walker further

141 *Roach, 9/11 Effect*, 252
142 s. 1(7)
143 *Roach, 9/11 Effect*, 252
144 *Ryder, Financial War on Terrorism*, 100
145 C. 4
146 C. 22
147 *Ryder, Financial War on Terrorism*, 102
148 C. 11
149 Clive Walker, *Blackstone's Guide to the Anti-Terrorism Legislation* (2nd edn, Oxford University Press, 2009) [hereinafter "*Walker, Blackstones*"] 23–4
150 Ibid, 23

notes, it is important to discuss this legislation in the context of the passage of the *Human Rights Act* (*HRA*) of 1998,[151] an event which had material consequences for the ways in which certain pieces of legislation, including those pertaining to detention without trial, control orders and TPIMs have been developed, implemented, scrutinized by courts and subsequently abolished or amended.[152] It has been noted that the *Terrorism Act* 2000 allows for a broad and intricate system for executive proscription of terrorist groups,[153] and was followed up with the subsequent creation of the Proscribed Organization Appeals Commission and a variety of new offences pertaining to terrorist financing found in sections 15–18 of the Act.[154]

2.4.2 Post-9/11 aftermath and the Anti-Terrorism, Crime and Security Act

As aforementioned, the UK was not immune to the pressures associated with the mobilization of the international community following 9/11, despite the fact that it had just passed expansive and thorough pre-9/11 legislation in the form of the *Terrorism Act* 2000. By 15 October 2001 it had outlined the *ATCSA*, and by 14 December 2001 the Act had received Royal Assent, although not without extensive commentary from the Home Affairs Select Committee. The Home Affairs Committee report starts by stating that the country has more anti-terrorism legislation on its books than any other developed country, noting that much of it had been rushed through in the wake of atrocities and has proved ineffective in some cases.[155] It also explicitly noted early on its report that detention without trial mechanisms were of the greatest concern,[156] illustrating that there was concern with these measures from the Bill's infancy. As was also the case in Canada, many questioned why existing legislation could not be used. Professor Conor Gearty asked, 'Why cannot they bring criminal proceedings under section 56, directing terrorist activities, or incitement to commit terrorist acts abroad?'[157] Gearty's sentiment echoes the arguments made by Canadian academics and parliamentarians in the aftermath of 9/11 pertaining to the use of normal criminal proceedings, foreshadowing the problematic nature of anti-terrorism measures outside of the normal criminal justice process in both Canada and the UK.

In reaching its conclusions, the Home Affairs Committee made several points that provide context for some of the problems that have ensued since the passage

151 C. 42 [hereinafter "*HRA*"]
152 This process is discussed extensively below and in the case law analyses in Chapter 3
153 *Roach, 9/11 Effect*, 257
154 *Ryder, Financial War on Terrorism*, 103
155 United Kingdom Home Affairs Committee, *First Report: The Anti-Terrorism, Crime and Security Bill 2001* (HC 351 19 November 2001) [hereinafter "*Home Affairs Report*"] para. 1
156 Ibid, para. 5
157 Ibid, para. 26

of the Act. The first pertained to the speed with which a bill that carried major implications for civil liberties moved through the legislative stages.[158] This was also a concern raised with regard to Canada's *ATA* and amendments to the *IRPA*. The second point pertained to the need to concentrate on prosecution. On that issue, the Committee stated that 'We are concerned that the power of detention is exercised only as a last resort, i.e., in circumstances where it is clearly not possible to proceed with prosecution, extradition or deportation'.[159] Finally, the third and final conclusion pertains to an argument that was raised in the Canadian context for these post-9/11 measures to be temporary. The Home Affairs Committee argued that the immigration and asylum provisions in Part four of the Bill should expire after five years and any revival or continuance of the powers would require full parliamentary consideration given to a bill and not just the 90-minute debate in a standing committee required for an annual renewal order.[160] Nonetheless, despite the concerns of the Home Affairs Committee pertaining to the detention without trial provisions and the derogation order they would require, the Bill was passed and on 18 December 2001, the derogation order[161] was registered by the Council of Europe Secretariat.

2.4.3 Detention without trial begins and undergoes scrutiny

It did not take long for the saga of the detention without trial provisions to begin. On 19 December 2001, one day after the derogation order was registered, eight suspected terrorist suspects, Djamel Ajouaoum, Abu Rideh and A, C, D, E, F and G were detained in London, Luton and Birmingham, only two days after they had been certified under the new powers. Months after, in the period dating from 5 February to 22 April 2002, suspects B, H and I were certified and detained. Detainee F, an Algerian, voluntarily left the UK for France. It did not take long for these certifications to make their way through to the courts. On 30 July 2002, SIAC ruled that the law governing detention without trial was discriminatory and disproportionate because it only allowed for the internment of foreign nationals. A Court of Appeal decision on 25 October 2002 overturned the SIAC judgment by ruling that the government was entitled to believe there was a public emergency threatening the UK.[162] Despite expressing the belief that SIAC had correctly approached the issue of whether there existed a public emergency threatening the life of nation within the meaning of Article 15 of the ECHR, the Court decided that it had to defer to the Home Secretary's conclusion that the action that was necessary in the interests of national security, and was limited to removing or detaining suspected terrorists who had no right to remain in the UK but could

158 Ibid, para. 68, note (b)
159 Ibid, note (e)
160 Ibid, note (h)
161 Human Rights Act 1998 (Designated Derogation) Order 2001 (S.I. 2001/3644)
162 *A and Others v. Secretary of State for the Home Department* [2002] EWCA Civ 1502

not be deported.[163] Ultimately, it was found that section 23 of the 2001 Act was not incompatible with the Convention and the detention without trial regime lived on. By 3 October 2003, SIAC had officially released its first rulings on individual detainees, upholding the Home Secretary's decision in all ten it considered.[164]

As these cases were making their way through the judicial process, they attracted fierce criticism and debate. The climate of the time is illuminated well by the Newton Committee Report,[165] which was released on 18 December 2003. The report, written by the Privy Counsellor Review Committee, is a sprawling, 121-page document that fiercely denounces detention without trial. Early on in the report, the Committee stated that its 'starting point is that the ordinary criminal justice system and established security methods must remain the preferred approach to tackling the crime of terrorism'.[166] Here again we see the suggestion to use the normal criminal law. The review also touches on another recurring theme, that is, concern with the speed with which the legislation came to exist and some of the issues raised by the enacting of emergency legislation.[167] The Committee also expressed concern that Part four was an adaptation of existing immigration and asylum legislation, rather than being designed expressly for the purpose of meeting the threat from international terrorism.[168] After detailing the various issues it had with the detention without trial regime, the Committee argued that Part four should be replaced as soon as possible. It stated its belief that the shortcomings of the provisions were serious enough that the regime should be replaced by new legislation that dealt with all terrorism, whatever its origin or the nationality of its perpetrators, and not require derogation from the ECHR.[169]

Criticism of detention without trial provisions only continued to grow after the Newton Report. On 18 March 2004, detainee M was released from prison after a SIAC ruling that his detention was unjustified was upheld by Chief Justice Lord Woolf.[170] Scrutiny of the measures continued to escalate, culminating on 5 August 2004 with the release of the Joint Select Committee on Human Rights' (JCHR's)

163 Ibid, para. 1

164 For a list of all outcomes of SIAC before 2007, see www.siac.tribunals.gov.uk/outcomespre2007.htm

165 Privy Counsellor Review Committee, *Anti-Terrorism, Crime and Security Act 2001 Review* (HC 100, 18 December 2003). This review was required by the *ATCSA* s. 122, which was added during passage

166 Ibid, para. 4

167 Ibid, para. 5: 'By definition, an emergency timetable does not allow the normal opportunities for full and detailed Parliamentary scrutiny. Enacting provisions in this way . . . ran the risk of undermining the usual consensus for recognizing the responsibility of the Government of the day for public safety and for giving it greater discretion when approving legislation presented under emergency conditions'

168 Ibid, para. 52

169 Ibid, para. 56

170 *M and Secretary of State for the Home Department*, SC/17/2002, para. 20

Review of Counter-Terrorism Powers.[171] The report began by affirming the central conclusion of the Newton Report, stating that indefinite detention should be replaced with new legislation that did not require derogation from the ECHR.[172] The report again placed emphasis on legislation enacted in emergency situations, noting that derogations from human rights are permitted in times of emergency but they are meant to be temporary. It argued that since the government and the security service now agreed that the UK faced a near-permanent emergency, it was imperative to find means to combat terrorist not requiring long-term derogations that would have a corrosive effect on human rights and diminish the UK's standing in the international community.[173] Not surprisingly, the report goes on to extensively discuss alternatives that stress the need to rely on prosecution of criminal offences to combat terrorism. Weeks after it was released, detainee D was freed from Belmarsh on the order of the Home Secretary, with no explanation given for the release after three years of custody. This left nine detainees who looked to the House of Lords to overturn the Court of Appeal ruling from October 2002. The case began on 4 October 2004.

2.4.4 A. v. Secretary of State for the Home Department[174] *and the subsequent* Prevention of Terrorism Act *2005*[175]

On 16 December 2004 the House of Lords ruled in a landmark decision that the detention without trial scheme was disproportionate and discriminatory and issued a declaration of incompatibility under section 3 of the *HRA* in what is now famously known as the *Belmarsh* case. The judgment, discussed further below, was immediately the source of much academic and political commentary. Dickson argued that the House of Lords 'much to its credit, has ensured that the rule of law prevails even when very few people, including non-British nationals, have their fundamental rights breached'.[176] Tomkins argued that what was most welcome about the decision was that it marked the first significant occasion in which the judiciary did not defer to the executive in a national security case.[177] That said, Tomkins was keen to note that unprecedented invasions of liberty and privacy in the *ATCSA* were left unscathed, stating that 'This is a telling reminder of the limitations inherent within the adjudicative process, even with a Bill of Rights,

171 Joint Committee on Human Rights, *Eighteenth Report: Review of Counter-Terrorism Powers* (HL 158, HC 713, 4 August 2004)

172 Ibid, 5

173 Ibid, 6

174 *A v. Secretary of State for the Home Department* [2004] UKHL 56 [hereinafter "*Belmarsh*"]

175 Prevention of Terrorism Act 2005 c. 2

176 Brice Dickson, 'Law Versus Terrorism: Can Law Win?' [2005] *European Human Rights Law Review* 11, 25

177 Adam Tomkins, 'Readings of A v Secretary of State for the Home Department' [2005] *Public Law* 259

no matter how progressive the judges'.[178] Nonetheless, Feldman argued that, at the time, 'It was unprecedented for UK judges to adjudicate on the legitimacy of measures adopted in good faith on national security grounds'.[179]

The *Belmarsh* judgment contains three rulings, pertaining to: 1) the lawfulness of the derogation from Article 5; 2) the proportionality of the interference with the right to liberty; and 3) whether or not the nature of the section 23 power was discriminatory in nature such that it violated Article 14. In the first ruling, the majority argued that there was a public emergency threatening the life of the nation, but that the power to detain without trial did not meet the 'strictly required by that emergency' standard. Lord Bingham used ECtHR case law to show that governments have considerable discretion in determining whether an emergency exists and characterized the question as to whether the UK was experiencing such an emergency as a political one that should be left to the executive.[180] However, the Court ruled that the power to detain without trial could not be said to be strictly required because if methods used to combat international terrorism were sufficient for British citizens then they must be sufficient for non-nationals as well. In addition, if those detained without trial were free to leave the country and possibly carry out terrorist activities, it could not be said that it was strictly required to hold them in the UK. As such, the interference with the right to liberty was disproportionate. Finally, the court ruled that section 23 was discriminatory in nature because of the way in which it made the distinction between nationals and non-nationals.

It became clear that the government would have to accept that 'derogation is not sustainable as the sole front-line policy . . . certainly not on a legal basis and probably not on a political basis'.[181] Walker sheds some light on the government's post-*Belmarsh* decision-making process, noting that after some hesitation it decided to respond to the Court's declaration of incompatibility in a manner that would not require a notice of derogation. He describes the legislative process behind the subsequent *Prevention of Terrorism Act* as 'often bitter' and suffering from the inevitable pressure placed on the government by a tight deadline for legislation before the expiration of the detention without trial provisions.[182] The *Prevention of Terrorism Act* 2005 received Royal Assent on 11 March 2005, at least in part as a result of the decision in the *Belmarsh* case. The Act was passed amidst much controversy in only 17 days,[183] and allowed for the making of derogating and non-derogating control orders that can include a number

178 Ibid, 265

179 David Feldman, 'Proportionality and Discrimination in Anti-Terrorism Legislation' (2005) 64 *Cambridge Law Journal* 271, 272

180 *Belmarsh*, paras. 28–9

181 Clive Walker, 'Prisoners of "War All the Time"' [2005] *European Human Rights Law Review* 50, 74

182 *Walker, Blackstones*, 29

183 Ed Bates, 'Anti-Terrorism Control Orders: Liberty and Security Still in the Balance' (2009) 29 *Legal Studies* 99 [hereinafter "*Bates, Anti-Terrorism Control Orders*"] 99

of restrictions.[184] It did not take long for the control order system to continue the work of the previous detention without trial regime. By 13 March 2006, 11 control orders were in place. However, what the government could not have known at the time it enacted the *Prevention of Terrorism Act* 2005 was that the UK would soon experience a domestic terrorist attack of its own.

2.4.5 The 7/7 London bombings and the Terrorism Act *2006*[185]

On 7 July 2005, suicide bombers using the public transit system engaged in a series of coordinated attacks during the morning rush hour, killing 56 people and injuring about 700. Security across the UK was raised to the highest alert level and media coverage of the events was intense. Drafts of a new terrorism bill were released on 15 September and 5 October 2005, respectively. The Terrorism Act 2006 came into force on 30 March 2006, nearly nine months after the attacks occurred. Lord Carlile, the government's former independent reviewer of terrorism legislation opined that the bombings 'rightly and inevitably catalyzed an earlier examination of potential additional legislation than had been envisaged at the time of the enactment of the *Prevention of Terrorism Act* 2005'.[186] While he seemed encouraged by the fact that there was a full public debate on the possible changes that might be made to the law,[187] he did note his concern 'about the recent detention for deportation of former subjects of control orders, in the absence of current Memoranda of Understanding with the countries to which they would be deported'.[188] The 2006 *Terrorism Act* did not itself make material changes or additions to the control order regime. The most controversial changes it introduced pertained to a new offence of the glorification of terrorism and a new maximum detention period. The context surrounding the passage of the Act is worth noting. It appears as though there was not the same rush to enact emergency legislation following the 7/7 attacks in the UK as there was following the 9/11 attacks, when both Canada and the UK quickly enacted emergency legislation. Moreover, in the post-9/11 period, the UK has amassed a number of reviews of anti-terrorism provisions,[189] which may have aided in the consultation process.

184 *Walker, Blackstones*, 18

185 C. 11

186 Lord Carlile, *Proposals by Her Majesty's Government for Changes to the Laws Against Terrorism* (Home Office, 2005) para. 6

187 Ibid, para. 7

188 Ibid, para. 115

189 Lord Carlile has engaged in annual reviews of the control order system and the JCHR has released several reports on the annual renewal of control order legislation. The JCHR, Home Office Affairs Committee and Privy Counsellor Review Committee have all released several reports on the functioning of terrorism legislation, two of which have been discussed at length in this chapter.

2.4.6 Control orders and the Counter-Terrorism Act 2008

Despite the fact that the *Terrorism Act* 2006 did not make any consequential amendments to the control order regime, this did not mean that the following months would not provide several challenges to the measures. They survived their first sunset clause on 15 February 2006, but were soon the focus of a trilogy of crucial House of Lords judgments.[190] In *JJ*, the House of Lords were asked to decide on two main issues raised on appeal, that is, whether Sullivan J was right to hold that obligations imposed by control orders amounted to a deprivation of liberty within the meaning of Article 5(1) of the ECHR and whether he was right to conclude that the Secretary of State did not have the power to make non-derogating control orders. The House of Lords subsequently held that a control order imposing an 18-hour curfew was sufficiently severe that it could be said to constitute a deprivation of the controlee's liberty.[191] Curfews of 12 and 14 hours were found not to constitute such a deprivation of liberty in *E* and *MB*, respectively. Nonetheless, academics expressed serious concern about the curfews and other restrictions on liberty that were imposed on those subject to control orders at the time. Bonner argued that 'Even if invalidity is confirmed by the House of Lords, the process of restriction could continue in "cat and mouse" fashion by reducing the degree of restriction or transferring the controlee to the deportation sector'.[192] Relatedly, Bates notes that the government interpreted *JJ* as effectively indicating that control orders with a 16-hour curfew would not engage Article 5, pointing to four control orders that were subsequently modified to change curfew hours from 12 to 16.[193]

The *MB* case also raised other issues outside of the deprivation of liberty considerations, most significantly the question pertaining to whether the use of closed material as the basis for the case leading to an order would lead to a violation of the right to a fair trial provided by Article 6 of the ECHR. The majority stopped short of finding that the use of the special advocate procedure would be sufficient to comply with Article 6 in every case, but argued that the controlled person should be afforded a sufficient measure of procedural protection, and that the judge conducting the hearing would be best able to discern whether this had occurred. Lord Bingham argued for a concept of fairness that imported 'a core irreducible minimum of procedural protection'.[194] This core minimum

190 *Secretary of State for the Home Department v. E* [2007] UKHL 47 [hereinafter "*E*"]; *Secretary of State for the Home Department v. JJ* [2007] UKHL 45 [hereinafter "*JJ*"]; *Secretary of State for the Home Department v. MB* [2007] UKHL 46 [hereinafter "*MB*"]

191 Walker has explained why the same lengthy period of curfew would be allowed under the Australian system of control orders. See Clive Walker, 'The Reshaping of Control Orders in the United Kingdom: Time for a Fairer Go, Australia!' (2013) 37 *Melbourne University Law Review* 143

192 *Bonner, Executive Measures,* 245

193 *Bates, Anti-Terrorism Control Orders*, 104

194 *MB*, para. 43

would not be fulfilled when the applicant was unable to see the closed material justifying their detention. This meant that it would be up to the judge conducting the hearing to conduct the difficult task of deciding whether such a core minimum had been fulfilled. The essence of the judgment in *MB* was that Article 6(1) of the ECHR required that the controlee should be sufficiently informed so as to be capable of rebutting the argument that the controlee was reasonably suspected of involvement in terrorist-related activity.[195]

Despite the modifications made to the regime by this trilogy of cases, control orders continued and were renewed again by Parliament on 21 February 2008. However, the issue of the special advocate and secret evidence was an issue that was not going away. Despite the fact that the *Counter-Terrorism Act* 2008,[196] which came into force on 26 November 2008, made no consequential amendments to the control order regime, tensions were rising in the lower courts that were now charged with the responsibility of deciding whether a sufficient measure of procedural protection had been afforded to controlees in their hearings. As was the case in Canada, it was only a matter of time until this issue made its way to the highest legal authority.

2.4.7 **A. v. United Kingdom**[197] ***and*** **Secretary of State for the Home Department v. AF**[198]

On 19 February 2009, the ECtHR court issued a landmark decision in *A v. UK*. The Court first had to decide whether the risk of terrorist attack faced by the UK constituted a public emergency threatening the nation. On this issue, the Court sided with the majority of the House of Lords, arguing that national authorities were better placed than international judges to decide if there was such an emergency, and stated that a wide manner of appreciation should left to these authorities.[199] Second, the Court had to determine whether the scheme for indefinitely detaining foreign terrorist suspects was strictly required by the exigencies of the situation. Again, the Court agreed with the majority of the House of Lords in deciding that it was not, noting many of the same reasons. This affirming of the House of Lords judgment was particularly significant because of the ECtHR's argument that domestic courts are 'part of the national authorities to which the Court affords a wide margin of appreciation under Article 15'.[200] This is a crucial difference between the rights adjudication processes in Canada and the UK. The Supreme Court of Canada's decision in *Charkaoui* would not have had

195 *Bates, Anti-Terrorism Control Orders*, 116
196 C. 28
197 *A v. United Kingdom*, App No 3455/05 [2009] ECHR 301 [hereinafter "*A v. UK*"]
198 *Secretary of State for the Home Department v AF (No 3)* [2009] UKHL 28 [hereinafter "*SSHD v. AF No 3*"]
199 *A v. UK*, para. 173
200 Ibid, para. 174

a higher rights adjudication body to challenge or affirm it, whereas the ECtHR affirmed the House of Lords' role in making key national security decisions, something the UK courts had been hesitant to do in the past. Although the British Government in *A v. UK* argued that the House of Lords should have afforded a wider margin appreciation to the executive and Parliament, the ECtHR disagreed by stating that 'The question of proportionality was ultimately a judicial decision, particularly in cases where the applicants were deprived of their fundamental right to liberty over a long period of time'.[201]

The ECtHR was also invited to comment on the issue of secret evidence by the appellants, who launched attacks on the special advocate procedure and on the non-disclosure of sensitive evidence through an Article 5(4) challenge. In response to this challenge, the Court found that it was unlawful to deny a party knowledge of the essence of the case against them in control order cases.[202] Granted, the special advocate could mitigate some of the problematic issues raised by the use of closed material by putting arguments forward for the controlee and testing the government's evidence, but no contact could be made afterwards with the controlee and, as such, the controlee could not give the advocate information to counter the allegations against them. For the ECtHR this fact, coupled with a situation where the open case against a controlee consisted of general assertions, meant that there was a breach of the convention right.[203] Section 2(1) (a) of the *Human Rights Act* 1998 requires UK courts to take decisions of the ECtHR 'into account' but does not strictly prevent the House of Lords from preferring its own view.

That being said, there is a strong imperative for the UK courts to take ECtHR judgments into account, something that was discussed by the House of Lords in *SSHD v. AF No 3*. The case essentially raised the same fair trial argument pertaining to the closed evidence that the ECtHR had ruled on and that had been raised earlier in the *MB* case. The House of Lords in *SSHD v AF No 3,* after summarizing the arguments made in *MB,* eventually concluded that the ECtHR had provided the 'definitive resolution'[204] of the closed material issue and, as such, decided that

> Where the open material consists purely of general assertions and the case against the controlee is based solely or to a decisive degree on closed materials, the requirements of a fair trial will not be satisfied, however cogent the case based on the close materials may be.[205]

Lord Hoffman wrote a lengthy dissent touching on the issue of acquiescence to the ECtHR decision. Despite his view that the ECtHR decision was wrong and

201 Ibid, para. 183
202 Ibid, paras. 216–20
203 Ibid, para. 220
204 *SSHD v. AF No 3*, para. 50
205 Ibid

damaging to the country's defences against terrorism, Hoffmann argued that the UK was bound as a matter of international law to accept the decision, stating that to reject such a decision would almost certainly put the country in breach of its international obligations.[206] Nonetheless, after the *SSHD v. AF No 3* decision, the government found itself in a very similar position to the Canadian Government post-*Charkaoui*. It was forced to either divulge more of its sensitive information or withdraw that information and risk losing the control order based on significantly weaker open material.

2.4.8 The Supreme Court rules on 1267 listing regulations: the **Ahmed** *case*[207]

Amidst the state of flux that control orders found themselves in following the judicial decisions noted above, the use of secret evidence was also being considered with regard to the same 1267 listing process that was at issue in *Abdelrazik*. In *Ahmed*, the UK Supreme Court held that regulations enacted by the UK Government to give effect to international instruments to suppress terrorist financing[208] were *ultra vires* because the executive had implemented them by executive order without any kind of parliamentary scrutiny, raising 'fundamental questions about the relationship between Parliament and the executive and about judicial control over the power of the executive'.[209] As noted by Daniel,

> As a result of this decision the government hastily passed the Al-Qaida and Taliban (Asset Freezing) Regulations on 5 February, the day after the judgment was handed down. The intention was to remedy the gaps exposed by the Supreme Court's judgment.[210]

Nonetheless, it has been argued that as a result of the decision in *Ahmed*, the 'ability of HM Treasury to freeze the assets of terrorists was dealt a monumental blow'.[211] It has been further suggested that it was inevitable that national measures introduced under 'such far-reaching instruments such as *Resolutions 1267* and *1373* should provoke widespread debate and legal challenges, once the international outrage sparked by the events of 9/11 had died down'.[212] The decision in *Ahmed* can be usefully compared with that of the Canadian Supreme Court in *Abdelrazik*, with both cases providing an example of a national court working within its legal structure to provide due process protections against the 1267 listing process.

206 Ibid, para. 70
207 *HM Treasury v. Ahmed* [2010] UKSC 2 [hereinafter "*Ahmed*"]
208 Terrorism (United Nations Measures) Order 2006 (S.I. 2006/2657); Al-Qaida and Taliban (United Nations Measures) Order 2006 (S.I. 2006/2952)
209 *Ahmed*, para. 5
210 *Daniel, International Cooperation*, 269
211 *Ryder, Financial War on Terrorism*, 127
212 *Daniel, International Cooperation*, 270

2.4.9 The repeal of control orders and the enactment of TPIMs

After the 2010 general election resulted in a hung Parliament, the Conservatives and Liberal Democrats formed a coalition government and set out a coalition agreement which, amongst other things, promised the repeal of control orders and a wider review of the UK's counter-terrorism framework. On 13 July 2010, the Home Secretary announced intentions to set up a Review of Security and Counter-Terrorism Powers, which was completed on 26 January 2011.[213] In regards to control orders, the review made a number of recommendations, namely: that the current regime should be repealed and replaced with a less intrusive system that ends forced relocation and lengthy curfews;[214] that new measures will be seen as a temporary alternative to prosecution, which remains the priority, and will be limited to a two-year maximum; and,[215] finally, that the new measures will have a number of key features, including a requirement for the Home Secretary to have reasonable grounds that an individual is involved in terrorist activity, a mandatory review attached to the measures, that the measures will require no derogation from the ECHR and that enhancements will be made to the special advocate regime.[216]

Lord Macdonald released a report that commented on the review broadly and also contained some analysis specific to control orders.[217] He argued for the abolition of relocation, called curfews and tagging disproportionate, unnecessary and objectionable and stated that telephone and internet bans are counter-productive because both are forms of communication that are easy to intercept and, as such, a ban of them limits what could be an easily accessible form of evidence.[218] In concluding his discussion on the restrictions, Macdonald argued that the various prohibitions placed on controlees in the past had in effect made them 'evidence neutral',[219] acting as a severe limit to the use of prosecution. Finally, he laid out five points pertaining to the process of how the control order regime's replacement should work in the future: 1) except in an emergency, restrictions should only be available after an application by the Home Secretary to the High Court; b) the test should be the Home Secretary's reasonable *belief* that an individual is engaged in terrorist activity; 3) there should be a further test that the Director of Public Prosecutions (DPP) is satisfied *that a criminal*

213 Secretary of State for the Home Department, *Review of Security and Counter Terrorism Powers* (Cm 8004, 26 January 2011). The review is analysed extensively in Chapter 4, particularly with regard to how it may be argued to be a result of coalition compromise and how this may have had an impact on the substance of the review and the ensuing TPIMs legislation

214 Ibid, recommendation 23, 41

215 Ibid, recommendation 24, 41–2

216 Ibid, recommendation 26, 42–3

217 Lord Macdonald, *Review of Counter-Terrorism and Security Powers* (Cm 8003, January 2011)

218 Ibid, 13

219 Ibid, 14

investigation is justified; 4) the restrictions permitted by the High Court should only last for as long as the criminal investigation continues, up to a maximum of two years; and, finally, 5) that the restrictions available to the state should be listed in, and limited by, statute.[220]

Analysis of whether Macdonald's recommendations are evident in the TPIMs legislation (which repealed control orders and established Terrorism Prevention and Investigation Measures) is given significant attention in Chapter 4.[221] Most academic commentary on the new measures still focuses on the need to rely on normal criminal prosecutions and expresses continued concerns about the use of secret evidence. Middleton notes that the use of such evidence will likely continue to come under scrutiny as 'there is growing tension amongst special advocates themselves, and the Independent Review of Terrorism Legislation'.[222] Tulich laments that 'The "pre-crime" focus of the intelligence-led model has merged intelligence and evidence while stimulating an extension of surveillance practices outside of the criminal justice system'.[223] Nonetheless, the TPIMs legislation[224] received Royal Assent and became law on 14 December 14 2011. According to Walker and Horne, the legislation 'appears set for a lengthy life'[225] despite the fact that many of the human rights issues raised in court in relation to control orders over the last six years, particularly in regards to the use of secret evidence, are likely to be re-raised.[226]

2.5 More recent significant developments in the United Kingdom

2.5.1 The Justice and Security Act *2013*

Post-*SSHD v. AF (No 3)*, the continued use of secret evidence in a variety of legal contexts, including those outside of TPIMs and particularly in relation to the use

220 Ibid, 16

221 These pages also include analysis of several sections of the legislation, as well as discussion of the JCHR reports and Public Bill Committee debates pertaining to the Act. There is also considerable academic commentary on the legislation. For an in-depth comparison of parliamentary scrutiny of the Prevention of Terrorism Act 2005 and TPIMs Act 2011, see Alexander Horne and Clive Walker, 'Lessons Learned for Political Constitutionalism?' [2014] *Public Law* 268. For a more general comparison of control orders and TPIMs, see Adrian Hunt, 'From Control Orders to TPIMs' (2013) 62 *Crime, Law and Social Change* 289

222 Ben Middleton, 'Terrorism Prevention and Investigation Measures' (2013) 71 *Journal of Criminal Law* 562, 567

223 Tamara Tulich, 'Adversarial Intelligence?' (2012) 12 *Oxford University Commonwealth Law Journal* 341, 369

224 Terrorism Prevention and Investigation Measures Act 2011 c. 23

225 Clive Walker and Alexander Horne, 'The Terrorism Prevention and Investigation Measures Act 2011' [2012] *Criminal Law Review* 421, 437

226 Helen Fenwick, 'Preventive Anti-Terrorist Strategies in the UK and ECHR' (2011) 25 *International Review of Law, Computers and Technology* 129

of Closed Material Proceedings (CMPs) in civil litigation, has proved problematic. Chapter 5 contains detailed analyses of judicial decisions pertaining to the use of secret evidence in wider national security contexts, including *Tariq*,[227] *Al Rawi*[228] and *Binyam Mohamed*.[229] Chapters 4 and 6 extensively detail and analyse the process behind the consultation, debate, amendment and implementation of the *Justice and Security Act* 2013[230] that became a controversial part of the UK's counter-terrorism framework on 25 April 2013. The legislation, which some argue was a direct response to the *Al Rawi* and *Binyam Mohamed* decisions,[231] has been referred to as 'further evidence, if more be needed, of the normalization of exceptional legal measures'.[232] Jackson expresses concern that Part 2 of the Act 'goes much further than existing statutes by extending the use of CMPs to *any* civil proceedings',[233] while Ip has noted that 'The use of CMPs and special advocates remains controversial, largely because of questions concerning whether special advocates can effectively mitigate the prejudice resulting from the non-disclosure of evidence'.[234] As was the case with more recent developments in Canada, the passage of the *Justice and Security Act* signals that, despite the successful challenges to the control order regime and the relative improvements of TPIMs, the use of secret evidence will continue to be prevalent (and problematic) going forward into the future.

2.5.2 The Counter-Terrorism and Security Act *2015*

The 7 January 2015 terrorist attacks at the offices of the satirical magazine *Charlie Hebdo* in Paris and the subsequent state of terror in the days that followed sparked renewed media attention and political condemnation of terrorism in the UK.[235] Although what would become the *Counter-Terrrorism and Security Act* (*CTSA*) 2015[236] had been introduced before these attacks, it was subject to a semi-fast-track procedure that saw it pass from Report stage in the House to full Royal Assent in just over a month, continuing a past trend of hastily passing omnibus legislation with multiple human rights implications without proper legislative

227 *Home Office v. Tariq* [2011] UKSC 35
228 *Al Rawi and Others v. the Security Service and Others* [2011] UKSC 34
229 *Mohamed, R (on the application of) v. Secretary of State for Foreign & Commonwealth Affairs* [2010] EWCA Civ 65
230 C. 18.
231 Tim Otty, 'The Slow Creep of Complacency and the Soul of Justice' [2012] *European Human Rights Review* 267
232 Greg Martin and Rebecca Scott Bray, 'Discolouring Democracy?' (2013) 40 *Journal of Law & Society* 624, 634
233 John Jackson, 'Justice, Security and the Right to a Fair Trial' [2013] *Public Law* 720
234 John Ip, 'Al Rawi, Tariq and the Future of Closed Material Procedures and Special Advocates' (2012) 75 *Modern Law Review* 606, 617
235 BBC News, 'Charlie Hebdo Attack: Three Days of Terror' (14 January 2015) available at: http://www.bbc.com/news/world-europe-30708237 [accessed 20 January 2015]
236 C. 6 [hereinafter "*CTSA*"]

scrutiny.[237] The *CTSA* makes provision for a number of new controversial anti-terrorism powers, including: 1) temporary exclusion orders (TEOs) allowing British citizens suspected of engaging in terrorist-related activity abroad to be barred from returning to the UK; 2) increased sanctions for airline carriers, requiring the supply of advanced passenger and crew information and allowing refusal of boarding to anyone on a government list; 3) compulsions that make previously voluntary measures to implement the government's PREVENT strategy mandatory, raising concerns about the chilling of free speech and expression; and 4) travel bans allowing a police or immigration officer to seize a person's passport in order to prevent them from leaving the country, if they reasonably suspect that the person intends to leave in connection with terrorism-related activity.[238]

At the time the measures were enacted, then Prime Minister David Cameron (who was heading a fragile coalition government established in 2010) would have very likely been cognizant of the political value of enacting this legislation ahead of a general election on 7 May 2015.[239] Following a trend evidenced both in relation to the *ATCSA* in 2001 and the *Prevention of Terrorism Act* 2005, it can be argued that the *CTSA* evidences a repetition of mistakes made in the aftermath of 9/11, namely the passage of sprawling counter-terrorism legislation carrying significant human rights concerns without an appropriate level of legislative scrutiny. In the aftermath of the *CTSA*'s passage, it has been noted that the legislation's provisions that allow for the stopping of a British citizen's re-entry into the country violate international law.[240] It has also been noted that the provisions pertaining to bans on travel and deradicalization are perhaps the most controversial and are the 'most likely to spawn ongoing controversy'.[241] As this chapter and subsequent analyses of post-9/11 measures in this book will show, the evolution of this legislation will likely be a long and protracted process that will involve considerable judicial scrutiny and parliamentary amendment, with those subject to the legislation bearing the financial and human costs.

237 The legislation became law on 12 February 2015 after introduction in Parliament in November 2014. See http://www.legislation.gov.uk/ukpga/2015/6

238 Ibid

239 Cameron's Conservative government subsequently won a majority in Parliament on 7 May 2015: http://www.bbc.com/news/election/2015/results

240 Taylor Brailey, 'UK Enacts Strict Anti-Terror Legislation' (13 February 2015) *The Jurist*, available at: http://jurist.org/paperchase/2015/02/uk-enacts-strict-anti-terror-legislation.php [accessed 15 February 2015]

241 Shahid Fatima, 'Travel Bans and Due Regard: The UK's New Counter-Terrorism and Security Act' (11 March 2015) *Just Security*, available at: https://www.justsecurity.org/20467/uk-law-counter-terrorism-security-act-2015/ [accessed 22 March 2015]

2.6 Conclusion

This chapter has further reinforced a justification for focusing on *Resolution 1373* by providing academic perspectives and concrete legislative examples of the impact of that international instrument. It has been noted that *Resolution 1373* further reinforced other international instruments, including *Resolutions 1267* and *1333* and the *1999 Convention* that had been sparsely ratified prior to 9/11. It was also argued that Canada's enactment of the *ATA* and the UK's enactment of the *ATCSA* in 2001 can be conceptualized as a direct response to the 9/11 attacks and the compulsion provided for by *Resolution 1373*, despite the fact that both countries had previously experienced terrorism and already had (particularly in the case of the UK) several existing legal provisions to combat terrorism. A detailed account of the historical evolution of those post-9/11 measures was provided, with an eye towards analyses in subsequent chapters pertaining to how this evolution can be said to be the product of domestic legal and political structures and cultures. Lastly, it was argued that although both security certificates and control orders (or their new incarnation, TPIMs) have been heavily modified through the courts and legislative amendments since 2001, concerns about the prevalence and problematic nature of the use of secret evidence still remain. This is particularly true in light of more recent significant developments that were discussed, particularly the 2015 passage of the *PCTA* and the *ATA* in Canada, and the 2013 *Justice and Security Act* and 2015 *Counter-Terrorism and Security Act* in the UK.

Bibliography

A and Others v. Secretary of State for the Home Department [2002] EWCA Civ 1502; [2004] QB 335

A v. Secretary of State for the Home Department (No 2) [2005] UKHL 71

A v. Secretary of State for the Home Department [2004] UKHL 56

A v. United Kingdom, App No 3455/05 [2009] ECHR 301

Abdelrazik v. Canada (Minister of Foreign Affairs) [2010] 1 F.C.R. 267

Al-Qaida and Taliban (United Nations Measures) Order 2006 (S.I. 2006/2952)

Anand, A. 'Combating Terrorist Financing: Is Canada's Legal Regime Effective?' (2011) 61 *University of Toronto Law Journal* 59

Anti-Terrorism Act, S.C. 2001, c. 41

Anti-Terrorism Act, S.C. 2015, c. 20

Anti-Terrorism, Crime and Security Act 2001, c. 24

Banerjee, S. 'Suspect Launches Suit after Terror Case Ordeal' (27 March 2010) *Toronto Star*, available at: https://www.thestar.com/news/canada/2010/03/13/suspect_launches_suit_after_terrorcase_ordeal.html [accessed 27 March 2010]

Barber, J. 'Canada's New Anti-Terror Legislation Prompts Civil Liberties Fears' (30 January 2015) *Guardian*, available at: http://www.theguardian.com/world/2015/jan/30/canadas-anti-terror-legislation-civil-liberties-fears [accessed 2 February 2015]

Bates, E. 'Anti-Terrorism Control Orders: Liberty and Security Still in the Balance' (2009) 29 *Legal Studies* 99

BBC News, 'Charlie Hebdo Attack: Three Days of Terror' (14 January 2015) available at: http://www.bbc.com/news/world-europe-30708237 [accessed 20 January 2015]

Bonner, D. *Executive Measures, Terrorism and National Security* (Ashgate, 2007)

Brailey, T. 'UK Enacts Strict Anti-Terror Legislation' (13 February 2015) *The Jurist,* available at: http://jurist.org/paperchase/2015/02/uk-enacts-strict-anti-terror-legislation.php [accessed 15 February 2015]

Canada (Citizenship and Immigration) v. Harkat [2014] 2 S.C.R. 33

Canada Evidence Act, R.S.C., 1985, C-5

Canadian Press, 'Hassan Almrei Wants Speedy Lawsuit Judgment' (CBC *News Canada*) available at: http://www.cbc.ca/news/canada/toronto/hassan-almrei-wants-speedy-lawsuit-judgment-1.1227881 [accessed 10 September 2012]

Canadian Security Intelligence Service Act, R.S.C., 1985, c. C-23

Charities Registration (Security Information) Act, S.C. 2001, c. 41, s. 113

Charkaoui v. Canada (Citizenship and Immigration) [2007] 1 S.C.R. 350

Charkaoui v. Canada (Citizenship and Immigration) [2009] 2 S.C.R. 326

Clement, D. 'The October Crisis of 1970: Human Rights Abuses Under the War Measures Act' (2008) 42 *Journal of Canadian Studies* 160

Commission of Inquiry into the Investigation of the Bombing of Air India Flight 182, *Air India Flight 182: A Canadian Tragedy* (Public Works and Government Services Canada, 2010) available at: http://publications.gc.ca/site/eng/371132/publication.html [accessed 2 October 2010]

—. Research Studies, vols 1–4 (Canadian Government Publishing, 2010)

Convention for the Protection of Human Rights and Fundamental Freedoms (European Convention on Human Rights, as Amended)

Counter-Terrorism Act 2008, c. 28

Counter-Terrorism and Security Act 2015, c. 217

Daniel, T. 'International Cooperation in Counteracting Terrorist Financing,' in Van Den Herik, L. and Schrijver, N. (eds), *Counter-Terrorism Strategies in a Fragmented International Legal Order* (Cambridge University Press, 2013) 240

Daniels, R., Macklem, P. and Roach, K. (eds), *The Security of Freedom: Essays on Canada's Anti-Terrorism Bill* (University of Toronto Press, 2001)

Dickson, B. 'Law Versus Terrorism: Can Law Win?' [2005] *European Human Rights Law Review* 11

Fatima, S. 'Travel Bans and Due Regard: The UK's New Counter-Terrorism and Security Act' (11 March 2015) *Just Security,* available at: https://www.justsecurity.org/20467/uk-law-counter-terrorism-security-act-2015 [accessed 22 March 2015]

Feldman, D. 'Proportionality and Discrimination in Anti-Terrorism Legislation' (2005) 64 *Cambridge Law Journal* 271

Fenwick, H. 'Preventive Anti-Terrorist Strategies in the UK and ECHR' (2011) 25 *International Review of Law, Computers and Technology* 129

Forcese, C. National *Security Law: Canadian Practice in International Perspective* (Irwin Law, 2008)

—. 'A Distinction with a Legal Difference: The Consequences of Non-Citizenship in the War on Terror' in Edwards, A. and Ferstman, C. (eds), *Human Security and Non-Citizens: Law, Policy and International Affairs* (Cambridge University Press, 2010)

—. 'The Judicialization of Extraterritorial Spying: Gaps and Gap-Fillers in the World of CSIS Foreign Operations' (2014) 61 *CLQ* 440

Forcese, C. and Roach, K. *False Security: The Radicalization of Canadian Anti-Terrorism* (Irwin Law, 2015)
Friedland, M. 'Police Powers in Bill C-36' in Daniels, R., Macklem, P. and Roach, K. (eds), *The Security of Freedom: Essays on Canada's Anti-Terrorism Bill* (University of Toronto Press, 2001)
HM Treasury v. Ahmed [2010] UKSC 2
Horne, A. and Walker, C. 'Lessons Learned for Political Constitutionalism?' (2014) *Public Law* 268
Hudson, G. 'As Good as It Gets? Security, Asylum and the Rule of Law after the Certificate Trilogy' (2015) 52 *Osgoode Hall Law Journal* 905
Human Rights Act 1998 (Designated Derogation) Order 2001, S.I. 2001/3644
Human Rights Act 1998 c. 42
Hunt, A. 'From Control Orders to TPIMs' (2013) *Crime, Law and Social Change*
Immigration and Refugee Protection Act, S.C. 2001, c. 27
Ip, J. 'Al Rawi, Tariq and the Future of Closed Material Procedures and Special Advocates' (2012) 75 *Modern Law Review* 606
Jackson, J. 'Justice, Security and the Right to a Fair Trial' (2013) *Public Law* 720
Joint Committee on Human Rights, *Eighteenth Report: Review of Counter-Terrorism Powers* (HL 158, HC 713, 4 August 2004)
Justice and Security Act 2013 c. 18
Library of Parliament, *Bill C-3: An Act to Amend the Immigration and Refugee Protection Act (Certificate and Special Advocate): Legislative Summary* (Parliamentary Information and Research Service, LS-567-E, 2008)
——. *Bill S-3: An Act to Amend the Criminal Code (Investigative Hearing and Recognizance with Conditions): Legislative Summary* (Parliamentary Information and Research Service, LS-574-E, 2008)
——. Legislative *Summary of Bill C-17: An Act to Amend the Criminal Code (Investigative Hearing and Recognizance with Conditions)* (Parliamentary Information and Research Service, 40-3-C17, March 2011)
——. *Legislative Summary of Bill S-7: An Act to Amend the Criminal Code, the Canada Evidence Act and the Security of Information Act* (Parliamentary Information and Research Service, 41-1-S7-e, June 2012)
Lord Carlile. *Proposals by Her Majesty's Government for Changes to the Laws Against Terrorism* (Home Office, 2005)
Lord Macdonald. *Review of Counter-Terrorism and Security Powers* (Cm 8003, January 2011)
Macklin, A. 'Stuck at the Border: Ten Years After 9/11' in Forcese, C. and Crepeau, F. (eds), *Terrorism, Law and Democracy: 10 Years after 9/11* (Canadian Institute for the Administration of Justice, Montreal, 2012)
Martin, G. and Bray, R.S. 'Discolouring Democracy?' (2013) 40 *Journal of Law & Society* 624
Middleton, B. 'Terrorism Prevention and Investigation Measures' (2013) 71 *Journal of Criminal Law* 562
Northern Ireland (Emergency Provisions) Act 1996 c. 22
Otty, T. 'The Slow Creep of Complacency and the Soul of Justice' (2012) *European Human Rights Review* 267
Powell, C. 'Defining Terrorism: How and Why' in LaViolette, N. and Forcese, C. (eds), *The Human Rights of Antiterrorism* (Irwin Law, 2008) 138

Press Release, Government of Canada. 'The Government of Canada Introduces Protection of Canada from Terrorists Act' (27 October 2014), available at: http://news.gc.ca/web/article-en.do?nid=897129 [accessed 3 April 2017]
Prevention of Terrorism (Temporary Provisions) Act 1974 s. 1(7)
Prevention of Terrorism (Temporary Provisions) Act 1989 c. 4
Prevention of Terrorism Act 2005 c. 2
Privy Counsellor Review Committee, *Anti-Terrorism, Crime and Security Act 2001 Review* (HC 100, 18 December 2003)
Proceeds of Crime (Money Laundering) and Terrorist Financing Act, S.C. 2000, c. 17
Protection of Canada from Terrorists Act, S.C. 2015, c. 9
Roach, K. 'Sources and Trends in Post-9/11 Anti-Terrorism Laws' in Goold, B. and Lazarus, L. (eds), *Security and Human Rights* (Hart Publishing, 2007)
—. 'The Air India Report and the Regulation of Charities and Terrorism Financing' (2011) 61 *University of Toronto Law Journal* 45
—. The *9/11 Effect: Comparative Counter-Terrorism* (Cambridge University Press, 2011)
—. 'A Comparative Assessment of Canadian Counter-Terrorism Laws and Practices' in Forcese, C. and Crepeau, F. (eds), *Terrorism, Law and Democracy: 10 Years after 9/11* (Canadian Institute for the Administration of Justice, Montreal, 2012)
—. 'The Problems with the New CSIS Human Source Privilege in Bill C-44' (2014) 61 *CLQ* 451
Ryder, N. *The Financial War on Terrorism: A Review of Counter-Terrorist Financing Strategies Since 2001* (Routledge, 2015)
Secretary of State for the Home Department, *Review of Security and Counter Terrorism Powers* (Cm 8004, 26 January 2011)
Secretary of State for the Home Department v. E [2007] UKHL 47
Secretary of State for the Home Department v. JJ [2007] UKHL 45
Secretary of State for the Home Department v. MB [2007] UKHL 46
Security of Canada Information Sharing Act, S.C. 2015, c. 20, s. 2
Special Immigration Appeals Commission Act 1997 c. 68
Special Senate Committee on the Anti-Terrorism Act, *Fourth Report* (Special Senate Committee on the Anti-Terrorism Act, 28 March 2007)
—. *Fundamental Justice in Extraordinary Times: Main Report of the Special Senate Committee on the Anti-Terrorism Act* (Special Senate Committee on the Anti-Terrorism Act, February 2007)
Subcommittee on the Review of the Anti-Terrorism Act. *Review of the Anti-Terrorism Act Investigative Hearings and Recognizance with Conditions: Interim Report of the Standing Committee on Public Safety and National Security* (Standing Committee on Public Safety and National Security, October 2006)
—. *Rights, Limits, Security: A Comprehensive Review of the Anti-Terrorism Act and Related Issues* (Standing Committee on Public Safety and National Security, March 2007)
Terrorism (United Nations Measures) Order 2006 (S.I. 2006/2657)
Terrorism Act 2000 c. 11
Terrorism Act 2006 c. 11
Terrorism Prevention and Investigation Measures Act 2011 c. 23
The Canadian Charter of Rights and Freedoms, Part I of the Constitution Act 1982, Being Schedule B to the Canada Act 1982 (UK), 1982, c. 11

Tomkins, A. 'Readings of A v Secretary of State for the Home Department' (2005) *Public Law* 259
Treaty on European Union (EU), 7 February 1992, 1992 O.J. (C 191) 1, 31 I.L.M.
Tulich, T. 'Adversarial Intelligence?' (2012) 12 *Oxford University Commonwealth Law Journal* 341
United Kingdom Home Affairs Committee, *First Report: The Anti-Terrorism, Crime and Security Bill 2001* (HC 351 19 November 2001)
UN Security Council. *Security Council resolution 1267 (1999) [Afghanistan]*, 15 October 1999, S/RES/1267 (1999)
UN Security Council. *Security Council resolution 1373 (2001) [on threats to international peace and security caused by terrorist acts]*, 28 September 2001, S/RES/1373 (2001)
Valverde, M. 'Governing Security, Governing through Security' in Daniels, R., Macklem, P. and Roach, K. (eds), *The Security of Freedom: Essays on Canada's Anti-Terorism Bill* (University of Toronto Press, 2001)
Waldman, L. 'An Evaluation of the Special Advocates Program in Canada' in Forcese, C. and Crepeau, F. (eds), *Terrorism, Law and Democracy: 10 Years after 9/11* (Canadian Institute for the Administration of Justice, Montreal, 2012)
Walker, C.'Terrorism and Criminal Justice: Past, Present and Future' (2004) *Criminal Law Review* 311
—. 'Prisoners of "War All the Time"' [2005] *European Human Rights Law Review* 50
—. Blackstone's *Guide to the Anti-Terrorism Legislation* (2nd edn, Oxford University Press, 2009)
—. 'The Reshaping of Control Orders in the United Kingdom: Time for a Fairer Go, Australia!' (2013) 37 *Melbourne University Law Review* 143
War Measures Act, R.S.C. 1970, c. W-2
Walker, C. and Horne, A. 'The Terrorism Prevention and Investigation Measures Act 2011' (2012) *Criminal Law Review* 421

3 Canada and the United Kingdom's domestic legal structure

Comparisons of Canada and the UK's legal structure focus on the operation of the Human Rights Act 1998[1] (*HRA*) in the UK, which gives effect to the European Convention on Human Rights[2] (*ECHR*), and on the Canadian Charter of Rights and Freedoms in Canada.[3] The *Charter* is a constitutionally entrenched Bill of Rights document that gives Canadian courts a formal power to strike down legislation, adjudicated at the highest level by the Supreme Court of Canada. By contrast, the *HRA* allows resort to the European Court of Human Rights (ECtHR) only once adjudication in the domestic courts has been exhausted and UK courts are only required under to 'take into account' Strasbourg jurisprudence.[4] While Kavanagh has argued that the powers of the courts under these two systems are not dissimilar,[5] others argue that the UK form of legislation for human rights is not as strong as the Canadian model.[6] Important questions are connected to this difference in legal structure that lead to analyses of how, and to what extent, the difference may have led to variation in the evolution of counter-terrorism measures. Specifically, two questions are raised: 1) How, and to what extent, are domestic legal decisions on counter-terrorism influenced by the structure of the rights adjudication systems in each jurisdiction?; and 2) How, and to what extent, do domestic legal structures allow for international legal instruments to impact domestic legal decisions on counter-terrorism?

1 Human Rights Act (1998) c. 42 [hereinafter "*HRA*"]

2 Council of Europe, *European Convention for the Protection of Human Rights and Fundamental Freedoms,* as amended by Protocols No. 11 and 14, 4 November 1950 [hereinafter "*ECHR*"]

3 *Canadian Charter of Rights and Freedoms,* s. 15, Part I of the *Constitution Act,* 1982 [hereinafter "*Charter*"]

4 *HRA,* s. 2(1) (a)

5 Aileen Kavanagh, *Constitutional Review under the UK Human Rights Act* (Cambridge University Press, 2009) [hereinafter "*Kavanagh, Constitutional Review*"] 163

6 Helen Fenwick, Gavin Phillipson and Roger Masterman, 'The Human Rights Act in Contemporary Context' in Fenwick, H., Phillipson, G. and Masterman, R. (eds), *Judicial Reasoning under the UK Human Rights Act* (Cambridge University Press, 2007) [hereinafter "*Fenwick et al*"] 2

This chapter analyses the key elements of the formal rights adjudication frameworks in Canada and the UK. It then analyses the case law pertaining to security certificates in Canada and detention without trial and control order provisions in the UK. In doing so, it explores how national courts operate within their respective legal structures and analyses how, and to what extent, these structures influence how judges engage in their examinations and come to their decisions. While authors such as Slaughter and Burke-White,[7] Feldman,[8] Nollkaemper,[9] Benvenisti and Downs[10] and Hudson[11] all agree to some extent that the terrain of international law has shifted and greater attention must be paid to the operation of domestic institutions, they all have different conceptions of how national courts are interacting with one another, and with the international legal order. This chapter assesses the extent to which each of these conceptions applies in order to help answer the second research question.

3.1 Canada's rights adjudication framework: the *Canadian Charter of Rights and Freedoms*[12]

There are four sections of the *Charter* that are specifically relevant to the operation of security certificates in Canada. The majority of the *Charter* challenges to the constitutionality of the security certificate regime are raised through section 7, which states that 'Everyone has the right to life, liberty, and security of the person and the right not to be deprived thereof *except in accordance with the principles of fundamental justice*' (emphasis added). A considerable and complex case law has been generated pertaining to what constitutes *principles of fundamental justice*, but the leading authority is *Re: B.C. Motor Vehicle Act*,[13] in which the Supreme Court argued that principles of fundamental justice 'are to be found in the basic tenets of our legal system' and 'do not lie in the realm of general public policy but

7 Anne-Marie Slaughter and Burke-White, 'The Future of International Law is Domestic' in Nollkaemper, A. and Nijman, J. (eds), *New Perspectives on the Divide between International and National Law* (Oxford University Press, 2007); Anne-Marie Slaughter, *A New World Order* (Princeton University Press, 2004)

8 David Feldman, 'The Internationalization of Public Law and Its Impact on the United Kingdom' in Jowell, J. and Oliver, D. (eds), *The Changing Constitution* (6th edn, Oxford University Press, 2007)

9 André Nollkaemper, *National Courts and the International Rule of Law* (Oxford University Press, 2011) [hereinafter "Nollkaemper"]

10 Eyal Benvenisti and George Downs, 'National Courts, Domestic Democracy, and the Evolution of International Law' (2009) 20 *European Journal of International Law* 59 [hereinafter "*Benvenisti and Downs*"]

11 Graham Hudson, 'Neither Here Nor There: The (Non) Impact of International Law on Judicial Reasoning in Canada and South Africa' (2008) 21 *Canadian Journal of Law and Jurisprudence* 329 [hereinafter "Hudson"]

12 Part I of the Constitution Act 1982, Being Schedule B to the Canada Act 1982 (UK), 1982, c. 11 [hereinafter "Charter"]

13 [1985] 2 S.C.R. 486

in the inherent domain of the judiciary as guardian of the justice system'.[14] Section 7 provides both substantive and procedural rights,[15] including other rights within the *Charter*, such as the section 8 unreasonable search and seizure rights, section 11 rights to a fair trial and section 12 rights against cruel and unusual punishment. Finally, principles of fundamental justice must: 1) be legal principles that provide meaningful content for the section 7 guarantee to avoid the adjudication of policy matters; 2) evidence sufficient consensus that the principle is vital to our societal notion of justice; and 3) be capable of being identified with precision and applied to situations in a manner that yields predictable results.[16]

When deciding if a section 7 right can be breached in accordance with the principles of fundamental justice, Canadian courts engage in a three-part analysis pertaining to the legislation in question. The first part of this analysis is to consider if the rights limitation is arbitrary to the legislative objective.[17] In the second part, Canadian courts engage in overbreadth analysis, considering if the legislation in question limits rights more than is necessary to achieve the legislative objective.[18] Finally, Canadian courts consider if there is gross disproportionality between the legislative objective and the harmful effects of the legislation.[19] Canadian courts have also generated other principles of fundamental justice that are relevant to

14 Ibid, para. 31

15 Ibid. This principle was also reaffirmed in *Suresh v. Canada (Minister of Citizenship and Immigration)*, [2002] 1 S.C.R. 3 [hereinafter "*Suresh*"] which is discussed further below

16 *Canadian Foundation for Children, Youth and the Law v. Canada (Attorney General)* [2004] 1 S.C.R. 76

17 The jurisprudence on arbitrariness is currently not entirely settled. According to *Rodriguez v. British Columbia (Attorney General)* [1993] 3 S.C.R. 519, a law is arbitrary where it bears no relation to, or is inconsistent with, the objective that lies behind it. In *Chaoulli v. Quebec (Attorney General)*, 2005 SCC 35, a case dealing with the provision of private health care in Quebec, three justices preferred an approach that asked if the limit was *necessary* to further the state's objective, whereas three other justices preferred to avoid necessity and follow the standard established in *Rodriguez*. Most recently, the Supreme Court in *Canada (Attorney General) v. PHS Community Services Society*, 2011 SCC 44, found that a provincial health minister's decision not to renew an exemption that would allow employees at a Safe Injection Site in Vancouver to legally provide health services to drug addicts was 'arbitrary regardless of which test for arbitrariness is used because it undermines the very purposes of the *CDSA* – the protection of health and public safety' (paras. 129–32)

18 The leading constitutional authority on overbreadth is *R v. Heywood* [1994] 3 S.C.R. 761: The state must not use means to pursue a legislative objective that are broader than necessary to accomplish that objective

19 In *R v. Malmo-Levine; R v. Caine* [2003] 3 S.C.R. 571, a landmark case pertaining to Canada's marijuana prohibition, gross disproportionality was described as 'state actions or legislative responses to a problem that are so extreme as to be disproportionate to any legitimate government interest' (para. 143). This standard was utilized and reaffirmed in the aforementioned *PHS Community Services / Society* case, where the Supreme Court also found that 'the effect of denying the services of Insite to the population it serves is grossly disproportionate to any benefit that Canada might derive from presenting a uniform stance on the possession of narcotics' (para. 133)

security certificates, such as the right to make full answer and defence,[20] and the 'shock the conscience' standard pertaining to extradition decisions.[21]

Section 1 of the *Charter*, often referred to as the reasonable limits clause, is the second key provision pertaining to the use of security certificates within Canada's rights adjudication framework. This section states that 'The *Canadian Charter of Rights and Freedoms* guarantees the rights and freedoms set out in it subject only to such reasonable limits *prescribed by law* as can be *demonstrably justified in a free and democratic society*' (emphasis added). Once the courts have found that a piece of legislation has violated a person's rights, the Crown must show, on a balance of probabilities standard, that the limitation was: 1) prescribed by law – the conduct that results in the rights limitation must have a legal basis;[22] and 2) justified in a free and democratic society. The second arm of this analysis is often referred to as the *Oakes* test.[23] The first part of the *Oakes* test, that there must be a *pressing and substantial objective*, is almost always fulfilled, especially in cases that involve national security. The second part of the *Oakes* test requires that the means must be proportional: 1) there must be a *rational connection* between the rights limitation and the legislative objective; 2) there must not be less intrusive means to justify the limitation (often referred to as a *minimal impairment* standard); and 3) overall balance between the legislative objective and the harm to rights.

The last two sections of the *Charter* that are specifically relevant to the operation of security certificates are sections 11(d) and 24(1). According to 11(d), 'Any person charged with an offence has the right to be presumed innocent until proven guilty according to law in a fair and public hearing by an independent and impartial tribunal'. In essence, the section protects the right to full answer and defence which, as aforementioned, has also been interpreted by the courts as a principle of fundamental justice. Section 24(1) states that 'Any one whose rights or freedoms, as guaranteed by this Charter, have been infringed or denied may apply to a court of competent jurisdiction to obtain such remedy as the court considers appropriate and just in the circumstances'. This section allows the courts to grant a variety of remedies to those whose rights have been shown to be violated, including striking down provisions of rights-violating legislation. Aside from these sections of the *Charter*, other legal provisions relevant to the operation of security certificates are found within the Immigration and Refugee Protection

20 This right is also protected under the *Charter's* section 11(d) rights to a fair trial, further discussed below.

21 According to *Canada v. Schmidt* [1987] 1 S.C.R. 500, punishments one might face when extradited to another country that would 'shock the conscience' of the Canadian public would breach principles of fundamental justice. This principle of fundamental justice is further elucidated in *Suresh*

22 *Little Sisters Book and Art Emporium v. Canada (Minister of Justice)* [2000] 2 S.C.R. 112

23 *R v. Oakes* [1986] 1 S.C.R. 103

Act (*IRPA*),[24] and in section 12 of the *CSIS Act*.[25] That section states that The Service shall collect, by investigation or otherwise, to the extent that is strictly necessary, and analyze and retain information and intelligence respecting activities that may on reasonable grounds be suspected of constituting threats to the security of Canada and, in relation thereto, shall report and advise the Government of Canada.

3.2 Security certificate case law analyses

This section analyses the case law pertaining to security certificates in Canada. In doing so, it explores how national courts operate within their respective legal structures and analyses how, and to what extent, these structures influence how judges engage in their analyses and come to their decisions. Although not principally concerned with the security certificate regime, it is necessary to analyse the decision in *Suresh* because it: 1) illustrates how Canadian courts used both Canadian and international perspectives to delineate the aforementioned 'shock the Canadian conscience' principle of fundamental justice; 2) concerns a constitutional challenge to the terms 'danger to the security of Canada' and 'terrorism' that are today used in the security certificate context; 3) contains useful jurisprudence on the procedural protections guaranteed by section 7 of the *Charter*; and 4) illustrates the balancing act that courts engage in under section 1 of the *Charter* in cases pertaining to national security. Mr Suresh was a convention refugee from Sri Lanka who was denied immigrant status in Canada and ordered to be deported because he constituted a danger to the security of Canada under section 53(1) (b) of the *Immigration Act*, R.S.C., 1985.[26] He appealed to the Supreme Court of Canada against decisions of the Federal Court and Federal Court of Appeal that had upheld the deportation order against him.

The Supreme Court in *Suresh* first analysed whether deportation 'to a country where the person's life or freedom would be threatened' would violate section 7 of the *Charter*. It began its inquiry into whether such a violation could be in accordance with the principles of fundamental justice by stating that it would be 'informed not only by Canadian experience and jurisprudence, but also by international law, including *jus cogens*'.[27] As such, it engaged in this inquiry first by looking at the Canadian perspective, and then from the perspective of the international norms that inform section 7. It is in the analysis of the former that

24 The relevant sections of the Immigration and Refugee Protection Act, S.C. 2001, c. 27 [hereinafter "*IRPA*"] are discussed in Chapter 2, 77–8

25 Canadian Security Intelligence Service Act, R.S.C., 1985, c. C-23 [hereinafter "*CSIS Act*"]

26 *Suresh*, paras. 16–23: This was largely based on the assertions of the intelligence services that he was a supporter of the Liberation Tigers of Tamil Eelam (LTTE), a Sri Lankan terrorist group.

27 Ibid, para. 46

the 'shock the conscience' principle was more fully elucidated, as the Court noted that torture is prohibited by section 269.1 of the Canadian Criminal Code, and argued that the government affirmed the Canadian people's opposition to torture by proscribing cruel and unusual punishment in section 12 of the *Charter*.[28] As such, the Court concluded that Canadians view torture as fundamentally unjust, finding that deportation to torture in this case would violate the principles of fundamental justice because it would be outrageous to the values of the Canadian community. The Court then turned to considering the international perspective, stating that 'The principles of fundamental justice expressed in s 7 of the *Charter* and the limits on rights that may be justified under s. 1 of the *Charter* cannot be considered in isolation from the international norms which they reflect'.[29] While the Court also noted that deportation to torture is prohibited by both the International Covenant on Civil and Political Rights (ICCPR),[30] ratified by Canada in 1976, and the Convention Against Torture and Other Cruel, Inhuman or Degrading Treatment or Punishment (CAT),[31] which was ratified in 1987, it concluded that:

> Insofar as Canada is unable to deport a person where there are substantial grounds to believe he or she would be tortured on return, this is not because Article 3 directly constrains the actions of the Canadian Government, but because the fundamental justice balance under s.7 of the *Charter* generally precludes deportation to torture.[32]

This aspect of the *Suresh* decision offers several possible answers to the question of how, and to what extent, do domestic legal structures allow for international legal instruments to impact domestic legal decisions on counter-terrorism? One could argue that the Court's reasoning above is an example of how national courts operate in a mixed zone, one that is neither fully domestic nor international, where they are subject to competing loyalties and obligations.[33] An argument could also be made that the Court's emphasis on the Canadian experience and Canadian values is the Court's way of asserting its independence and relying on its own human rights obligations under the *Charter*. By contrast, it could be argued that the Supreme Court's invocation of international law is part of an 'informal bargaining process in which they, their legislatures, and the respective

28 Ibid, paras. 50–1

29 Ibid, para. 59

30 UN General Assembly, *International Covenant on Civil and Political Rights*, 16 December 1966, United Nations, Treaty Series, vol 999, p. 171

31 UN General Assembly, *Convention Against Torture and Other Cruel, Inhuman or Degrading Treatment or Punishment*, 10 December 1984, United Nations, Treaty Series, vol 1465, p. 85

32 Ibid, para. 78

33 *Nollkaemper*, 14

civil societies are relatively equal partners'.[34] Hudson specifically utilizes the *Suresh* decision, among others, in his argument against the impact of international law on Canada, stating his belief that it is only used to add rhetorical weight to decisions which have been reached on other grounds.[35] This argument is particularly forceful, considering how the Court emphasizes above that it is the fundamental justice balance under the *Charter* that precludes deportation to torture, and not the constraining force of the Convention Against Torture.[36]

The Court then had to decide whether the terms 'danger to the security of Canada' and 'terrorism', both used today in the issuance and adjudication of security certificates under the *IRPA*, were unconstitutionally vague. It found that the former was not, concluding that to insist on direct proof of a specific threat would be to set the bar too high, namely because 'Canada's national security may be promoted by reciprocal considerations between Canada and other states in combating international terrorism'.[37] The Court also noted the dicta of Lord Slynn in *Secretary of State for the Home Department v. Rehman,* when arguing that courts may now conclude that the support of terrorism abroad raises a possibility of adverse repercussions for Canada's security.[38] This is the kind of judicial dialogue that Benvenisti and Downs argue national courts are frequently engaging in when they use comparative analysis to seek support from other jurisdictions for their judgments.[39] Turning to the definition of 'terrorism', the Court noted that the *Immigration Act* does not define the term and there is no single definition that is accepted internationally.[40] It argued that the definition found within the *International Convention for the Suppression of Financing of Terrorism*[41] employs a useful definition which was within the scope of nine other international treaties that are listed in the Convention's annex and, as such, 'this definition catches the essence of what the world understands by "terrorism"'.[42] Here, there was no conflict between domestic law and international law and, as such, the Court chose to fill a gap in its legal structure by recourse to an international instrument. Hudson's argument loses some of its explanatory power here, although the clear difference is that in this part of the decision the Court lacked a domestic approach to prioritize in its reasoning. The implication is that national courts may be more willing to look to international law when their national law is silent and there is an available legal instrument that provides useful guidance. This usefully illustrates

34 *Benvenisti and Downs,* 68
35 *Hudson*, 329
36 UN General Assembly, *Convention Against Torture and Other Cruel, Inhuman or Degrading Treatment or Punishment,* 10 December 1984, United Nations, Treaty Series, vol 1465, p. 85 [hereinafter *Convention Against Torture*]
37 *Suresh,* para. 88
38 Ibid, para. 87
39 *Benvenisti and Downs,* 66
40 Ibid, 94
41 GA Res. 54/109, 9 December 1999
42 *Suresh,* para. 98

how, and to what extent, domestic legal decisions on counter-terrorism are influenced by the structure of the rights adjudication systems in each jurisdiction. When making decisions on counter-terrorism legislation, courts may be more willing to engage in international or comparative law analysis to fill in aspects of their legal structure that are lacking or incomplete.

Finally, the Court addressed the procedural protections Mr Suresh was entitled to under section 7 of the *Charter*. In doing so, the Court argued that:

> The greater the effect on the life of the individual by the decision, the greater the need for procedural protections to meet the common law duty of fairness and the requirements of fundamental justice under s. 7 of the *Charter*.[43]

Although the Court stopped short of ordering a full oral hearing or a complete judicial process, they found that the procedural protections required by section 7 meant that the refugee must be informed of the case to be met and given an opportunity to challenge the information against them, and no such opportunities had been available to Mr Suresh.[44] As such, the Court argued that this lack of basic procedural protections could not be justified by section 1 because 'valid objectives do not, without more, suffice to justify limitations on rights'.[45] As a result, the Supreme Court remanded the cases back to the Minister for reconsideration in accordance with the procedures they had set out in their reasons.

In *Charkaoui v. Canada (Citizenship and Immigration)*,[46] the Supreme Court issued its first ruling on the constitutionality of the security certificate regime, once again engaging in section 7 and 1 analysis. The Court cited a number of factors to argue that the security certificate process engages section 7 rights, most notably the possible deportation and loss of liberty associated with detention.[47] It further bolstered this claim by citing the findings of the Maher Arar Commission pertaining to potential consequences of deportation combined with allegations of terrorism.[48] Ultimately, the Court decided that the deprivation was not in accordance with the principles of fundamental justice because the scheme denied the named person the opportunity to know the case against them and challenge it accordingly.[49] As such, it engaged in section 1 analysis, where the legislation failed the 'minimal impairment' arm of the *Oakes* test, largely because of the existence of the special advocate system in the UK.[50] This aspect of the

43 Ibid, para. 118
44 Ibid, paras. 121–2
45 Ibid, para. 128
46 [2007] 1 S.C.R. 350 [hereinafter *Charkaoui I*]
47 Ibid, paras. 12–18
48 Ibid, para. 26
49 Ibid, paras. 52–65
50 Ibid, para. 69: 'The United Kingdom uses special counsel to provide a measure of protection to the detained person's interests, while preserving the information that must be kept secret. These alternatives suggest that the IRPA regime, which places on the judge the entire

decision offers some insight into the question pertaining to the impact of legal structure on judicial decision-making. Here, the 'minimal impairment' aspect of Canada's rights adjudication system offered the Court the opportunity to consider ways in which the security certificate system could more minimally impair the right in question, inviting comparisons with the special advocate system in the UK. This is an example of how national courts 'learn from each other's legal systems how to balance amongst the competing common interests and how to manage the conflicting common risks to their societies'.[51] The structure of the rights adjudication system in Canada, namely section 1's minimal impairment test, allowed the Court to look elsewhere for a solution.

The government was also found to fail the section 1 minimal impairment test when the Court considered the *IRPA* provisions that provided for mandatory detention review. If a permanent resident could receive a detention review within 48 hours, how could the same system, which took 120 days for a foreign national, be said to pass a less intrusive means standard?[52] Interestingly, the Court had engaged in this section 1 analysis after finding a breach in sections 9 and 10(c) of the *Charter*, which pertain to the right against arbitrary detention and the right to prompt review of detention. In the UK jurisprudence, a similar argument was raised in the *Belmarsh*[53] case in reference to the detention of non-nationals. This argument was won by the appellants on discrimination grounds, among others, because there was no similar provision made for the detention of UK citizens. A similar argument was raised in *Charkaoui I*, but since section 6 of the *Charter* provides for differential treatment of citizens and non-citizens in deportation matters, the security certificate scheme was found not to infringe equality rights in section 15 of the *Charter*. This provides another illustration of how Courts hear, and decide on, certain legal issues in a different manner as a result of differences in the legal structures within which they work.

Having found that the *IRPA*'s procedure for the judicial confirmation of certificates and review of detention violated section 7 of the *Charter* and had not been shown to be justified under section 1, the Court moved to remedy the violations. The Court did so within the structure in which it operates, namely, by striking down section 78(g) of the *IRPA* and declaring it to be of no force or effect because it allowed for 'the use of evidence that is never disclosed to the named person without adequate measures to compensate for the non-disclosure and the constitutional problems it causes'.[54] However, by suspending this declaration for one year, the Court's formal strike down power in effect operated

burden of protecting the person's interest, does not minimally impair the rights of non-citizens'

51 *Benvenisti and Downs*, 68

52 *Charkaoui I*, paras. 90–4

53 *A v. Secretary of State for the Home Department* [2004] UKHL 56 [hereinafter "*Belmarsh*"]. This case is more fully analysed and discussed in the UK section below

54 *Charkaoui I*, para. 139

similarly to the declaration of incompatibly mechanism at the disposal of UK courts, albeit with a specified time period to amend the procedure attached. The Court then turned to the second defect of the legislation, that section 84(2) of the *IRPA* denied a prompt hearing to foreign nationals, and reasoned that the appropriate remedy was to strike the impugned provision and read foreign nationals into section 83 in a manner which would ensure that they receive the same timely detention review as permanent residents.[55] Here again we see an example of the Court operating within its legal structure, utilizing available powers to read down legislation and modify the existing statutory framework under the *IRPA*.

Within a year of this decision, the Supreme Court heard a second appeal from the Federal Court with regard to Mr Charkaoui.[56] This case centred on whether he had a right to obtain notes from interviews that CSIS had conducted with him in 2002. He was informed that this disclosure would not be possible because these notes had been destroyed in accordance with section 12 of the *CSIS Act*. Justice Noel of the Federal Court, in the judgment that was at issue in the appeal, had argued that security certificates were not criminal proceedings warranting protection of the *Charter*, and that CSIS was not a police agency subject to disclosure obligations.[57] The Supreme Court disagreed with Noel's characterization of CSIS, primarily by using the Arar Inquiry's finding that CSIS and the RCMP frequently interact with respect to national security-related intelligence.[58] Moreover, the Court decided that Charkaoui should have access to the original interview notes, because the CSIS's operational policy under section 12 of the *CSIS Act* rested 'on an erroneous interpretation of that provision'.[59] Finally, the Supreme Court reaffirmed its stance in *Charkaoui I* that the security certificates can place rights in serious jeopardy and, as such, the application of the *Charter* should not turn on a formal distinction between the different areas of law, but rather on the serious consequences of the state's actions for the individual.[60] The sum of these findings was that disclosure of the entire file at issue was ordered and CSIS was sent a strong message that the intelligence it collects could be subject to disclosure in subsequent proceedings. Here again, structure is important because the ordering of the disclosure depended heavily on the characterization of the relationship between CSIS and the RCMP, and on the erroneous interpretation of an institutional policy. If the two agencies had a different institutional relationship, or if the structure of the policy CSIS relied on had been different, the Court may have come to a different conclusion.

55 Ibid, paras. 141–2
56 [2009] 2 S.C.R. 326 [hereinafter "*Charkaoui II*"]
57 *Re Charkaoui* [2005] F.C.J. 139, para. 17
58 *Charkaoui II*, para. 27
59 Ibid, paras. 38–43
60 Ibid, para. 53

As a result of the disclosure ordered in *Charkaoui II*, CSIS disclosed original operational notes to the Ministers that were then disclosed to the Federal Court and the special advocates, who carried out their duties under the *IRPA* of scrutinizing and challenging claims against disclosure on the part of the Ministers. When the Federal Court then found that disclosure of certain evidence would not be injurious to national security, the Ministers disagreed with the Court's determinations and chose to withdraw the evidence in accordance with their right to do so under the *IRPA*, stating that the evidence remaining was not sufficient to prove the reasonableness of the certificate against Mr Charkaoui.[61] Subsequently, the Court declared his certificate to be void and held that there would be no further appeals in his case. Shortly after, Hassan Almrei's certification was dismissed by Justice Richard Mosley in a 185-page judgment.[62] In *Almrei*, Mosley found that there was no longer any reason to believe that Almrei was a security threat and, in doing so, stated that the intelligence services and involved Ministers had breached their duty of candour to the court by providing information that was shown to be inconsistent and incomplete after the *Charkaoui II* ruling ordered the production of additional material.[63] The government has chosen not to pursue possible appeals stemming from the decision.

The most recent Supreme Court decision on security certificates came in the *Harkat*[64] case. In that case, the Supreme Court of Canada decided that the security certificate scheme was constitutional, arguing that Parliament had responded to *Charkaoui* in a manner that conferred upon judges a discretion and flexibility to fashion a fair process in each particular case before them.[65] Referencing the UK Supreme Court's decision in *Secretary of State for the Home Department v AF (No 3)* [2009] UKHL 28, the Court found that this fair process would generally occur when the named person was provided with sufficient information about the allegations against them, i.e. more than purely general assertions.[66] The Court had previously developed this standard in *Charkaoui*, and used the UK House of Lords decision to add further rhetorical weight to its decision. This aspect of the decision is another good example of Benvisiti and Downs' conceptualization. The Court also noted that the level of disclosure required in any case would be case-specific, and that ultimately the judge in the case 'is the arbiter of whether this standard has been met'.[67] It has been argued that the Supreme Court ruled this way because of the performance of the Federal Court, and much of the judgment reads as an affirmation of the work that had been done by the Federal

61 *Charkaoui (Re)* [2010] 4 F.C.R. 448; 2009 FC 1030 [hereinafter "*Charkaoui III*"]
62 *Almrei (Re)* [2011] 1 F.C.R. 163; 2009 FC 1263 [hereinafter "*Almrei*"]
63 Ibid, paras. 501–3
64 *Canada (Citizenship and Immigration) v. Harkat* [2014] 2 S.C.R. 33 [hereinafter "*Harkat*"]
65 Ibid, para. 4
66 Ibid, para. 56
67 Ibid, para. 57

Court in these cases.[68] This leads to another important observation about legal structure. The Supreme Court ruling in this case may have been different if there had been significant questions about the ability of Federal Court judges to ensure a fair process on a case-by-case basis.

Another important aspect of the Court's judgment in *Harkat* pertained to restrictions on the ability of the special advocate to communicate with the named person once they have seen closed material, which has long been regarded as a difficult aspect of the process. Ultimately, the Supreme Court was satisfied that restrictions on communication are not absolute (a judge can allow them, subject to any conditions, via section 85.4(2) of the *IRPA*) and found that the availability of this judicial authorization meant that special advocates were able to perform their role in a constitutionally sufficient manner.[69] Again, this leads to an important observation about the impact of legal structure. Here the Supreme Court focused on an aspect of legal structure – i.e. the ability of a judge to authorize communication under section 85.4(2) – in order to confidently rule that the availability of this provision and its appropriate use by Federal Court judges would go a long way towards ensuring the effectiveness of the special advocate and, in turn, allowing for an overall fair process. In its concluding remarks on the constitutionality of the *IRPA* scheme, the Court acknowledged that 'these provisions remain an imperfect substitute for full disclosure in an open court' but also pointed to the ability of judges to grant remedies (including a stay of proceedings under section 24(1) if necessary) based on their assessment of the overall fairness of the proceedings.[70] Here again the Supreme Court is pointing to an element of legal structure – i.e. the availability of a stay of proceedings under section 24(1) – to develop its argument that the security certificate scheme under *IRPA* is constitutional. One might fairly argue that if this element of legal structure was absent, the Supreme Court may have come to a different conclusion in the *Harkat* case.

This section has used the analysis of the case law on security certificates in Canada to explore how national courts operate within their legal structure and to analyse how, and to what extent, this structure has influenced how judges engage in their analysis and come to their decisions. In the *Suresh* analysis, the Supreme Court argued that it was an element of its own legal structure, namely, the fundamental justice balance under section 7 of the *Charter* that precluded deportation to torture, rather than the ICCPR and CAT. Conversely, the Court used an international instrument to fill a void in Canada's legal structure by adopting the *International Convention for the Suppression of Financing of Terrorism*'s definition of terrorism. The discrimination argument that had been successfully raised against differential treatment of non-citizens in *Belmarsh* did

68 Graham Hudson, 'As Good as It Gets? Security, Asylum and the Rule of Law after the Certificate Trilogy' (2015) 52 *Osgoode Hall Law Journal* 905

69 Ibid, paras. 69–70

70 Ibid, para. 77

not succeed in *Charkaoui I* because the structure of the Canadian legal system, namely section 6 of the *Charter*, provides for this differential treatment. Moreover, the 'minimal impairment' aspect of Canada's rights adjudication system gave the Court the opportunity to consider ways in which the security certificate system could more minimally impair the right in question, inviting comparisons with the special advocate system in the UK. This is an example of how national courts learn how to balance competing common interests in their societies from each other's legal systems.[71] The structure of the rights adjudication system in Canada, namely section 1's minimal impairment test, allowed the Court to look elsewhere for a solution. In *Harkat,* the impact of legal structure was once again evident, as the presence of both the communication authorization power under section 85.4(2) and the availability of a stay of proceedings under section 24(1) were pointed to by the Supreme Court in deciding that these powers, properly exercised by a Federal Court judge on a case-by-case basis could lead to an overall fair process. Finally, the case law analyses in this section suggested several answers to the question of how, and to what extent, domestic legal structures allow for international legal instruments to impact decision-making on counter-terrorism. Hudson's argument that international law is often only used by courts to add rhetorical force to a decision they would have reached anyway was most forceful in the *Suresh* analysis, where the Court emphasizes that it is the fundamental justice balance under the *Charter* that precludes deportation to torture, and not the constraining force of the *Convention Against Torture.* However, the *Suresh* analysis also suggested that national courts may be more willing to look to international law when their national law is silent and there is an available legal instrument that provides useful guidance as to how to fill a gap in domestic law. Moreover, Benvenisti and Downs' conceptualization was also applicable in several of the cases analysed.

3.3 United Kingdom's rights adjudication framework: the *European Convention on Human Rights*[72] and the *Human Rights Act*[73]

The *ECHR* is given domestic effect in the UK by the Human Rights Act, analysed earlier in this book. This section focuses on the provisions of the *ECHR*, specifically those relevant to the operation of detention without trial, control orders and TPIMs. There are a number of *ECHR* articles that are relevant to the challenges that have been brought against these measures. The first to be discussed is the Article 3 torture prohibition, which is one of the most fundamental provisions of the Convention.[74] The prohibition of torture is an absolute right, from which

71 *Benvenisti and Downs*, 68
72 *ECHR*
73 Human Rights Act 1998 c. 42 [hereinafter "*HRA*"]
74 *Pretty v. UK*, App No 2346/02 [2002] ECHR 423, para. 49

no derogation can be made,[75] regardless of the individual's conduct, including whether it is argued that the person poses a threat to national security.[76] The Article places both negative and positive duties on the state to ensure that this treatment is not endured.[77] The scope of Article 3 was further articulated in *Ireland v UK*,[78] where it was held that treatment must attain a minimum level of severity to fall within the article, with this level being based on criteria such as duration, physical and mental effects.[79] Moreover, states may not extradite an individual to a country where there are substantial grounds for believing that there is a real risk the individual would be subject to torture or ill-treatment.[80]

Article 5 of the *ECHR* has several similarities to section 7 of the *Charter* and is perhaps the article most relevant to the challenges to the aforementioned measures that this section will discuss. Article 5(1) states that 'Everyone has the right to liberty and security of the person. No one shall be deprived of his liberty save in the following cases and in accordance with a procedure prescribed by law.' Its main focus is to ensure that nobody is deprived of liberty in an arbitrary fashion.[81] In order for a procedure to be prescribed by law, the legislation in question must be both adequately accessible, and formulated with sufficient precision to enable the citizen to regulate his conduct.[82] What constitutes a deprivation of liberty is a difficult question with an extensive case law behind it. The ECtHR has distinguished between deprivations of, and restrictions on, liberty.[83] The distinction depends on a question of degree or intensity, rather than nature or substance.[84] Finally, *Guzzardi v. Italy*[85] states that a range of factors pertaining to the concrete situation of the person involved must be taken account of, including type, duration and effects.[86]

In contrast to Article 3, Article 5 is not an absolute right and is subject to exceptions.[87] Moreover, the Article provides a number of procedural rights to those who are deprived of their liberty.[88] Of these procedural rights, Article 5(4) is of particular relevance for this section's case analysis. It states that:

75 This was reaffirmed in *Saadi v. Italy*, App No 37201/06, 28 February 2008, para. 127

76 *Chahal v. UK*, App No 22414/93 [1996] ECHR 54 [hereinafter "*Chahal*"]

77 The obligation not to do harm is absolute, but the positive obligation requires the state to do all that it reasonably can to prevent harm from occurring: *Re E* [2008] UKHL 66

78 *Ireland v. UK*, App No 5310/71 [1978] ECHR 1

79 Ibid, para. 162

80 *Soering v. UK*, App No 14038/88 [1989] ECHR 14

81 *Brogan v. UK*, App No 11266/84 [1988] ECHR 24 [hereinafter "*Brogan*"]

82 *Sunday Times v. UK*, App No 6538/74 [1979] ECHR 1 [hereinafter "*Sunday Times*"]

83 *Engel v. Netherlands*, App No 5370/72 [1976] ECHR 3 [hereinafter "*Engel*"]

84 *Ashingdane v. UK*, App No 8225/78 [1985] ECHR 8 [hereinafter "*Ashingdane*"]

85 *Guzzardi v. Italy*, App No 7367/76 [1980] ECHR 5

86 Ibid, para. 92

87 These are laid out in Article 5(1) (a)–(f). Of particular relevance is the exception under 5(1) (f), which pertains to the lawful arrest or detention of a person against whom action is being taken with a view to deportation or extradition.

88 These are laid out in Articles 5(2)–(4)

> Everyone who is deprived of his liberty by arrest or detention shall be entitled to take proceedings by which the lawfulness of his detention shall be decided speedily by a court and his release ordered if the detention is not lawful.

The court referenced in this article need not be a traditional court of law, so long as it: 1) exhibits necessary judicial procedures and safeguards; 2) is independent of the executive and the parties; and 3) is able to decide the lawfulness of the detention and, if not, order release.[89] As a result of the liberty issues at stake, Article 5(4)'s expediency requirement has been held to be more exacting than Article 6(1),[90] to which focus now turns.

Article 6 of the *ECHR* enshrines the right to a fair trial. The Court's main task under this article is to examine whether proceedings, taken as a whole, were fair. Although the right to a fair trial is absolute, it is subject to a number of limitations, most specifically the fact that Article 6(1) pertains to legal proceedings generally, but Articles 6(2) and 6(3) pertain to criminal cases only. As such, Article 6(1) is most relevant to this section's case analysis. The component aspects of Article 6(1) have a considerable case law behind them. What constitutes a *determination* has been defined as: 1) requiring there to be a dispute and a resolution procedure;[91] 2) including all proceedings that have a *decisive* result for civil rights and obligations;[92] or 3) in relation to a criminal charge, involving the individual concern being substantially affected.[93] The ECtHR has elucidated what it means by civil rights and obligations by stating that, 'Whether or not a right is to be regarded as civil within the meaning of this expression in the Convention must be determined by reference to the substantive content and effects of the right – and not for its legal classification – under the domestic law of the state concerned'.[94] Moreover, a number of entitlements have been held to be implicit under Article 6(1) including: 1) access to a court, which is real and effective; 2) a hearing before an independent and impartial tribunal established by law; 3) that this hearing be public in nature and within a reasonable time; 4) that it present a real opportunity for the case to be made; and 5) that there be a reasoned decision.

Article 14 of the *ECHR* states that:

> The enjoyment of the rights and freedoms set forth in this Convention shall be secured without discrimination on any ground such as sex, race, colour, language, religion, political or other opinion, national or social origin, association with a national minority, property, birth or other status.

89 *Benjamin and Wilson v. UK*, App No 28212/95 [2002] ECHR 636, para. 33
90 *Reid v. UK* [2003] ECHR 94, para. 79
91 *Konig v. Germany*, App No 6232/73 [1978] ECHR 3 [hereinafter "*Konig*"]
92 *Ringeisen v. Austria*, App No 2614/65 [1971] ECHR 2
93 *Heaney and McGuinness v. Ireland* [2001] 33 EHRR 12
94 *Konig*, para. 89

Although the article is not a general guarantee to equal treatment, it can apply without the breach of another article if the facts of the case come within the ambit of another article.[95] It has been argued to be of crucial importance, because discriminatory law breeds resentment, brings the law into disrepute and fosters inequality that is demeaning to those unfairly benefitted and those unfairly prejudiced.[96] Discrimination is held to have occurred when the individuals facing the detrimental treatment were in relevantly similar or analogous situations,[97] and when no objective or reasonable justification for the differential treatment exists.[98] The test for this justification is that the state must advance a legitimate aim to justify the differential treatment, and it must show proportionality between the aim and the means chosen to pursue it.[99] Finally, while the ECtHR does afford a certain margin of appreciation in these cases, greater deference is paid in cases that involve the absence of a common standard among the contracting states.[100]

Article 15(1) of the *ECHR* allows states to take measures that derogate from its Convention obligations '*to the extent strictly required by the exigencies of the situation,* in times of war or *other public emergency threatening the life of the nation*' (emphasis added). This Article only relates to rights that are derogable (i.e. no derogation is permitted from Articles 2, 3, 4(1) and 7). A public emergency threatening the life of the nation has been defined as 'an exceptional situation of crisis or emergency that affects the whole population and constitutes a threat to the organized life of the community of which the state is composed'.[101] A wide margin of appreciation has been afforded to states in these determinations and, as such, the ECtHR has never rejected the existence of such a public emergency.[102] In elucidating what is meant by *strictly required by the exigencies of the situation*, the ECtHR has held that:

> There must be a link between the facts of the emergency on the one hand and the measures chosen to deal with it on the other hand. Moreover, the obligations under the Convention do not entirely disappear. They can only be suspended or modified to the extent that is strictly required as provided in Article 15.[103]

95 *Abdulaziz, Cabales and Balkandali v. UK*, App No 9473/81 [1985] ECHR 7
96 *Ghaidan v. Godin Mendoza* [2004] UKHL 30, para. 9
97 *National and Provincial Building Society v. UK*, App No 21319/93 [1997] ECHR 87
98 *Fredin v. Sweden* (1991) 13 EHHR 784
99 *Belgian Logistics (No 2)*, App No 2126/64 (1968) 1 EHRR 252
100 *Petrovic v. Austria*, App No 20458/92 [1998] ECHR 21
101 *Lawless v. Ireland*, App No 332/57 (A/3) [1961] ECHR 2
102 The ECtHR did reject such a claim in the *Greek Case* (1969) 12 YB 1, in which the features of such an emergency were laid out as: 1) actual or imminent; 2) having effects that involve the whole nation; 3) continuance of organized life of the community is threatened; and 4) the danger or crisis is exceptional, such that normal measures or restrictions are inadequate
103 *Ireland v. UK*, App No 5310/71 [1978] ECHR 1, 588

Here too, the ECtHR affords a wide margin of appreciation, but still retains a supervisory role,[104] specifically with regard to the nature of the rights affected, the nature and duration of the emergency, and any safeguards against arbitrary state behavior.[105]

Lastly, Article 13 of the *ECHR* provides the right to an effective remedy. However, the Article does not provide a free-standing right to this remedy, and it must be brought in conjunction with an alleged breach of another Convention right. The ECtHR has found that both domestic procedures for dealing with the substance of an arguable complaint and for granting relief in cases of actual breaches are necessary for an effective remedy.[106] Article 13 was not included in the *HRA* because it was believed that provisions of the *HRA* itself provided for effective remedies. However, the declaration of incompatibility has been roundly criticized by the ECtHR, mostly because of its inability to place a binding legal obligation on the executive or legislature to amend law once a breach has been found.[107] Although the Article was not included in the *HRA*, English courts have considered the right by virtue of section 2 of the *HRA*, under which they are required to take Strasbourg case law into account.

3.4 Detention without trial and control order case law analyses

This section analyses the case law pertaining to detention without trial and control order mechanisms in the UK. In doing so, it explores how national courts operate within their respective legal structures and analyses how, and to what extent, these structures influence how judges engage in their analyses and come to their decisions. *Chahal* is an important starting point for consideration of the detention without trial and control order jurisprudence for a number of reasons: 1) it resulted in the creation of SIAC, which has become an important national court intrinsically involved in the adjudication of control orders; 2) it argues that Article 3 of the *ECHR* provides wider protections than UN Conventions; and 3) it contains useful statements on Articles 5(1) (f) and 5(4) of the *ECHR*, both relevant articles in the challenges to be discussed. Mr Chahal had been detained in custody for deportation purposes on the basis that he was a threat to national security. He argued, amongst other things, that his deportation to India would expose him to a real risk of torture or inhuman or degrading treatment, that his detention was not lawful under Article 5 and that he had no effective domestic remedy because of the national security elements in his case. While no violation of Article 5(1) was found, he was successful in his Article 3, 5(4) and 13 claims.

104 Ibid

105 *Brannigan and Mcbride v. UK*, App No 14553 [1993] ECHR 21

106 *Askoy v. Turkey*, App No 21987/93 [1996] ECHR 68

107 *Dodds v. UK*, App No 59314/00, 8 April 2003; *Walker v. UK*, App No 37212/02, 16 March 2004; *Pearson v. UK*, App No 8374/03, 27 April 2004

In consideration of the Article 3 claim, the ECtHR reaffirmed the absolute nature of Article 3 of the Convention, arguing that the protection offered by the Article was 'wider than that provided by Articles 32 and 33 of the United Nations 1951 Convention on the Status of Refugees'.[108] The ECtHR also found a violation of Article 5(4), arguing that neither the proceedings for judicial review of the decision to detain Chahal, nor the advisory panel procedure satisfied the article's requirements.[109] In arriving at this finding, the Court stated that:

> In Canada, a more effective form of judicial control has been developed in cases of this type. This example illustrates that there are techniques which can be employed which both accommodate legitimate security concerns about the nature and sources of intelligence information and yet accord the individual a substantial measure of procedural justice.[110]

The presence of the Canadian system under the *IRPA* was once again noted when the Court found a violation of the Article 13 right to an effective remedy.[111] As a result of the judgment, SIAC was created and has since functioned in a manner similar to the Federal Court of Canada under the *IRPA*.[112] In essence, a gap in the UK's legal structure was recognized by the UK courts and was subsequently filled, based on the decision of a court that looked to the solution developed in a foreign jurisdiction.

The events following *Chahal* and the UK's subsequent derogation from Article 5(1) of the *ECHR*[113] led to the ruling of the House of Lords in *Belmarsh*. In *Belmarsh* the House of Lords begins its judgment by noting that the domestic definition of terrorism, found within section 1 of the *Terrorism Act* 2000, would be used in the appeal at hand.[114] As such, the House of Lords did not engage in an analysis of international definitions of terrorism, as the Canadian Supreme Court had done in *Suresh*, because a definition already existed within their legal framework. The House of Lords then turned its consideration to the derogation from Article 5(1) (f), made under Article 15(1) of the *ECHR*. After Lord Bingham

108 *Chahal*, para. 80
109 Ibid, para. 132
110 Ibid, para. 131
111 Ibid, para. 144: 'The interveners were all of the view that judicial review did not constitute an effective remedy in cases involving national security. Article 13 required at least that some independent body should be appraised of all the facts and evidence and entitled to reach a decision which would be binding on the Secretary of State. In this connection, Amnesty International, Liberty, the Aire Centre and the JCWI drew the Court's attention to the procedure applied in such Cases in Canada'
112 SIAC was fully discussed in Chapter 2
113 These events, namely the terrorist attacks of 11 September 2001, the passage of the *Anti-Terrorism, Crime and Security Act 2001* and the UK's derogation order in relation to this act were discussed in Chapter 1
114 *Belmarsh,* para. 5

found there to be a public emergency threatening the nation,[115] the Court engaged in a proportionality analysis in order to discern if the derogation was strictly required by the exigencies of the situation.[116] Whilst doing so, it noted: the Newton Committee findings pertaining to the real threat coming from UK citizens;[117] a number of critical comments made by the European Commissioner for Human Rights;[118] and, finally, the appellants' argument that the fundamental importance of the right to personal freedom drew on a long libertarian tradition of English law, dating back to Chapter 39 of the Magna Carta.[119]

The House of Lords found that the appellants' proportionality challenge to the Order and section 23 was 'sound, for all the reasons they gave and also for those given by the European Commissioner for Human Rights and the Newton Committee'.[120] This also occurred during analysis of the Article 14 claim, where Lord Bingham examined if section 23 was discriminatory because it provided for the detention of suspected terrorists who were foreign nationals, but not for the detention of UK nationals. Here again, a variety of international instruments and opinions of international bodies were referred to in order to assess the Article 14 claim, including: 1) the Parliamentary Assembly, and the Committee of Ministers of the Council of Europe, as well as the European Commission against Racism and Intolerance;[121] 2) the United Nations Human Rights Committee, which pointed to non-discrimination provisions in the Universal Declaration of Human Rights, the Declaration on the Human Rights of Individuals who are not Nationals of the Country in which they live, and Article 4 of the ICCPR;[122] and c) the United Nations Security Council.[123]

115 Ibid, paras. 27–9. Lord Hoffman disagreed with the finding of a public emergency, paras. 88–97

116 Ibid, para. 30

117 Ibid, para. 32: 'The Newton Committee recorded the Home Office argument that the threat from Al-Qaeda terrorism was predominantly from foreigners, but drew attention to accumulating evidence that this is not now the case . . . Almost 30% of Terrorism Act 2000 suspects in the past year have been British. We have been told that, of the people of interest to the authorities, because of their suspected involvement in international terrorism, nearly half are British nationals'

118 Ibid, para. 34: 'It would appear, therefore, that the derogating measures of the Anti-Terrorism, Crime and Security Act allow both for the detention of those presenting no direct threat to the United Kingdom and for the release of those of whom it is alleged that they do. Such a paradoxical conclusion is hard to reconcile with the strict exigencies of the situation'

119 Ibid, para. 36

120 Ibid, para. 43

121 Ibid, para. 57: states had a responsibility 'to review legislation and regulations adopted in connection with the fight against terrorism to ensure that these do not discriminate directly or indirectly against persons or a group of persons, notably on grounds of race, colour, language, religion, nationality or national or ethnic origins, and to abrogate any such discriminatory legislation'.

122 Ibid, paras. 58–62

123 Ibid, para. 61

After noting these materials, Lord Bingham stated that while they are not 'legally binding on the United Kingdom', there is 'no European or other authority to support the Attorney General's submission' against the appellants' argument.[124] As a result, Bingham found the decision to detain one group of suspected international terrorists, and not another, to be in violation of Article 14 as well as 'article 26 of the ICCPR and so inconsistent with the United Kingdom's other obligations under international law within the meaning of article 15 of the European Convention'.[125] Again, this decision helps to answer this chapter's question pertaining to how, and to what extent, domestic legal structures allow international legal instruments to impact decisions on counter-terrorism. The decision lends support to the argument that this was one of the cases where although international law considerations are among many that support a particular interpretation, it is unlikely that the interpretation would otherwise have been different if the court had not considered international law.[126] Hudson's argument would fairly further suggest that the Court here used international law to add rhetorical force to a decision it would have reached anyway.[127] As a result, the majority quashed the derogation order and found that section 23 of the Anti-Terrorism, Crime and Security Act (*ATCSA*) was incompatible with Articles 5 and 14 of the *ECHR* insofar as it was both disproportionate and discriminatory. Having reached these conclusions, Lord Bingham found it unnecessary to address arguments on alleged breaches of Articles 3 and 6 of the *ECHR*, nor did he find it necessary to express an opinion relating to the admissibility of evidence obtained by torture.[128]

The latter issue was the primary subject in *A v. Secretary of State for the Home Department (No 2)*.[129] The House of Lords held unanimously that evidence which had been obtained through torture had long been viewed as unreliable and agreed with the appellants' submission that the common law forbids the admission of such evidence.[130] The House of Lords, in granting the appeals, drew not only on the common law but also on Article 3 and international law jurisprudence.[131] On behalf of the majority, Lord Bingham stated that:

> I accept the broad thrust of the appellants' argument on the common law. The principles of the common law, standing alone, in my opinion compel the exclusion of third party torture evidence as unreliable, unfair, offensive to

124 Ibid, para. 63
125 Ibid, para. 68
126 *Nollkaemper*, 18
127 *Hudson*, 329
128 *Belmarsh*, para. 71
129 [2005] UKHL 71 [hereinafter "*A v. SSHD No 2*"]
130 Ibid, para. 11
131 Ibid, paras. 23–7 are exclusively dedicated to analysis of the *ECHR*, while paras. 28–45, dedicated to analysis of public international law, draw on a number of international instruments and bodies

> ordinary standards of humanity and decency and incompatible with the principles which should animate a tribunal seeking to administer justice. *But the principles of the common law do not stand alone.* Effect must be given to the European Convention, which itself takes account of the all but universal consensus embodied in the Torture Convention. (emphasis added)[132]

Despite the fact that the Court was of the opinion that the common law of its own country compelled the exclusion of evidence adduced through torture, it also recognized that other international instruments further re-enforced this exclusion,[133] adding further rhetorical force to its decision.

The House of Lords rulings in a trilogy of control order cases[134] were primarily concerned with what constitutes a deprivation of liberty and how the use of closed material impacts on the right to a fair trial. They ruled in *JJ* that imposing an 18-hour curfew on the controlled person constituted a deprivation of liberty, whereas curfews of 12 and 14 hours, respectively, were held not to constitute deprivations in *E* and *MB*. In *MB*, the Court considered whether the procedures provided by the Prevention of Terrorism Act (PTA) 2005 c. 2 were compatible with Article 6 in cases where they resulted in the case being made almost entirely in closed material. It began this analysis by quoting case law from a variety of countries on the absolute nature of the right to a fair trial, including passages from *Charkaoui I*.[135] This can be viewed as another example of the applicability of Benvenisti and Downs' conceptualization. The Court also engaged in a lengthy analysis of the role that the special advocate can play in enhancing the measure of procedural justice available to a controlled person.[136] Lord Bingham noted the view of Lord Woolf in *Roberts* that the use of the special advocate is 'never a panacea for the grave disadvantages of a person affected not being aware of the case against him'.[137] MB had not had the thrust of the case effectively conveyed to him and, as such, the Court had difficulty accepting that the very essence of a right to a fair hearing had not been impaired.

132 Ibid, para. 52

133 Para. 44 also notes concern following the judgment of the Court of Appeal in these appeals by the International Commission of Jurists and the Council of Europe Commissioner for Human rights, who stated that 'During the 2004 visit, several persons whom the delegation met were very concerned that the SIAC could apparently take into consideration evidence that might have been obtained elsewhere by coercion, or even by torture. Such an approach would contravene universal principles governing the protection of human rights and the prohibition of torture and other forms of ill-treatment, to which the United Kingdom has adhered'

134 *Secretary of State for the Home Department v. E* [2007] UKHL 47 [hereinafter "*E*"]; *Secretary of State for the Home Department v. JJ* [2007] UKHL 45 [hereinafter "*JJ*"]; *Secretary of State for the Home Department v. MB* [2007] UKHL 46 [hereinafter "*MB*"]

135 Ibid, para. 30

136 Largely based on the domestic case of *R (Roberts) v Parole Board* [2005] UKHL 45; [2005] 2 AC 738

137 *MB*, para. 35

The question then became the appropriate remedy within the legal framework that the Court operates. Lord Bingham noted the suggestion that the provisions be read down under section 3 of the *HRA* so that 'they would take effect only when it was consistent with fairness for them to do so', which would be a possible course because the provisions do no operate unfairly in all cases.[138] He questioned this remedy, wondering whether it would 'fly in the face of Parliament's intention' and if it might instead be desirable to issue a declaration of incompatibility.[139] However, he noted that there was strong support for reading down the legislation in the opinions of Baroness Hale,[140] Lord Carswell[141] and Lord Brown.[142] As such, he chose not to press his opinion to the point of dissent and agreed that section 3 should be applied. Here we find another answer to the question of how, and to what extent, are domestic legal decisions on counter-terrorism influenced by the structure of the rights adjudication system in a jurisdiction. This is an excellent example of how Courts make decisions within their domestic legal structures. The rights adjudication system under which the House of Lords operates mandates them to read down legislation where it is possible to do so.[143] As such, declarations of incompatibility were not issued and the cases were referred back for individual consideration.

The findings of the Strasbourg Court in *A. v United Kingdom,*[144] namely, that the House of Lords was correct to find a public emergency threatening the nation, that the provisions at issue were not strictly required by the exigencies of the situation because they were disproportionate and discriminatory and that Article 5(4) would be violated when the essence of the case lay in closed materials, have been previously discussed.[145] That said, it is important to analyse more closely the dicta in *A v UK* because, taken together with the House of Lords judgment in *Secretary of the State for the Home Department v. AF (No 3),*[146] it illustrates how the legal structure that decision-makers work within has an impact on the analyses that

138 Ibid, para. 44

139 Ibid

140 She noted that the court was required by Parliament under section 3(1) of the *HRA* to take this course of action if it was possible to do so (para. 71). She also argued that by interpreting the Act compatibly it gave the greatest possible incentive to all parties involved to conduct the proceedings in a way that afforded sufficient and substantial measures of procedural justice, whereas a declaration of incompatibility 'would allow all of them to conduct the proceedings in a way which they knew to be incompatible' (para. 73)

141 He argued that the declaration of incompatibility is to be regarded as a measure of last resort, to be avoided unless it is plainly impossible to do and, as such, the provisions should simply be read in to include 'a qualification that the powers conferred do not extend to withholding particulars of reasons or evidence where to do so would deprive the controlee of a fair trial' (para. 84)

142 Brown simply states his support for invoking section 3 in the manner, and with the consequences suggested by Hale and Carswell (para. 92).

143 As noted in previous discussions throughout this book pertaining to s. 3 of the *HRA*

144 *A v. United Kingdom,* App No 3455/05 [2009] ECHR 301 [hereinafter "*A v. UK*"]

145 See Chapter 2.4.7

146 [2009] UKHL 28 [hereinafter *SSHD v. AF No 3*]

those decision-makers engage in and the judgments that they make. This becomes especially clear when comparisons are made to the Canadian legal structure.

In *A v. UK*, the government challenged the decision of its own highest court, a process that cannot occur within the Canadian rights adjudication framework. The ECtHR recognized that while it was unusual for governments to resort to challenging the decisions of their own highest courts, there was no prohibition on a government making such a challenge.[147] The ECtHR affirmed the House of Lords decision that the derogating measures were disproportionate in that they discriminated unjustifiably between nationals and non-nationals.[148] While this reasoning was uncontroversial, the ECtHR's ruling that the procedural requirements of Article 5(4) would not be satisfied where open material in control order cases consisted purely of general assertions and SIAC's decision to uphold the certification was based solely or to a decisive degree on closed material[149] was a subject of discussion when the case returned to the House of Lords. In *SSHD v. AF (No 3)*, Lord Phillips made it clear that the ECtHR had authoritatively resolved the issue raised in the appeal, and that the *HRA* required the House of Lords to take into account the Strasbourg jurisprudence.[150] In doing so, he operated within the confines of the applicable legal structure, i.e. section 2 of the *HRA*. As such, he allowed the appeals in each case, stating that the disclosure required by the decision of the ECtHR had not been given.[151]

A number of judges commented additionally on the ECtHR's decision and their need to take it into account including, most forcefully, Lord Hoffmann in dissent.[152] Lord Carswell, who also cited the *MB* decision, nonetheless noted that whatever latitude there may be within section 2(1) of the *HRA*, 'the authority of a considered statement of the Grand Chamber is such that our courts have no option but to accept and apply it'.[153] Finally, although he was also unequivocal about the fact that the Court was bound to apply the *A v. UK* decision, Lord Brown also appeared to maintain his support for the solution suggested in *MB*.[154] *A v. UK* and *SSHD v. AF (No 3)* taken together demonstrate how legal decision-makers act within the constraints of their domestic legal structures. While some

147 *A v. UK*, para. 157
148 Ibid, para. 190
149 Ibid, para. 220
150 *SSHD v. AF (No 3)*, para. 64
151 Ibid, para. 69
152 Ibid, para. 70: Hoffman refers to the decision in *A v. UK* as 'wrong' and laments the fact that the Lordships 'have no choice but to submit' to it, because to 'reject such a decision would almost certainly put this country in breach of the international obligation which it accepted when it acceded to the Convention'
153 Ibid, para. 108
154 Ibid, paras. 116–17: 'In short, Strasbourg has decided that the suspect must always be told sufficient of the case against him to enable him to give effective instructions to the special advocate . . . Was this what the majority of the Committee (Baroness Hale of Richmond, Lord Carswell and myself) held in *Secretary of State for the Home Department v MB* [2008] AC 440? I do not think so'

of the Lords in the latter case may have very well preferred the approach of deciding appropriate disclosure obligations in control order cases that they developed in *MB*, they were all unequivocal that they were bound by the constraints of their legal structure. They recognized that they operate within the rights adjudication framework under the *ECHR* and the *HRA*. That the ECtHR was even able to consider a government's challenge to its own highest court's ruling is a marked example of how the difference in legal structure between Canada and the UK can shape the analysis engaged in, and the decisions reached by, national courts.

3.5 Conclusion

This chapter has analysed the case law on security certificates in Canada and detention without trial and control orders in the UK to explore how national courts operate within their respective legal structures. In doing so, it has analysed how, and to what extent, these structures influence how judges engage in their analyses and come to their decisions, including how these structures allow for international legal instruments to impact on decisions. In the *Suresh* analysis, the Supreme Court argued that it was an element of its own legal structure, namely, the fundamental justice balance under section 7 of the *Charter* that precluded deportation to torture, rather than the ICCPR and CAT. Conversely, the Court used an international instrument to fill a void in Canada's legal structure by adopting the *International Convention for the Suppression of Financing of Terrorism's* definition of terrorism. The same void was not present in *Belmarsh* and, as such, the UK House of Lords proceeded in its analysis on the basis of its own domestic definition. Conversely, the discrimination argument that had been successfully raised against differential treatment of non-citizens in *Belmarsh* did not succeed in *Charkaoui I* because the structure of the Canadian legal system, namely section 6 of the *Charter*, legally provides for this differential treatment. SIAC was created as a result of a gap in the UK's legal structure that was recognized by *Chahal*, a case that turned on the existence of a similar system in Canada. Despite favorable discussion towards the issuing of a declaration of incompatibility, the majority in *MB* decided that they were essentially mandated by section 3(1) of the *HRA* to read down legislation. Similarly, the majority in *SSHD v. AF (No 3)* spoke clearly about how they were essentially bound to take into account *A. v UK* by their legal constraints under the *ECHR* and the *HRA*. These analyses illustrate how, and to what extent, domestic legal decisions on counter-terrorism are influenced by the structure of a rights adjudication system in a jurisdiction.

Moreover, the question of how, and to what extent, domestic legal structures allow for international legal instruments to impact domestic legal decisions on counter-terrorism was answered by the analyses in this chapter. The argument that international legal instruments are often invoked to add rhetorical force to a decision was most forceful in the *Suresh* analysis, when the Supreme Court used both the Canadian and international experience to engage in its section 7 analysis but made clear that it was the fundamental justice balance under the *Charter* that precludes deportation to torture, and not the constraining force of the *Convention Against Torture.* It was also useful in the *Belmarsh* analysis, where it seems reasonable to argue that the Court's consideration of international sources was largely rhetorical backing for a decision that was already strongly based on a domestic definition of terrorism and a long English law tradition. The argument that Courts are open to looking to solutions in other jurisdictions to fill in gaps in their own legal structure was also very applicable, most especially in the *Charkaoui I* analysis, where the Supreme Court of Canada placed strong emphasis on the case law pertaining to control orders and system of special advocates present in the UK.

Bibliography

A and Others v. Secretary of State for the Home Department [2002] EWCA Civ 1502; [2004] QB 335
A v. Secretary of State for the Home Department (No 2) [2005] UKHL 71
A v. Secretary of State for the Home Department [2004] UKHL 56
A v. United Kingdom, App No 3455/05 [2009] ECHR 301
Abdelrazik v. Canada (Minister of Foreign Affairs) [2010] 1 F.C.R. 267
Abdulaziz, Cabales and Balkandali v. UK, App No 9473/81 [1985] ECHR 7
Al-Khawaja v. United Kingdom, App No 26766/05 [2009] ECHR 11
Almrei (Re) [2011] 1 FCR 163; 2009 FC 1263
Al-Qaida and Taliban (United Nations Measures) Order 2006 (S.I. 2006/2952)
Anti-Terrorism Act, S.C. 2001, c. 41
Anti-Terrorism Act, S.C. 2015, c. 20
Anti-Terrorism, Crime and Security Act 2001 c. 24
Ashingdane v. UK, App No 8225/78 [1985] ECHR 8
Askoy v. Turkey, App No 21987/93 [1996] ECHR 68
Belgian Logistics (No 2), App No 2126/64 (1968) 1 EHRR 252
Benjamin and Wilson v. UK, App No 28212/95 [2002] ECHR 636
Benvenisti, E. and Downs, G. 'National Courts, Domestic Democracy, and the Evolution of International Law' (2009) 20 *European Journal of International Law* 59
Brannigan and Mcbride v. UK, App No 14553 [1993] ECHR 21
Brogan v. UK, App No 11266/84 [1988] ECHR 24
Canada (Attorney General) v. PHS Community Services Society, 2011 SCC 44
Canada (Citizenship and Immigration) v. Harkat [2014] 2 SCR 33
Canada Evidence Act, R.S.C., 1985, C-5
Canadian Foundation for Children, Youth and the Law v. Canada (Attorney General) [2004] 1 SCR 76
Canadian Security Intelligence Service Act, R.S.C., 1985, c. C-23
Chahal v. UK, App No 22414/93 [1996] ECHR 54
Charities Registration (Security Information) Act, S.C. 2001, c. 41, s. 113
Charkaoui v. Canada (Citizenship and Immigration) [2007] 1 SCR 350
Charkaoui v. Canada (Citizenship and Immigration) [2009] 2 SCR 326
Counter-Terrorism Act 2008 c. 28
Counter-Terrorism and Security Act 2015 c. 6
Dodds v. UK, App No 59314/00, 8 April 2003
Engel v. Netherlands, App No 5370/72 [1976] ECHR 3
Esbester v. United Kingdom, App No 18601/91 [1993] ECHR 64

European Convention for the Protection of Human Rights and Fundamental Freedoms (European Convention on Human Rights, as Amended)

Feldman, D. 'The Internationalization of Public Law and Its Impact on the United Kingdom' in Jowell, J. and Oliver, D. (eds), *The Changing Constitution* (6th edn, Oxford University Press, 2007)

Fenwick, H., Phillipson, G. and Masterman, R. 'The Human Rights Act in Contemporary Context' in Fenwick, H., Phillipson, G. and Masterman, R. (eds), *Judicial Reasoning under the UK Human Rights Act* (Cambridge University Press, 2007)

GA Res. 54/109, 9 December 1999

Ghaidan v. Godin Mendoza [2004] UKHL 30

Greek Case (1969) 12 YB 1

Guzzardi v. Italy, App No 7367/76 [1980] ECHR 5

Handyside v. UK, App No 5493/72 [1976] ECHR 5

HM Treasury v. Ahmed [2010] UKSC 2

Hudson, G. 'As Good as It Gets? Security, Asylum and the Rule of Law after the Certificate Trilogy' (2015) 52 *Osgoode Hall Law Journal* 905

Hudson, G. 'Neither Here Nor There: The (Non) Impact of International Law on Judicial Reasoning in Canada and South Africa' (2008) 21 *Canadian Journal of Law and Jurisprudence* 329

Human Rights Act 1998 (Designated Derogation) Order 2001, S.I. 2001/3644

Human Rights Act 1998 c. 42

Immigration and Refugee Protection Act, S.C. 2001, c. 27

Ireland v. UK, App No 5310/71 [1978] ECHR 1

Justice and Security Act 2013 c.18

Kavanagh, A. *Constitutional Review under the UK Human Rights Act* (Cambridge University Press, 2009)

Kennedy v. United Kingdom, App No 26839/05, 18 May 2010

Konig v. Germany, App No 6232/73 [1978] ECHR 3

Lawless v. Ireland, App No 332/57 (A/3) [1961] ECHR 2

Leander v. Sweden, App No 9248/81 [1987] ECHR 4

Little Sisters Book and Art Emporium v. Canada (Minister of Justice) [2000] 2 SCR 112

National and Provincial Building Society v. UK, App No 21319/93 [1997] ECHR 87

Nollkaemper, A. *National Courts and the International Rule of Law* (Oxford University Press, 2011)

Pearson v. UK, App No 8374/03, 27 April 2004

Petrovic v. Austria, App No 20458/92 [1998] ECHR 21

Pretty v. UK, App No 2346/02 [2002] ECHR 423

Prevention of Terrorism (Temporary Provisions) Act 1974 s. 1(7)

Prevention of Terrorism (Temporary Provisions) Act 1989 c. 4

Prevention of Terrorism Act 2005 c. 2

Proceeds of Crime (Money Laundering) and Terrorist Financing Act, S.C. 2000, c. 17

Protection of Canada from Terrorists Act, S.C. 2015, c. 9

R (Anufrijeva) v. SSHD [2003] UKHL 36

R (Roberts) v. Parole Board [2005] UKHL 45; [2005] 2 AC 738

R (Ullah) v. Special Adjudicator [2004] UKHL 26

R v. Horncastle [2009] UKSC 14

R v. Heywood [1994] 3 S.C.R. 761
R v. Malmo-Levine; R. V. Caine [2003] 3 S.C.R. 571
R v. Oakes [1986] 1 S.C.R. 103
Re E [2008] UKHL 66
Re B.C. Motor Vehicle Act [1985] 2 S.C.R. 486
Ribic v. Canada (Attorney General) [2005] 1 FCR 33
Ringeisen v. Austria, App No 2614/65 [1971] ECHR 2
Rodriguez v. British Columbia (Attorney General) [1993] 3 S.C.R. 519
Saadi v. Italy, Appl No 37201/06, 28 February 2008
Secretary of State for the Home Department v. E [2007] UKHL 47
Secretary of State for the Home Department v. JJ [2007] UKHL 45
Secretary of State for the Home Department v. MB [2007] UKHL 46
Secretary of the State for the Home Department v. AF (No 3) [2009] UKHL 28
Security of Canada Information Sharing Act, S.C. 2015, c. 20, s. 2
Slaughter, A-M., *A New World Order* (Princeton University Press, 2004)
Slaughter, A.-M. and Burke-White, W. 'The Future of International Law Is Domestic' in Nolkaemper, A. and Nijman, J. (eds), *New Perspectives on the Divide between International and National Law* (Oxford University Press, 2007)
Soering v. UK, App No 14038/88 [1989] ECHR 14
Special Immigration Appeals Commission Act 1997 c. 68
Sunday Times v. UK, App No 6538/74 [1979] ECHR 1
Suresh v. Canada (Minister of Citizenship and Immigration) [2002] 1 S.C.R. 3
Terrorism (United Nations Measures) Order 2006 (S.I. 2006/2657)
Terrorism Act 2000 c. 11
Terrorism Act 2006 c. 11
Terrorism Prevention and Investigation Measures Act 2011 c. 23
The Canadian Charter of Rights and Freedoms, Part I of the Constitution Act 1982, Being Schedule B to the Canada Act 1982 (UK), 1982, c. 11
Treaty on European Union (EU), 7 February 1992, 1992 O.J. (C 191) 1, 31 I.L.M.
UN General Assembly, *Convention Against Torture and Other Cruel, Inhuman or Degrading Treatment or Punishment*, 10 December 1984, United Nations, Treaty Series, vol 1465, p. 85
UN General Assembly, *International Covenant on Civil and Political Rights*, 16 December 1966, United Nations, Treaty Series, vol 999, p. 171
UN Security Council, *Security Council resolution 1267 (1999) [Afghanistan]*, 15 October 1999, S/RES/1267 (1999)
UN Security Council, *Security Council resolution 1373 (2001) [on threats to international peace and security caused by terrorist acts]*, 28 September 2001, S/RES/1373 (2001)
Walker v. UK, App No 37212/02, 16 March 2004

4 Canada and the United Kingdom's domestic political structure

This chapter analyses Canada and the UK's political structures, including government types[1] and mechanisms for parliamentary oversight of anti-terrorism measures. Canada and the UK have both had experience of minority (or coalition) governments in the years since 9/11, albeit at different times, and there is much academic debate about how legislation may evolve differently under minority (or coalition) or majority governments.[2] This raises the following question: Has the existence of minority (or coalition) governments had an impact on domestic counter-terrorism legislation? Both sections in this chapter begin with a discussion of how, and to what extent, the country's government type influenced the evolution of security certificates or Terrorism Prevention and Investigation Measures (TPIMs). Moreover, a significant difference in the UK and Canada's political structure is the comparative abundance of parliamentary oversight and review of counter-terrorism provisions in the UK and the glaring lack of these review mechanisms in Canada.[3] This leads to the following question: How, and to what

1 Richard Conley, 'Legislative Activity in the Canadian House of Commons: Does Majority or Minority Government Matter?' (2011) 41 *American Review of Canadian Studies* 422 [hereinafter "*Conley*"]: this is the term used by Conley to distinguish between minority (or coalition) and majority governments in his analysis of how institutional structures and governing contexts intersect to account for variation in legislative outcomes

2 The impact of political structures on domestic decision-making is discussed in Chapter 2 of this book, specifically by: Christopher Knill and Dirk Lehmkuhl, 'Private Actors and the State: Internationalization and Changing Patterns of Governance' (2002) 5 *Governance* 41 [hereinafter "*Knill and Lehmkuhl*"]; Andrew Cortell and James Davis, Jr., 'How Do International Institutions Matter? The Domestic Impact of International Rules and Norms' (1996) 40 *International Studies Quarterly* 451 [hereinafter "Cortell and Davis"]

3 Several authors in Chapter 1.3.2 make arguments about the importance of these scrutiny mechanisms, and have also noted a significant gap between the two jurisdictions: Clive Walker, 'Keeping Control of Terrorists without Losing Control of Constitutionalism' (2007) 59 *Stanford Law Review* 1395; Craig Forcese, 'Fixing the Deficiencies of Parliament Review of Anti-Terrorism Law: Lessons from the United Kingdom and Australia' (2008) 14:4 *IRPP Choices* 2; Kent Roach, 'A Comparative Assessment of Canadian Counter-Terrorism Laws and Practises' in Forcese, C. and Crepeau, F. (eds), *Terrorism, Law and Democracy: 10 Years After 9/11* (Canadian Institute for the Administration of Justice, Montreal, 2012)

extent, have systems for parliamentary review and oversight of counter-terrorism measures had an impact on domestic counter-terrorism legislation? It is then argued that mechanisms for parliamentary oversight suggest improvements to counter-terrorism measures that: reinforce the recommendations of other domestic committees or inquiries; make the case for additional domestic scrutiny mechanisms; and make targeted recommendations for amendments that may be taken up in public bill committee debates. As such, parliamentary scrutiny and oversight mechanisms are a crucial part of a state's domestic political structure, but the extent to which they actually influence those decision-makers operating within this structure needs to be further analysed. Both sections conclude by judging the tangible influence that can be attributed to parliamentary oversight mechanisms, and discuss the issue of whether there is a need for an annual review of security certificates or TPIMs.

4.1 Impact of minority government instability in Canada

Up until 2 May 2011 Canada had a conservative minority government led by Prime Minister Stephen Harper. Harper's victory on that day brought an end to two consecutive minority government terms, which began in 2006 when he was a narrow 30 seats short of a majority. That government lasted 2 years and 207 days before Parliament was dissolved on 7 September 2008, leading to another election on 14 October of that year. Harper again won a conservative minority, which would last 2 years and 142 days until the 2 May 2011 election. In that election, Harper's Conservative Party finally won a majority and formed a majority government in resounding fashion.[4] There are three major ways in which the instability of Canada's minority government influenced the manner in which security certificates have evolved over the course of the last decade. The first of these pertains to the stalling of major anti-terrorism reviews. As the House of Commons Subcommittee on the Review of the Anti-Terrorism Act notes, 'The predecessor to this Subcommittee was established in the autumn of 2004 and commenced its work in December of that year. At the same time, the Senate established a special committee to carry out this same review. The work of both committees was interrupted by the November 2005 dissolution of Parliament.'[5] Both of these reviews were in the process of scrutinizing the operation of Canada's entire national security apparatus, including security certificates under the Immigration and Refugee Protection Act (*IRPA*). The dissolution of Parliament

4 Stephen Harper's reign as Prime Minister of Canada came to an end after the 19 October 2015 General Election, when he was defeated by current Prime Minister Justin Trudeau, the leader of the Liberal Party. See http://www.cbc.ca/news2/interactives/results-2015 [accessed 22 October 2015]

5 Subcommittee on the Review of the Anti-Terrorism Act, ***Rights, Limits, Security: A Comprehensive Review of the Anti-Terrorism Act and Related Issues*** (Standing Committee on Public Safety and National Security, March 2007) [hereinafter "*House Final Report*"] 84

delayed the completion of the reviews, and also caused some to call into question their consistency. For example, when amendments to the security certificate regime were being discussed in the Senate, Senator Joyal noted that only four of the seven members of the House of Commons Subcommittee had remained constant during the delayed review of the Anti-Terrorism Act (ATA).[6] Senator Joyal also stated, 'It seems to me that it is common sense when dealing with such exceptional provisions . . . that Parliament has an obligation to review them and not to put those obligations in competition with other demands that the politics of the day might put on Parliamentarians'.[7] Measures as exceptional as security certificates, which pose serious threats to the human rights of those who are subject to them, need to be scrutinized in a timely fashion. The instability of Canada's minority government during this time precluded the expedient exercise of this scrutiny and oversight.

Another way in which the instability of Canada's minority government influenced the evolution of security certificates occurred when Bill C-81 (An Act to Establish a National Security Committee of Parliamentarians) died on the order paper, also as a result of the 2005 dissolution of Parliament. The Bill, which had cross-party support,

> would have established a committee made up of no more than three senators and six MPs, with a mandate to review the legislative, regulatory and administrative framework for national security, the activities of national security departments and agencies, and any other matter relating to national security referred to it by the appropriate minister.[8]

As a result of the dissolution, Canada was left without a permanent parliamentary committee to review national security and human rights matters, as opposed to ad hoc committees set up on a sporadic basis. This committee could have proved to be one of the important 'veto points' that Knill and Lehmkuhl argue are crucial to prevent national governments from initiating and pushing through reform against political and societal resistance.[9] It could have very well suggested amendments to the security certificate regime before they were mandated by the

6 Canadian Senate Debate, Public Bill Committee, 3 December 2007. Anti-Terrorism Act, S.C., 2001, c. 41 [hereinafter "*ATA 2001*"]

7 Ibid

8 Standing Committee on Public Safety and National Security, *Review of the Findings and Recommendations Arising from the Iacobucci and O'Connor Inquiries* (Standing Committee on Public Safety and National Security, June 2009) [hereinafter "*House Review of Iacobucci and O'Connor*"] 16

9 *Knill and Lehmkuhl*, 47: institutional structures have an important impact on the capacity for governance by public actors because they affect the cost/benefit calculations of the actors within these structures

Supreme Court in *Charkaoui*[10] with a one-year deadline for legislative change. These recommendations could have been helpful during the swift consideration of Bill C-3 (An Act to Amend the Immigration and Refugee Protection Act), which was introduced to respond to the Supreme Court's deadline in the midst of the looming 2008 dissolution of Parliament.

Comparing the genesis of Bills S-3 (An Act to Amend the Criminal Code (investigative hearing and recognizance with conditions)) and C-3 also illustrates how the instability of Canada's minority government influenced the way in which amendments to the security certificate regime were discussed and passed. Both were introduced into Parliament at the same time, although the latter had the added impetus of having to be passed by the end of February 2008, as a result of the one-year deadline set by the Supreme Court in *Charkaoui*. Many believed that C-3, which contained minimalistic amendments to the security certificate regime, such as the provision for a special advocate, was rushed through the House of Commons.[11] It has also been suggested that the Bill only survived the House vote because the Conservative Government threatened to hold confidence votes and force an election if the Liberals did not support it and enable it to pass.[12] Several members of the Special Senate Committee on Anti-Terrorism expressed their displeasure that they did not have the proper amount of time to make serious and consequential amendments to Bill C-3.[13] Minority governments can allow this kind of posturing, with the end result being less carefully considered legislation and what some have argued was a democratic deficit that existed under Prime Minister Harper.[14] Nevertheless, the Bill was passed and the security certificate regime continued, despite not receiving the scrutiny that a committee such as that envisioned by Bill C-81 would have been able to provide. To contrast, Bill S-3

10 *Charkaoui v. Canada (Citizenship and Immigration)* [2007] 1 S.C.R. 35 [hereinafter "*Charkaoui*"]

11 For example, Paul Copeland, head of Lawyers' Rights Watch Canada, noted that 'it was a rush through the Committee process in the House' and also pointed to the fact that Bill C-3 received its First Reading in the Senate on the same day that it was passed in the House: Canadian Senate Debate, Public Bill Committee, 11 February 2008

12 Adil Charkaoui, Canadian Senate Debate, Public Bill Committee, 11 February 2008: 'Unfortunately, I was disappointed by the Liberals because what they said was that they did not want to go into an election and that they had to pass that legislation'. Added Mohammed Harkat: 'The problem is that the NDP and the Bloc Québécois voted against the Bill and the Liberals and Conservatives voted for it. We were put into a situation because it was a case of pass the Bill or go for an election'

13 Senator Baker stated: 'If I were to propose amendments to this Bill, which I certainly would wish to recommend to the Government, it would take me months to decide on the wording, get the proper translation and put the proposal forward . . . The Senate was given two weeks, and one of the weeks was a vacation on the part of the House of Commons.' Senator Joyal said: 'I think we have to recognize that there is a deadline. We have been put in an untenable position to adopt the Bill within a couple of days . . . I think the only sensible thing to do would be to pass the Bill as it is, with all the flaws that it might contain': Canadian Senate Debate, Public Bill Committee, 12 February 2008

14 *Conley*, 430

pertained to investigative hearing and recognizance with condition measures found within the Criminal Code. Although these measures had never been used and had expired by the end of 2006, they were subjected to careful scrutiny in the Senate. Moreover, both the aforementioned House Subcommittee and Special Senate Committee on the Anti-Terrorism Act had recommended the renewal of these measures in their respective reports. Despite this careful scrutiny, Bill S-3 did not become law before Parliament was once again dissolved on 7 September 2008. Absent the instability inherent in Canada's minority government during this time, it is likely that both Bills C-3 and S-3 would have received full and proper scrutiny before becoming law. It is important to note that the investigative hearing and bail with recognizance provisions contained in Bill S-7 would later be reinstated under a majority government led by Steven Harper.[15]

The three examples in this section illustrate how political instability can have an impact on the evolution of counter-terrorism measures. The instability of Canada's minority government has influenced the discussion, study and amendment of security certificates in three major ways. It has precluded the timely conclusion of reviews that made a number of suggestions for amendments to the security certificate regime. Moreover, it has resulted in the death of Bill C-81 which, if enacted, would have established a much-needed Committee of Parliamentarians to regularly review issues surrounding Canada's anti-terrorism framework, including the use of security certificates. Finally, it is fair to argue that the threat of non-confidence votes and an ensuing election likely, in combination with the *Charkaoui* deadline,[16] precipitated the swift passing of amendments to the security certificate regime through the House, despite real concerns with Bill C-3 noted in the Senate. Bill S-3, which contained carefully considered amendments, died as a result of the 2008 dissolution of Parliament just months after Bill C-3 became law. In this instance, minority government instability directly led to one set of amendments to security mechanisms passing, while another set failed.

It should also be noted that majority government types can also have a significant impact on the evolution of counter-terrorism mechanisms. For instance, it should not be viewed as a coincidence that some of the most significant, sprawling and omnibus counter-terrorism legislation has been passed in Canada by majority governments. As outlined in Chapter 1, the 2001 *ATA* was passed in record time in the aftermath of 9/11. While this book has suggested several reasons for this, particularly the impetus provided by Resolution 1373, it should also be noted that a Liberal *majority* government was in power at the time of its passage. Similarly, the passage of both the Protection of Canada from Terrorists Act (PCTA)[17] and

15 This process is extensively detailed in Chapter 6

16 The one-year deadline to amend the security certificate provisions imposed by the Supreme Court in the 2007 *Charkaoui* decision has been previously discussed in Chapters 1 and 3

17 S.C., 2015, c. 9

the Anti-Terrorism Act (ATA)[18] in 2015 in the direct aftermath of the October 2014 terrorist attacks occurred under a *majority* government led by Prime Minister Stephen Harper. Again, while the impact of the October 2014 attacks cannot be ignored as a driving force behind the legislation, this is another example of sprawling and contentious legislation passed in a relatively short time period under a majority government. Analyses in Chapter 6 illustrate that Stephen Harper also capitalized on his new majority government status after the 2011 General Election result to pass bail with recognizance and investigative hearing provisions that he had previously been successfully able to pass under a minority government. As such, the sum of analyses here points to the importance of understanding this aspect of a country's political structure when trying to understand the evolution of domestic laws.

4.2 The role of parliamentary committees within Canada's political structure

Given what was said in the last section, it is unsurprising that there are few parliamentary committee reviews of anti-terrorism mechanisms in Canada, especially in comparison to the wealth of material published in the UK. Since the 1980s, the Canadian Parliament has inserted clauses that require comprehensive reviews of the provisions and operation of selected legislation it has adopted, which have typically had to be commenced within three to five years of the legislation coming into force.[19] The committees charged with completing these reviews

> bring the issues underlying a particular Act back to public attention and encourage a reconsideration of any controversy by those who are both interested in, and affected by, it. This is done through the hearings held by Parliamentary committees and their consideration of briefs submitted to them.[20]

Canada's comprehensive anti-terrorism reviews have referred to views of international organizations, reinforced the views of other domestic committees or inquiries, made the case for implementing additional scrutiny mechanisms and, finally, made targeted recommendations for change that have been taken up in the public bill committee debates on amendments to the security certificate regime.

Cortell and Davis argue that international rules and norms can affect national policy choices by operating through the domestic political process, but that 'the structure of domestic political institutions plays an important role in determining whether and how an appeal to an international norm will influence policy choice'.[21] The House Subcommittee's report on the Anti-Terrorism Act referenced a variety

18 S.C., 2015, c. 20
19 *House Final Report*, 83
20 Ibid
21 *Cortell and Davis*, 471

of international organizations that had expressed concerns about the security certificate process, including the United Nations Working Group on Arbitrary Detention and United Nations Human Rights Committee (UNHRC),[22] as well as the International Civil Liberties Monitoring Group.[23] The Special Senate Committee's Report[24] did much of the same, noting that Canada's obligations to ensure the security of its citizens whilst respecting their civil liberties were enshrined in international instruments such as the Charter of the United Nations, the Universal Declaration of Human Rights and the Vienna Declaration.[25] Moreover, the UNHRC's comments regarding secret evidence and disclosure of information in its review of Canada's compliance with the International Covenant on Civil and Political Rights were quoted.[26] The Senate Committee also criticized the security certificate regime for not including an express prohibition on deportation to torture, noting that in May 2005, the United Nations Committee against Torture criticized Canada's failure 'to recognise, at the level of domestic law, the absolute nature of the protection of article 3 of the Convention that is subject to no exceptions whatsoever'.[27] Here we see international rules or norms operating through the domestic political process, but focus now turns to the domestic political institutions that Cortell and Davis argue determine whether and how an appeal to an international norm will influence policy choice.

The parliamentary committee reports on anti-terrorism have advanced several domestic solutions to the issues posed by security certificates. One way in which they have done this is by further reiterating and reinforcing the recommendations of other ad hoc domestic committees or inquiries:

> The Subcommittee believes that the imbalance between the state and the individual or entity can be redressed by developing a scheme whereby security-cleared counsel can challenge evidence in closed hearings, and adduce evidence of their own, and advocate on behalf of transparency and accountability in situations where the limited disclosure of information make it difficult, if not impossible, for affected persons to fully defend their interests. The comments by Justice O'Connor described earlier in this chapter capture the Subcommittee's view.[28]

22 *House Final Report*, 67
23 Ibid, 137
24 Special Senate Committee on the Anti-Terrorism Act, *Fundamental Justice in Extraordinary Times: Main Report of the Special Senate Committee on the Anti-Terrorism Act* (Special Senate Committee on the Anti-Terrorism Act, February 2007) [hereinafter "*Senate Main Report*"]
25 Ibid, 1
26 Ibid, 33: The April 2006 Report expressed concern that Canada's security certificate regime 'did not fully abide by the requirements of due process set out in article 14 of the Covenant' and argued that Canada had an obligation 'to guarantee the right of all persons to a fair trial, and in particular, to ensure that individuals cannot be condemned on the basis of evidence to which they, or those representing them, do not have full access'
27 Ibid, 109
28 *House Final Report*, 80

The Commission of Inquiry relating to Maher Arar, which itself can also be considered part of Canada's political structure, had recommended the creation of an enhanced review and complaints body to oversee the entire national security apparatus. The Senate Committee was disappointed that this recommendation had not yet been acted on.[29] Another committee found it 'regrettable that the government has not yet established the independent national security review framework recommended by Justice O'Connor' and argued that said framework was 'essential to prevent further human rights violations'.[30] This independent national security review framework may have provided for a forum through which appeals to international norms may have been made with an eye towards improving the protection of human rights in domestic anti-terrorism legislation.

Parliamentary committees can seek to improve anti-terrorism legislation by arguing for the implementation of additional domestic scrutiny mechanisms. These arguments are especially pertinent in Canada, where these mechanisms have been recognized as sorely lacking.[31] However, whether these arguments result in substantive change can be contingent on 'the actions of government officials . . . In other words, on some occasions the domestic structural context will make it difficult for domestic actors – be they state or societal – to get what they want'.[32] Unfortunately, the instability of a minority government provided for the structural context that led to the death of Bill C-81. This is especially disappointing given that mechanisms for conducting reviews and oversight of legislation are 'especially important in relation to activities intended to combat terrorist activity where pre-emptive, preventive, and punitive steps have to be taken in a manner respectful of rights and freedoms, due process, and natural justice'.[33] The Committee envisioned in Bill C-81 would be well equipped to carry on the ongoing compliance auditing of the Anti-Terrorism Act and security certificates, as the House Report noted when it stated that Much work was done in the last Parliament in developing the ideas that led to the tabling of Bill C-81. A multi-party consensus emerged in support of providing Parliamentarians and Parliament with an important means for overseeing the Canadian security and intelligence community. The momentum built up should not be lost: Bill C-81, or a variation of it, should be introduced in Parliament at the earliest opportunity.[34]

The Standing Committee on Public Safety and National Security reiterated this argument two years later, arguing that 'there was an urgent need for action' and that without an integrated structure for the full review of national

29 *Senate Main Report*, 117

30 *House Review of Iacobucci and O'Connor*, 11

31 *Senate Main Report*, 114: 'The lack of adequate oversight and review of matters relating to national security and anti-terrorism has been a recurring preoccupation since the time the Anti-terrorism Act was first tabled in Parliament'. House Final Report, 127: 'Canada is unique among western nations in its lack of a Security oversight committee'

32 *Cortell and Davis*, 454

33 *House Final Report*, 2

34 Ibid, 85

security issues, Canadians would be at further risk of violations of their rights and freedoms.[35]

The reports released by the parliamentary committees in Canada have made targeted recommendations for amendments. Increased parliamentary scrutiny of security certificates and other anti-terrorism measures was a prominent feature of each report, and has been officially recommended in every report canvassed.[36] There were also recommendations that went to the core of substantive issues with the security certificate regime, including that the special advocate should be able to communicate with the affected party and his or her counsel, *after* receiving confidential information in camera hearings.[37] Finally, it was also recommended that the *IRPA* be amended to provide that an individual will not be removed from Canada on the basis of a security certificate if there are reasonable grounds to believe that the individual would be subjected to torture in the country to which they would be removed (i.e. an express prohibition on deportation to torture).[38] Many of these recommendations were taken up during discussions of Bill C-3 in the Senate public bill committee debates.[39] Ziyaad Mia, head of the Canadian Muslim Lawyers Association, specifically reiterated the Senate's recommendation 8 pertaining to the ability of special advocates to communicate with the party affected after the disclosure, saying that the absence of such a provision in Bill C-3 was 'one of the biggest changes that needs to be made to the legislation'.[40] Senator Joyal also made specific mention of recommendation 40 pertaining to amending section 145 of the *ATA 2001* to ensure future review, and questioned the Minister of Justice as to why the recommendation had not been put in Bill C-3, along with various other recommendations pertaining to annual review.[41] Unfortunately,

35 House Review of Iacobucci and O'Connor, 11–17: Recommendation five of this report states that 'The Committee recommends, *once again*, that Bill C-81, introduced in the 38th Parliament, An Act to Establish the National Security Committee of Parliamentarians, or a variation of it, be introduced in Parliament at the earliest opportunity' (emphasis in the original)

36 *House Final Report*, 86: recommendation 58 mirrors recommendation five of the House Review of Iacobucci and O'Connor, with the above underlined 'once again' being the only difference in the latter recommendation

37 *Senate Main report*, 42: recommendation 8

38 Ibid, 110: recommendation 34

39 Senator Andreychuk, Senate Debate, Public Bill Commitee, 11 February 2008: After reading out recommendation 36 pertaining to engaging the UN on the issue of security certificates, the Senator further proceeds to press the Minister of Justice by saying, 'I do not know, in this year of reflection, whether you have gotten to Recommendation 36 in our report, but I would sincerely suggest that that is part of the answer in dealing fairly and adequately with this issue'

40 Ibid. Alex Neve, Secretary General of Amnesty International Canada, also flagged the same issue in this debate and noted the precise recommendation in the Committee's report before stating that 'There obviously are amendments that could go some distance in meeting these concerns and others. The question that arises is whether the special advocate model can be improved to such an extent that these serious flaws can be remedied'

41 Ibid, Senator Joyal

although a number of the House and Senate reports' recommendations were used to express concern about Bill C-3's amendments to the security certificate regime, the time constraints posed by the *Charkoui* deadline, and the possibility of an impending election, ultimately resulted in the Bill being passed without full and careful consideration of how those recommendations could have been better realized in the Bill.

4.3 Judging the tangible impact of Canadian parliamentary oversight

Bill C-3 received Royal Assent on 14 February 2008, containing virtually none of the amendments recommended by the House and Senate Committee reports, save for those which made basic provisions for a special advocate to be added to the *IRPA* regime to bring it in accordance with the Supreme Court's ruling in *Charkaoui*. Bill C-3's own legislative summary acknowledges that the 'Senate's opportunity to amend the Bill was limited by time' and states that 'Rather than consider amendments to Bill C-3 in haste, on 12 February 2008 the Special Senate Committee reported the Bill back to the Senate without amendment'.[42] In response to the general concern raised with the process whereby Bill C-3 became law, an Order of Reference was referred to the Special Senate Committee for a study on the security certificate process, as well as a 'review of the operation of that process in the context of Canada's anti-terrorism framework'.[43] Although the Committee began this task in the months after the passing of Bill C-3, it was indefinitely halted when Parliament was once again dissolved on 7 September 2008.

Since that time, no amendments to the security certificate scheme have been passed by the government, nor have any bills that would resemble C-81 and establish a National Security Committee of Parliamentarians. Moreover, no comprehensive review of security certificates or their operation within the context of Canada's anti-terrorism framework has been released. Given these facts, and the process whereby Bill C-3 passed without serious consideration or implementation of the House and Senate reports' recommendations, it is difficult to argue that the parliamentary committees in Canada that have reviewed security certificates and other related anti-terrorism mechanisms have had any tangible impact. This is partly because dissolutions of Parliament, caused by the instability of a minority government, delayed or prevented meaningful review of these provisions on two separate occasions. This instability also lead to the death of a bill that would have created a National Security Committee of Parliamentarians with the power to engage in the comprehensive and timely reviews of security

42 Library of Parliament, *Bill C-3: An Act to Amend the Immigration and Refugee Protection Act (Certificate and Special Advocate): Legislative Summary* (Parliamentary Information and Research Service, 9 July 2008, LS-567-E, 24)

43 Special Senate Committee on Anti-Terrorism, *Order of Reference* (11 March 2008)

certificates and other anti-terrorism provisions that this country has been sorely lacking for almost a decade.

Although Canada is no longer governed by a minority government, it is still without a proper parliamentary committee mechanism to review security certificates and other anti-terrorism measures. Just because parliamentary committees have not had a tangible impact in the past does not mean that this glaring hole in Canada's political structure does not need to be addressed. It is not hard to envision something along the lines of the 'precursor expert review' that Forcese argues distinguishes the UK from Canada.[44] Forcese makes a strong case for precursor expert review, or 'public assessment of anti-terrorism law by an independent expert or committee, either prior to enactment or on a periodic basis thereafter'.[45] Ideally, this would occur alongside specialized committees of parliamentarians created by statute mandated to review national security law.[46] This is similar to the mechanisms present in the UK that will be discussed in the following section. Precursor expert review would also help to develop what Roach refers to as the 'bank of sound policy advice and research'.[47] Many key Members of Parliament argued during the Senate Debate on Bill C-3 that a pre-set timetable for reviews of counter-terrorism measures was not needed, and that the issues posed by security certificates were sufficiently serious that members would start the debate on their own prerogative.[48] This simply has not been the case, possibly because of the instability suffered by Canada's minority governments over the last decade. While this instability is no longer a feature of Canada's political structure, a regular review and oversight mechanism along the lines of 'precursor expert review' for anti-terrorism mechanisms definitely needs to become part of this structure.[49]

44 Craig Forcese, 'Fixing the Deficiencies of Parliament Review of Anti-Terrorism Law: Lessons from the United Kingdom and Australia' (2008) 14:4 *IRRP Choices* 2 [hereinafter "*Forcese, Deficiencies*"] 13

45 Ibid, 26

46 Ibid

47 Senate Special Committee on the Anti-Terrorism Act, 5 March 2008

48 Senate Debate, Public Bill Debate, 11 February 2008: Stockwell Day, Minister of Public Safety and National Security said: 'I believe, Senator, that a review will happen, possibly on an annual basis or maybe every two or three years. I believe these cases are so important because they deal with basic elements of a person's liberty. Therefore, committees of Parliament should have the opportunity at any time to review. I believe that is what will happen.' Senator Andreychuk argued that 'If we are as concerned about anti-terrorism and the rights of individuals, I do not think we will let up on our vigilance to look after this. I do not think I need to be told to do it. I will want to do it'

49 For a further, rigorous and thorough discussion of different types of review and oversight of counter-terrorism activities and why they are desperately needed in Canada, see Craig Forcese and Kent Roach, *False Security: The Radicalization of Canadian Anti-Terrorism* (Irwin Law, 2015), specifically Chapters 11 and 12

4.4 Impact of the United Kingdom's coalition government

This section begins by analysing how, and to what extent, the coalition government within the UK has had an effect on the study, discussion and amendment of TPIMs. After the 2010 general election resulted in a hung Parliament, the Conservatives and Liberal Democrats formed a coalition government and made a coalition agreement, which set out a programme for government until 2015.[50] This programme promised the repeal of control orders and 'a wider review of counter-terrorist legislation, measures and programmes'.[51] Lord Carlile argued that this 'committed manifesto opposition of the Coalition parties to control orders has led to heavy scrutiny of the system', including Lord Macdonald's Counter-Terrorism Review, which was discussed in earlier chapters, published on 26 January 2011.

When Theresa May introduced TPIMs for the second reading of the TPIMs Bill on 7 June 2011, she argued that the coalition had done

> what we undertook to do as a coalition Government when we came to power. Both parties were committed to reviewing the control order regime. We did that, and what we have decided is that the right balance between civil liberties and national security is reflected in the Bill.[52]

However, in the debates on the Bill that followed, it would be made clear that several MPs did not agree with the balance that had been struck, and that there was scepticism about the process behind the Bill. Critics generally argued that TPIMs were simply a lighter version of control orders, with a different name.[53] Lord Hunt went so far as to argue that 'It is a flawed Bill, it is a fudged Bill. It seems to owe as much to the needs of the coalition as it does to national security'.[54] In fact, clause 1 of the Bill, which simply reads 'The Prevention of Terrorism Act 2005 (which gives powers to impose control orders) is repealed', was heavily debated during the Bill's reading, as opposition MPs argued that control orders had been repealed only in name. For example, Mark Tami argued that 'Surely the party political point—the fudge—is clause 1 itself, which is intended to give the Liberal Democrats the idea that control orders have somehow been abolished'.[55] Other MPs were more substantive in their criticisms, arguing that

50 The coalition lasted until 7 May 2015, when David Cameron's Conservative Party won a majority government

51 HM Government, *The Coalition: Our Programme for Government* (May 2010)

52 United Kingdom House of Commons, TPIMs Public Bill Committee, 7 June 2011, Col 72

53 Ibid, 'The only thing the Liberals have got out of it is a renaming of control orders', according to Pete Wishart (SNP)

54 Lord Hunt of Kings Heath, United Kingdom House of Lords, TPIMs Public Bill Committee, 5 October 2011, Col 1138

55 United Kingdom House of Commons, TPIMs Public Bill Committee, 23 June 2011, Col 85

the Bill represented a 'compromise that demonstrates the weakness of the Government . . . epitomised by a Liberal Democrat Deputy Prime Minister and a Conservative Home Secretary – trying to reconcile the irreconcilable'.[56] Critics of the Bill argued that it is evidence of a necessary compromise under the coalition, which echoes Conley's argument that under this government type, governments operate under a 'manifest uncertainty and fear of imminent defeat that threatens their stability and capacity to govern effectively',[57] causing them to compromise in ways they would not have done had they held a majority.

The views offered above suggest that the compromises required by a coalition government had negative effects on the amendment and implementation of anti-terrorism mechanisms. However, others offered less cynical views on how the new coalition government influenced the new TPIMs Bill. For instance, Lord Howard stated that:

> We live in a Parliamentary democracy and the Secretary of State is a member of a coalition Government, so what the Secretary of State brings forward to meet the important considerations that you have identified will inevitably be determined by discussions in government. I suppose that that is just as the position would have been determined by discussions within a single-party Government in which people might have different views about where precisely the balance should be struck.[58]

For Lord Howard, the accommodation between security and civil liberty that occurred as a result of coalition government was not too different from the same compromises that have to be achieved within governing majority parties. Lord Carlile, a long-time supporter of control orders, agreed with this statement, but called the Bill the 'sufficient lowest common multiple'.[59] When later pressed as to how this compromise was any different than the various compromises the previous government had made with the judiciary, and also with their own back benches, he responded:

> A coalition is a quite different structure from the other Governments we have had, certainly in my political life. There is a level of intense negotiation that takes place between Ministers within the coalition. All I said earlier was that I am aware of extremely intensive negotiation between various parts of the coalition on what should appear in the counter-terrorism review . . . The compromises were a necessary part of obtaining an agreement in the coalition. There is nothing wrong with that, but it is a factual observation

56 Lord Harris of Haringey, United Kingdom House of Commons, TPIMs Public Bill Committee, 5 October 2011, Col 1151

57 *Conley*, 7

58 United Kingdom House of Commons, TPIMs Public Bill Committee, 21 June 2011

59 Ibid

> one has to take into account in considering the Bill. It has not been produced by the Law Commission; it has been produced by the coalition, and that is a different process.[60]

Lord Carlile, Lord Howard and the critics above all make arguments that speak to how a country's government type impacts the substance of the measures it develops and implements.[61] This is because the process that produces them is different and because decision-makers responsible for carrying out these functions do so within the confines of the coalition.

That being said, accepting this fact does not entail foregoing proper scrutiny of the measures. Rather, it simply entails recognizing and being cognizant of the fact that in certain countries where there isn't a clear majority government, the process whereby the government develops and amends legislation like TPIMs will be different. As Stephen Phillips states:

> We cannot, of course, escape the fact that we are all members of political parties. However, the Bill's subject matter is important, and in striking the right balance, we are really concerned with the substance of the measures that should be put in place to deal appropriately with the small number of individuals who must, unfortunately, be controlled.[62]

A majority of those debating the Bill agreed, and clause 1 remained without amendment. While the substance of the amendments in the TPIMs regime is discussed in the pages that follow, it is important to note the process whereby this new Bill came to be. The Canadian minority government, and the instability inherent in it, frequently undermined reviews of, and changes to, security certificates and the wider anti-terrorism framework. In its early stages, the UK coalition government appeared to be more stable and able to reach compromises. The fact that reform of control orders was in the manifesto of both the Conservative and the Liberal parties before either had any notion of a coalition undoubtedly made this easier. Nonetheless, the government successfully engaged in the review that it set out in its coalition programme and created what it believed was a more liberal regime with the TPIMs Act 2011.[63]

60 Ibid

61 Lacey has also written on how the dynamics of bargaining under conditions of coalition government affect the environment for criminal justice policy-making, in the context of the prisoners' dilemma: Nicola Lacey, 'Political Systems and Criminal Justice: The Prisoners' Dilemma After the Coalition' [2012] *CLP* 1

62 United Kingdom House of Commons, TPIMs Public Bill Committee, 23 June 2011

63 Discussion of the passage of the Justice and Security Act 2013, a controversial and problematic piece of more recent legislation passed under the same minority government, is discussed extensively in Chapter 6 on political culture, as that piece of legislation is widely believed to be primarily the result of a decision in the *Binyam Mohamed* case, itself discussed in Chapter 5

4.5 The role of parliamentary committees within the United Kingdom's political structure

In comparison to Canada, the parliamentary committee review mechanisms pertaining to national security within the UK are extensive. The Joint Committee on Human Rights (JCHR) 'acts as a kind of buckler of the system in scrutinising compliance, questioning Ministers and reporting to Parliament'.[64] It should not be forgotten that there is no parallel to the Independent Reviewer in the Canadian political structure, which means that there is no person like Lord Carlile (or now, David Anderson, QC) who could make up for the glaring lack of regular mechanisms for parliamentary oversight of counter-terrorism measures. Up until the passage of the TPIMs Bill, both the JCHR and Independent Reviewer engaged in annual review of control orders, which provided for 'an opportunity for frequent Parliamentary scrutiny of the continuing necessity and justification for the powers in the light of the evidence of how the powers are being used in practice and any problems to which they are giving rise'.[65] The JCHR reported in detail on each of the six renewals of the control order regime, as did Lord Carlile in his capacity as Independent Reviewer. This section illustrates that the UK's anti-terrorism reviews have pointed to views of international organizations, but they have also referenced the views of other domestic committees or reviews, made the case for maintaining domestic scrutiny mechanisms and, finally, made targeted recommendations for change that have been discussed in the committee debates on TPIMs.

The JCHR's reports, like those of the aforementioned Canadian ad hoc committees have, on occasion, referred to the views of international organizations. Most recently, the JCHR endorsed the view of the UN Special Rapporteur on the protection of human rights and fundamental freedoms while countering terrorism, when it criticized the government for refusing to subject the TPIM measures to 'annual review and renewal like the control order regime it replaces'.[66] The Special Rapporteur, Martin Scheinin, had observed that 'Regular review and the use of sunset clauses are best practices helping to ensure that special powers relating to the countering of terrorism are effective and continue to be required, and to help avoid the "normalisation" or de facto permanent existence of extra-ordinary measures'.[67] The JCHR reiterated its view that TPIMs are an extraordinary departure from principles of due process, and stated that it supported amendments

64 Lord Lester of Herne Hill, *Human Rights Judgments: Oral Evidence Given to the JCHR* (15 March 2011) 19

65 Joint Committee on Human Rights, *Control Order Renewal 2011: 8th Report of Session 2010–11* (March 2011, HL 106, HC 838) [hereinafter "*JCHR Eighth Report*"] 10

66 Joint Committee on Human Rights, *Legislative Scrutiny: Terrorism Prevention and Investigation Measures Bill (Second Report)* (19 October 2011, HL 204, HC 1571) [hereinafter "*JCHR TPIMs Second Report*"] 10

67 Ibid

that would place a requirement of annual review and renewal in the TPIMs Bill.[68] On other occasions, the JCHR has published written evidence to demonstrate that the government's counter-terrorism policies have attracted criticism from the UN Committee Against Torture and the Eminent Jurists Panel on Counter-Terrorism and Human Rights.[69] As aforementioned, Cortell and Davis have argued that the activation of international legal norms depends on the actions of government officials and domestic structural conditions that prevail during a policy debate.[70] As such, despite the JCHR noting views espoused by the international organizations above pertaining to annual review, the onus still falls on the government officials tasked with passing the legislation. As will be argued below, it is questionable at best to suggest that parliamentary review has had a tangible impact on the substance of TPIMs legislation.

Parliamentary committees can suggest improvements to counter-terrorism measures that reinforce the recommendations of other domestic committees or reviewers. The JCHR has stated that it shares Lord Macdonald's concerns about TPIMs not going far enough to bring the restrictions back into the domain of criminal due process, adding that:

> As the Bill currently stands, it is clear that the overriding purpose of its provisions is prevention, not investigation and prosecution.[71] It also echoed the scepticism of Lord Carlile in designating TPIMs as an investigative measure because 'the investigation is over by the time the control order is made'.[72] Finally, the JCHR went so far as to propose an alternative to TPIMs which is 'designed to give effect to Lord Macdonald's alternative model'.[73] Here the JCHR in effect expressed its support for a solution put forward by a domestic actor, by supporting the recommendation of Macdonald's counter-terrorism review, itself an element of the UK's political structure. Moreover, the JCHR supported its view that TPIMs are serious interferences with a number of rights, and that the imposition of such restrictions on individuals can only ever be justified if they are the product of robust due process, by pointing to the fact that this view is also shared by the House of Lords Constitution Committee.[74] Finally, the JCHR has published additional written evidence submitted by the Equality and Human Rights Commission

68 Ibid

69 Joint Committee on Human Rights, *Justice and Security Green Paper, Written Evidence Submitted by the Equality and Human Rights Commission* (January 2012) 23

70 *Cortell and Davis*, 454

71 Joint Committee on Human Rights, *Legislative Scrutiny: Terrorism Prevention and Investigation Measures Bill* (11 July 2011, HL 180, HC 1432) [hereinafter "*JCHR TPIMs First Report*"] 10

72 Ibid, 11

73 Ibid. Lord Macdonald's report and his alternative model have been previously discussed in Chapter 1, 69–70

74 *JCHR TPIMs Second Report*, 5

pertaining to the link between TPIMs and Closed Material Proceedings (CMPs) being discussed in the Green Paper.[75]

Parliamentary committees can also make the case for additional scrutiny mechanisms, or the continuation of existing mechanisms. Whereas the House and Senate reports in Canada made the case for additional parliamentary scrutiny mechanisms that could engage in annual review, the JCHR made a strong case for it to continue its practice of annual renewal that had occurred under the control order regime:

> The control orders regime was renewed every year for six years. Notwithstanding the fact that renewal was agreed to on each occasion, this was a very important safeguard. On each of these occasions we and our predecessor Committee reported in detail on the renewal and Parliament had a full debate about the need for renewal, informed by the reports both of this Committee and the Government's reviewer of terrorism legislation who also reported annually on the operation of the regime. We remain disappointed by the Government's reluctance to expose its proposed replacement regime to the rigours of formal and regular post-legislative scrutiny which annual renewal entails. Although the TPIMs regime is less severe than the control orders regime, it remains an extraordinary departure from the ordinary principles of criminal due process, as Lord Macdonald's report makes clear. We recommend that the Bill be amended to require annual renewal, and so ensure that there is an annual opportunity for Parliament to scrutinise and debate the continued necessity for such exceptional measures and the way in which they are working in practice.[76]

Here the JCHR is campaigning for the continuation of what it believes to be a crucial domestic scrutiny mechanism. Given the Canadian experience, it is not surprising that the JCHR would want to maintain this annual review power. The JCHR quoted Baroness Neville-Jones as saying that 'We will put this legislation in place and it will then be in place . . . We believe that the regime we are putting in place is a good framework that ought to be able to operate on a stable basis indefinitely'.[77] There were similar pronouncements made by Canadian MPs in the

75 Joint Committee on Human Rights, *Justice and Security Green Paper: Written Evidence* (January 2012) 3: 'The Green Paper's proposals are being put forward without a clear indication of the extent of closed material currently being used. The Commission suspects that the great majority of cases involving secret evidence continue to be those before the Special Immigration Appeals Commission and the High Court in control order proceedings (previously under the Prevention of Terrorism Act 2005 but now under the Terrorism Prevention and Investigative Measures Act 2011). Nonetheless, the continuing lack of accurate information concerning the extent of closed proceedings remains a serious problem'

76 *JCHR TPIMs First Report*, 15–16

77 *JCHR Eighth Report*, 1

first section of this chapter. They argued that reviews of anti-terrorism mechanisms, which still haven't taken place, would occur because the issues associated with the measures were sufficiently serious that Parliamentarians would take up review on their own accord. The JCHR is rightly sceptical of such claims, which is why they have recommended amendments to the TPIMs regime on several occasions to provide for annual review.[78]

Parliamentary committees can also make targeted recommendations for amendments that may be taken up in public bill committee debates. Aside from those noted above pertaining to annual review, the JCHR has consistently tabled a number of targeted recommendations for amendments to the control order and TPIMs regimes. These have almost always included recommendations pertaining to the priority of prosecution, including receiving assurances from the Director of Public Prosecutions (DPP) (or relevant prosecuting authority) that they are satisfied that a criminal investigation into the individual's involvement in terrorism-related activity is justified, and that none of the control orders or TPIMs imposed on that individual will impede the investigation.[79] The recommendation that the TPIMs Bill be amended to require the Secretary of State, at the outset, to provide the individual with sufficient information about the allegations against him has also been consistently argued for by the JCHR.[80] The same is true for recommendations pertaining to the special advocate's ability to communicate with the individual whose interests he or she represents after having seen the closed material.[81] Finally, in its most recent report, the JCHR recommended that the standard of proof for the imposition of a TPIM – which had been raised in the TPIMs Bill to reasonable belief from the reasonable suspicion standard in control orders – should be raised to the balance of probabilities standard used in civil proceedings.[82]

The TPIMs Bill was debated from 23 May 2011 until it received Royal Assent on 14 December 2011 and, as such, there is a wealth of debate in Hansard pertaining to its provisions. Also, given the more extensive and robust nature of parliamentary oversight and review mechanisms in the UK, there was much more extensive discussion of the findings of these mechanisms in Hansard than there was in Canada. The JCHR and its recommendations were most often discussed in the context of the debate on annual review. Specifically noting recommendation 7 of the JCHR's *Eighth Report*, Shabana Mahmood supported an amendment to insert a requirement for annual review into the legilation, arguing that Parliament

78 *JCHR Eighth Report*, recommendation 7, p. 14; *JCHR TPIMs First Report*, recommendations 18 and 19, p. 21; *JCHR TPIMs Second Report*, recommendation 10, p. 12

79 *JCHR Eighth Report*, recommendations 5 and 6; *JCHR TPIMs First Report*, recommendations 3 to 13; *JCHR TPIMs Second Report*, recommendation 5

80 *JCHR TPIMs First Report*, recommendation 16; *JCHR TPIMs Second Report*, recommendation 9

81 *JCHR TPIMs First Report*, recommendation 17; *JCHR TPIMs Second Report*, recommendation 8

82 *JCHR TPIMs Second Report*, 11: recommendation 6

renewing the powers each year had an important symbolic value.[83] Lord Judd also noted that just because the new regime is less severe than control orders, there still 'should be a provision for Parliament to scrutinise annually the continued need for such exceptional measures and to evaluate how they work in practice'.[84] Lord Pannick, who moved the amendment for annual review, reminded MPs that it had the support of the JCHR, and went on to argue that annual review was crucial to keep government disciplined in its explaining of the necessity of the measures to Parliament and to the public.[85] Despite this strong support, there were a number of members that followed Lord Carlile's view that the annual renewal process had been 'a bit of a fiction'.[86] Lord Carlile's suggestions that the annual debates had been tokenistic, and that 'Parliament should have the courage of its convictions and decide whether it wants a regime like this or not',[87] were ultimately taken up by several members who voted to defeat the amendment pertaining to annual review in an incredibly close vote (168 to 165).[88] Further to Cortell and Davis's point, this vote may have had a different outcome if the role of the Independent Reviewer, who carried strong persuasive force during these debates, was not a part of the UK's political structure.

The JCHR and Lord Macdonald's recommendations pertaining to the priority of prosecution were often commonly discussed in tandem during the debates on the TPIMs Bill. Lord Judd went so far as to specifically summarize the points made by both the JCHR and Lord Macdonald:

> It may be helpful for the House to hear the specific response on this Bill to some of the observations that the committee makes. I shall try to summarise them. Why is there not an even stronger emphasis on bringing proposed restrictions back into the domain of criminal due process? The noble Lord, Lord Macdonald, spoke strongly on this. Why is there not a precondition

83 United Kingdom House of Commons, TPIMs Public Bill Committee, 5 July 2011. Mark Durhan also noted the important role of the JCHR in arguing for annual review: United Kingdom House of Commons, TPIMs Report and Third Reading, 5 September 2011

84 United Kingdom House of Lords, TPIMs Second Reading, 5 October 2011. Lord Rosser also makes a number of arguments for annual review using the JCHR's recommendations, including four direct references to the JCHR's *Twentieth Report*: United Kingdom House of Lords, TPIMs Public Bill Committee, 1 November 2011. He made similar arguments again at the House of Lords Report Stage on 15 November 2011

85 United Kingdom House of Lords, TPIMs Bill Report Stage, 15 November 2011, Col 630

86 Paul Goggins: United Kingdom House of Commons, TPIMs Report and Third Reading, 5 September 2011; James Brokenshire: United Kingdom House of Commons, TPIMs Public Bill Committee, July 5 2011; Richard Fuller: United Kingdom House of Commons, TPIMs Report and Third Reading, 5 September 2011; Lord Henley: United Kingdom House of Lords, TPIMs Report State, 15 November 2011

87 Lord Carlile, United Kingdom House of Commons, TPIMs Public Bill Committee, 21 June 2011

88 Nonetheless, it should be noted that the TPIMs Bill was eventually amended to include a sunset clause (s. 21), and it is expected that independent review will precede any renewal

> in the Bill that when restrictions are being imposed on an individual, the DPP or equivalent must be satisfied that a criminal investigation into that individual's involvement in terrorist-related activity is justified and that none of the specified terrorism and investigation measures to be imposed on the individual will impede a criminal investigation?[89]

This is only one example of several statements of support for the JCHR and Lord Macdonald's recommendations pertaining to the priority of prosecution. However, several opponents of these recommendations once again used Lord Carlile's comments to argue against the amendments. Keir Starmer noted that Lord Carlile had testified in his last report that no control order had been made where a prosecution for a terrorism offence would have been possible.[90] Mr Gerry Sutcliffe argued against some kind of system of police bail, noting that Lord Carlile and the police have argued that the balance should remain with the security services.[91] Ultimately, the TPIMs Bill passed without any explicit provisions linking the measures to ongoing criminal prosecution or anything resembling Lord Macdonald's or the JCHR's alternative method.[92] Again, the presence of an independent reviewer in the UK political structure had a crucial influence on how amendments to the TPIMs Bill were debated.

The JCHR's recommendations pertaining to closed material were also noted in the TPIMs debates. Lord Judd argued that:

> Surely, where secret evidence is relied on, there should be a provision in the Bill both for a statutory obligation that the Secretary of State give reasons for imposing the restrictions and for special advocates to take instructions from those whom they represent after having seen the closed material where the judge permits this. Why is this not in the Bill?[93]

Lord Pannick, who put forward amendments 38 and 49 to give effect to the JCHR's recommendations on disclosure of closed material and the ability of special advocates to communicate after having received closed material, noted specific paragraphs and lines of the JCHR's reports during his speech.[94] He was especially

89 Ibid

90 Keir Starmer: United Kingdom House of Commons, TPIMs Public Bill Committee, 21 June 2011

91 Ibid, 23 June 2011

92 Lord Macdonald expressed his view that the government 'have failed to grapple with the central issue' of his review: 'facilitate the prosecution of serious criminals . . . This stance has been supported by the JCHR and deserves more serious consideration than the Government have so far shown it': United Kingdom House of Lords, TPIMs Second Reading, 5 October 2011

93 United Kingdom House of Lords, TPIMs Second Reading, 5 October 2011, Col 1183

94 House of Lords, TPIMs Public Bill Committee,19 October 2011, Col 339

concerned that the *SSHD v AF No 3*[95] disclosure principle had not been explicitly stated in the Bill, which he believed would lead to further expensive litigation.[96] In response, Lord Henley argued that respect for the AF obligations was found in the Explanatory Notes, and that the need to put them on the face of the Bill was not necessary because 'the right to a fair trial of individuals subject to a TPIM notice is already fully protected by the provisions contained in the TPIMs Bill and the application of existing case law'.[97] In this instance, Lord Carlile's views were not noted, but the amendments that followed the JCHR's recommendations pertaining to closed material were still defeated and there remains no explicit recognition of the AF disclosure obligations in the TPIMs regime.[98]

4.6 Judging the tangible impact of UK parliamentary oversight

There have been a number of changes to the control order regime in the new TPIMs legislation that should be viewed as positive, especially the ending of controversial relocation, but also including the changing of the burden of proof to reasonable belief from reasonable suspicion, and the two-year time limit on the imposition of a TPIM. Moreover, Lord Dubs has noted that the restrictions that can be imposed are less serious than those which were available under control orders.[99] That said, many of the aspects of control orders that caused the most fundamental concern still remain. The measures are still outside of the remit of normal criminal due process, and issues still remain pertaining to disclosure and the usage of closed material. Furthermore, the annual renewal requirement and review engaged in by the JCHR no longer remains. This section has showed that these were all issues that the JCHR argued needed to be addressed in amendments to the TPIMs Bill, to no avail. That said, it is hard to argue that the JCHR has had significant tangible impact on the outcomes of the TPIMs legislation. By contrast, the views of the Independent Reviewer, Lord Carlile, have indeed carried great weight. This is perhaps unsurprising given that he 'has carried out 10 reviews. He has examined every control order in detail. He has seen the

95 *Secretary of the State for the Home Department v. AF (No 3)* [2009] UKHL 28

96 Ibid. During the same exchange, Lord Rosser also used the JCHR recommendations to support Lord Pannick's amendments. Lord Hunt also noted the release of the JCHR's *Twentieth Report* on the same day, arguing that the report made a strong case for the AF disclosure obligations to be written explicitly into the Bill. Similar concerns were raised by Lord Goodhart, who also noted the specific recommendations of the JCHR: United Kingdom House of Lords, TPIMs Report, 15 November 2011, Col 586

97 Ibid, Col 342

98 It should also noted that the JCHR's recommendation pertaining to the balance of probabilities burden of proof was discussed, although sparsely. The final TPIMs Bill did not incorporate this recommendation and, as such, the burden of proof in the Bill is one of reasonable belief.

99 United Kingdom House of Lords, TPIMs Second Reading, 5 October 2011

intelligence and talked to the agencies.'[100] Given his experience and access to information, his viewpoints have carried significant weight in the discussion around the amendment and implementation of TPIMs. It is not unreasonable to argue that if Lord Carlile's position of Independent Reviewer did not exist within the UK's political structure, the opinions of the JCHR would not have been countered as easily and may have carried greater weight in the debates on the amendments to TPIMs.

Despite similar arguments on both sides of the debate for annual renewal and review in the UK and Canada, the key difference is the comparative lack of review mechanisms in the latter country compared to the wealth of review mechanisms in the former. It is far easier to suggest that Canada needs additional mechanisms for parliamentary scrutiny of security certificates and other anti-terrorism mechanisms because, quite frankly, few exist within its political structure. Analysis here has shown that the recommendations of the JCHR, whilst acknowledged in public bill committee debates, have not had a tangible impact on most of the substance of the final TPIMs legislation. Moreover, it has also been shown that the Independent Reviewer played a crucial role in informing this debate. The presence of this additional scrutiny mechanism makes the case for foregoing annual renewal, which many thought was an important symbolic, yet tokenistic, exercise that much stronger. That said, this section has outlined a number of concerns that the JCHR and its advocates have with many of the elements that still remain within the TPIMs legislation. It is likely that these elements, especially the lack of any real change to provisions dealing with closed material, may soon give rise to another challenge to the constitutionality of the TPIMs regime. The Canadian experience has shown that it is best to have what Roach calls a considered 'bank' of knowledge[101] if, and when, a court imposes a deadline for amendments to legislation. While the UK is certainly not lacking in this area, given the various scrutiny mechanisms applicable to TPIMs that still remain, it will be interesting to follow how, and to what extent, the loss of the annual renewal and review mechanism will impact the future evolution of TPIMs.

4.7 Conclusion

The analyses in this chapter have provided clear answers to the two questions: 1) Has the existence of minority (or coalition) governments had an impact on domestic counter-terrorism legislation? and 2) How, and to what extent, have systems for parliamentary review and oversight of counter-terrorism measures had an impact on domestic counter-terrorism legislation? In response to the first question, it was argued that the instability of Canada's minority government resulted in the stalling of anti-terrorism reviews, the lack of a much needed domestic

100 Hazel Blears: United Kingdom House of Commons, TPIMs Public Bill Committee, 5 July 2011

101 Kent Roach, Senate Special Committee on the Anti-Terrorism Act, 5 March 2008

national security scrutiny mechanism and, at least partially, the rushed consideration of amendments to the security certificate regime. The current security certificate regime may have looked very different if none of these things had taken place. Similarly, the process behind the drafting, tabling and passing of TPIMs could have been different in a majority government that did not require any kind of compromise. This finding is further exacerbated by the fact that large and sprawling pieces of counter-terrorism legislation have passed in both countries under majority governments, both in the aftermath of 9/11 and more recently. With regard to the second question, it was argued that systems for parliamentary review and oversight of counter-terrorism measures often reinforced the recommendations of other domestic committees or inquiries, made the case for additional domestic scrutiny mechanisms and made targeted recommendations for amendments that were taken up in public bill committee debates. Nonetheless, analysis of domestic scrutiny mechanisms in Canada revealed that these mechanisms had very little influence on the evolution of security certificates, likely because the few mechanisms that exist have no regular mandate, and because the previous government type precluded their proper consideration of amendments to security certificates. By contrast, the UK has a wealth of parliamentary scrutiny mechanisms, although the views of the Independent Reviewer seemed to carry more weight than those of the JCHR. As a result, it is reasonable to argue that the discussion around, and vote regarding, annual renewal was very different from what it might have been had the Independent Reviewer not been a part of the country's domestic political structure. Similarly, it is fair to argue that several other debates on amendments recommended to the TPIMs Bill by the JCHR were swayed by the views of the Independent Reviewer.

Bibliography

Charkaoui v. Canada (Citizenship and Immigration) [2007] 1 SCR 350

Conley, R. 'Legislative Activity in the Canadian House of Commons: Does Majority or Minority Government Matter?' (2011) 41 *American Review of Canadian Studies* 422

Cortell, A. and Davis, J. 'How Do International Institutions Matter? The Domestic Impact of International Rules and Norms' (1996) 40 *International Studies Quarterly* 451

Forcese, C. 'Fixing the Deficiencies of Parliament Review of Anti-Terrorism Law: Lessons from the United Kingdom and Australia' (2008) 14:4 *IRPP Choices* 2

Forcese, C. and Roach, K. *False Security: The Radicalization of Canadian Anti-Terrorism* (Irwin Law, 2015)

HM Government. *The Coalition: Our Programme for Government* (20 May 2010) Cabinet Office, available at: https://www.gov.uk/government/publications/the-coalition-our-programme-for-government [accessed 3 April 2017]

JCHR TPIMs Second Report

Joint Committee on Human Rights. *Control Order Renewal 2011: Eighth Report of Session 2010–11* (March 2011, HL 106, HC 838)

___. *Legislative Scrutiny: Terrorism Prevention and Investigation Measures Bill* (11 July 2011, HL 180, HC 1432)

___. *Legislative Scrutiny: Terrorism Prevention and Investigation Measures Bill (Second Report)* (19 October 2011, HL 204, HC 1571)

___. *Justice and Security Green Paper, Written Evidence Submitted by the Equality and Human Rights Commission* (January 2012)

Knill, C. and Lehmkuhl, D. 'Private Actors and the State: Internationalization and Changing Patterns of Governance' (2002) 5 *Governance* 41

Lacey, N. 'Political Systems and Criminal Justice: The Prisoners' Dilemma After the Coalition' [2012] *CLP* 1

Library of Parliament. *Bill C-3: An Act to Amend the Immigration and Refugee Protection Act (Certificate and Special Advocate): Legislative Summary* (Ottawa: Parliamentary Information and Research Service, 9 July 2008, LS-567-E, 24)

Lord Lester of Herne Hill. *Human Rights Judgments: Oral Evidence Given to the JCHR* (15 March 2011)

Roach, K. 'A Comparative Assessment of Canadian Counter-Terrorism Laws and Practises' in Forcese, C. and Crepeau, F. (eds), *Terrorism, Law and Democracy: 10 Years After 9/11* (Canadian Institute for the Administration of Justice, Montreal, 2012)

Secretary of the State for the Home Department v. AF [2009] UKHL 28

Senate Special Committee on the Anti-Terrorism Act, 5 March 2008

Special Senate Committee on Anti-Terrorism, *Order of Reference* (11 March 2008)

Special Senate Committee on the Anti-Terrorism Act, *Fundamental Justice in Extraordinary Times: Main Report of the Special Senate Committee on the Anti-Terrorism Act* (Special Senate Committee on the Anti-Terrorism Act, February 2007)

Standing Committee on Public Safety and National Security. *Review of the Findings and Recommendations Arising from the Iacobucci and O'Connor Inquiries* (Standing Committee on Public Safety and National Security, June 2009)

Subcommittee on the Review of the Anti-Terrorism Act. *Rights, Limits, Security: A Comprehensive Review of the Anti-Terrorism Act and Related Issues* (Standing Committee on Public Safety and National Security, March 2007)

United Kingdom House of Commons, TPIMs Public Bill Committee, 7 June 2011, Col 72

United Kingdom House of Commons, TPIMs Public Bill Committee, 28 June 2011, Col 85

Walker, C. 'Keeping Control of Terrorists without Losing Control of Constitutionalism' (2007) 59 *Stanford Law Review* 1395

5 Canada and the United Kingdom's domestic legal culture

It has been argued that rhetoric about rights takes a different tone in different legal cultures because the histories and traditions of the countries being analysed have produced 'different conceptions about the right and the role of fundamental rights'.[1] Judicial decisions can contain reasoned statements pertaining to the judiciary's role in constitutional democracies, and can illustrate the prevalence of concepts such as the separation of powers and judicial deference within a country's legal culture.[2] While this book has previously analysed judicial decisions specifically with regard to control orders (now TPIMs) and security certificates, this chapter analyses key decisions pertaining to the wider use of secret evidence in criminal prosecutions, civil litigation and terrorist listing in order to make observations about differences in the legal culture between Canada and the UK in the wider national security realm. In doing so, it provides a useful basis of comparison for Chapter 6's analysis of political culture, which will focus on the decisions and statements of politicians, the mainstream media and the wider public with regard to human rights instruments and the courts charged with upholding them. The idea that judges should defer to the executive because they are unelected and, thus, cannot claim to have the same accountability and legitimacy as elected Members of Parliament ('the institutional legitimacy claim') and the idea that judges should defer because they don't have the same competence, expertise or access to information that the government does ('the institutional competence claim') were both previously discussed in Chapter 1.[3] Opinions vary widely about the role of the courts and the proper exercise of this deference. Hunt argues that

1 Liora Lazarus, *Contrasting Prisoner's Rights: A Comparative Examination of Germany and England* (Oxford University Press, 2004) [hereinafter "*Lazarus*"] 16

2 Academic literature on the nature of, and issues surrounding, the concepts of separation of powers, judicial deference and legal culture were discussed extensively in Chapter 1. More recently, David Nelken and other contributors have expressed a variety of opinions on the 'uses and usefulness' of the concept of legal culture, see David Nelken, 'Using Legal Culture: Purposes and Problems' in Nelken, D. (ed), *Using Legal Culture* (Wildy, Simmons and Hill, 2012) [hereinafter "*Nelken, Using Legal Culture*"]

3 Aileen Kavanagh, 'Judging the Judges under the Human Rights Act: Deference, Disillusionment and the War on Terror' [2009] *PL* 287, 304 [hereinafter "*Kavanagh, Judging*"]; Jeff A. King,

English courts should adopt a 'due deference' approach based on an idea of power shared amongst various actors in a democracy rather than organized by some rigid and outdated conceptualization of the separation of powers.[4] Dyzenhaus envisions a 'culture of justification', wherein Parliament should be 'required to earn judicial deference from the courts on human rights questions'.[5] This chapter analyses decisions in the wider national security realms of both countries in order to discern if, and to what extent, these concepts are evident in judicial decision-making with a view to answering the following question: How, and to what extent, do the judiciaries of Canada and the UK express deference to the executive in national security cases?

Moreover, this chapter begins to analyse if a 'rights culture' can be said to be a part of the legal culture in the two countries. As discussed in Chapter 1, it is difficult to analyse whether such a culture has emerged without taking into account 'surrounding attitudes, political climate and political receptivity'.[6] Whilst analysis that takes into account these political factors will be undertaken in Chapter 6, this chapter's analysis of judicial decisions in the wider national security realm can, in combination with judicial decisions analysed in the previous chapters, be used to analyse whether a 'rights culture' is part of the legal culture in the two countries. While Dyzenhaus argues that the Human Rights Act (*HRA*)[7] gave concrete institutional expression to a culture that was already developing,[8] Feldman notes that:

> No one body can establish a human rights culture. It demands the interaction of systems and institutions to achieve and maintain the delicate and unstable equilibrium between interests and values on which respect for human rights depends, making them part of the decision-making process in their different spheres and functions.[9]

As such, the analysis in this chapter seeks to answer the question: To what extent can judicial decisions in national security cases be argued to be indicative of a

'Institutional Approaches to Judicial Restraint' (2008) 28 *Oxford Journal of Legal Studies* 409 [hereinafter "*King, Judicial Restraint*"]

4 Murray Hunt, 'Sovereignty's Blight: Why Contemporary Public Law Needs the Concept of "Due Deference"' in Nicholas Bamforth and Peter Leyland (eds), *Public Law in a Multi-Layered Constitution* (Hart Publishing, 2003) 370 [hereinafter "*Hunt*"]

5 David Dyzenhaus, *The Constitution of Law: Legality in a Time of Emergency* (Cambridge University Press, 2006) 153 [hereinafter "*Dyzenhaus*"]

6 Lucia Zedner, 'Securing Liberty in the Face of Terror: Reflections from Criminal Justice' (2005) 32 *Journal of Law and Society* 507, 519 [hereinafter "*Zedner*"]

7 Human Rights Act 1998 c. 42 [hereinafter "*HRA*"]

8 *Dyzenhaus*, 145

9 David Feldman, 'The Internationalization of Public Law and Its Impact on the United Kingdom' in Jowell, J. and Oliver, D. (eds), *The Changing Constitution* (6th edn, Oxford University Press, 2007) 114–15

human rights culture in the two jurisdictions? This analysis of how, and to what extent, judicial decision-making in Canada and the UK can be said to be indicative of the existence of a rights culture will prove additionally useful when focus turns to the political sphere in Chapter 6.

5.1 Judicial decisions pertaining to the wider use of secret evidence in Canada

As is the case in the UK analysis in the next section, the case law pertaining to the wider use of secret evidence in the Canada illustrates judicial reasoning pertaining to the appropriate role of the courts and their relationship with Parliament and the executive within the separation of powers. This reasoning is analysed in relation to the decisions in *Ahmad*,[10] *Almalki*[11] and *Khadr SC*.[12] Similar to the cases in the UK analysis, these cases arise from the tension between national security confidentiality of potentially damaging information and the public interest in disclosure and open justice (in *Ahmad* and both *Almalki* cases), as well as the tension between the Court performing its role in upholding the Canadian Charter of Rights and Freedoms in Canada[13] whilst respecting the Crown prerogative over foreign relations (*Khadr SC*). Moreover, the *Abdelrazik*[14] case on terrorist listing deals with the same tension, albeit that which occurs between domestic courts and the executive of the United Nations (UN). Since there is no parallel in Canada to the interaction that occurs between the European Court of Human Rights (ECtHR) and UK domestic courts under the European Convention on Human Rights[15] (*ECHR*) and *HRA*, analysis of the Canadian case law will focus on judicial reasoning about the complex balancing that occurs in the wider national security realm between upholding *Charter* values, such as the right to a fair trial and to make full answer and defence, and the Crown prerogative over foreign affairs and national security (including the making of regulations to give effect to international obligations, such as the UN instruments on terrorist listing).

5.1.1 The Ahmad *case*

In *Ahmad*, the Supreme Court of Canada heard an appeal from the Ontario Superior Court of Justice pertaining to the validity of the section 38 scheme of

10 *R v. Ahmad* [2011] 1 S.C.R. 110 [hereinafter "*Ahmad*"]

11 *Canada v. Almalki*, [2010] FC 1106 refers to the main Federal Court decision [hereinafter "*Almalki*"]. The Federal Court of Appeal decision will also be discussed: *Canada v. Almalki* [2011] FCA 199 [hereinafter "*Almalki FCA*"]

12 *Canada (Prime Minister) v. Khadr* [2010] 1 S.C.R. 44 [hereinafter "*Khadr SC*"]

13 *The Canadian Charter of Rights and Freedoms*, Part I of the Constitution Act 1982, Being Schedule B to the Canada Act 1982 (UK), 1982, c. 11 [hereinafter "*Charter*"]

14 *Abdelrazik v. Canada (Minister of Foreign Affairs)* [2010] 1 F.C.R. 267 [hereinafter "*Abdelrazik*"]

15 Council of Europe, *European Convention for the Protection of Human Rights and Fundamental Freedoms, as amended by Protocols Nos. 11 and 14*, 4 November 1950 [hereinafter "*ECHR*"]

the Canada Evidence Act[16] (*CEA*), which grants jurisdiction to the Federal Court to determine questions of disclosure of information pertaining to international relations, national defence or national security. The Supreme Court had to decide if the exclusive jurisdiction of the Federal Court to make national security determinations under section 38 violated the inherent jurisdiction of the provincial superior courts, or the section 7 rights of the accused to a fair trial. The case concerned a group of 18 people who were arrested in June 2006 on the suspicion that they were plotting terrorist attacks, also known as the 'Toronto 18'. The Superior Court judge had found that the section 38 scheme was unconstitutional insofar as it violated section 96 of the *Constitution Act* by conferring the responsibility to rule on non-disclosure claims exclusively to the Federal Court.[17] Dawson J. also found that section 38 of the *CEA* violated section 7 because it violated the accused's right to a fair trial and could not be justified under section 1 of the *Charter* (minimal impairment test) because allowing trial judges to make non-disclosure decisions would be less of an impairment. The Supreme Court disagreed and held the section 38 *CEA* scheme to be constitutional.

In its reasons, the Supreme Court began by noting the delicate balance between safeguarding national security and protecting fair trial rights that these cases require, stating that 'Parliament has recognized that on occasion it may become necessary to choose between these objectives, but has laid out an elaborate framework to attempt, where possible, to reconcile them'.[18] In disposing of the claim that section 38 was unconstitutional because it gave the Federal Court exclusive jurisdiction over non-disclosure claims, the Court engaged in a lengthy historical analysis of the role of the courts at the time of Confederation.[19] The Court noted that 'In 1867, Crown claims to refuse disclosure of potentially injurious or sensitive information were generally considered by superior courts in Canada to be a matter of unreviewable executive prerogative'.[20] Here, the Court upheld the section 38 *CEA* scheme not out of some substantial deference, but rather by engaging in a historical analysis back of a time when that substantial deference existed. The Court's disposal of the section 7 claim was slightly more complex, as it looked specifically into Parliament's intent in the creation of the section 38 scheme.[21] Ultimately, the fact that the trial judge would have at their disposal a

16 R.S.C., 1985, C-5 [hereinafter "*CEA*"]

17 *R v. Ahmad* [2009] OJ No 6156

18 *Ahmad*, para. 1

19 Ibid. This was the test developed in *Re Residential Tenancies Act*, 1979, whereby the Court engages in a 'historical inquiry into whether the power or jurisdiction conforms to the power or jurisdiction exercised by superior, district our county courts at the time of Confederation' and 'if the power in question does not conform to one exercised by a superior court in 1867, the inquiry ends' at para. 59

20 Ibid, para. 60

21 Ibid, para. 68: The Court references an exchange between members of the Special Senate Committee on the subject matter of Bill C-36 which, among other things, made consequential amendments to the *CEA*. During the exchange, Mr Piragoff states that 'We are balancing

power to stay the proceedings under section 38.14 if they were concerned about the fairness of the trial led the Court to find that section 7 was not violated, despite some reservations.[22] This disposition is in line with some of the judicial reasoning in Chapter 3, where the courts pointed to aspects of their legal structure to rule on the constitutionality of security certificates. Nonetheless, the consequence of this ruling is that trial judges will be faced with ending proceedings in what could potentially be high-profile terrorism cases but, as the Court notes, 'It will ultimately be for Parliament to determine with the benefit of experience whether the wisdom of the bifurcated scheme should be reconsidered'.[23] The Court here has stated that it is limited to ruling on the overall fairness of the proceedings, but has also not refrained from suggesting proper consideration of the wisdom of the *CEA* scheme in Parliament.

5.1.2 The Almalki *cases*

Almalki was a case before the Federal Court arising out of a civil claim for damages pursuant to claims of torture or complicity in torture brought by Abdullah Almalki, Amhad Abou-Elmaati and Muayyed Nurredin, all of whom alleged that their *Charter* rights were violated when they were detained and tortured in Syria and Egypt. The government disclosed to the respondents' counsel approximately 500 documents, of which 290 were in redacted form. The respondents moved in the Superior Court for an action requiring production of the documents without redaction and, as such, the matter was referred to the Federal Court. In his judgment on the disclosure of the material, Justice Mosley engaged in *Ribic*[24] analysis. The *Ribic* analysis is a three-part test that: 1) considers the relevance of the material to the underlying proceeding; 2) considers whether its disclosure would be injurious to national security, international relations or national defence; and 3) decides whether the public interest in disclosure is outweighed by the public interest in non-disclosure. Whilst engaging in this analysis, Mosley noted that he must 'give considerable weight to the Attorney General's submission on the injury that would be caused by disclosure, given the access that

the interests of the state to protect information and the interests of the accused to have a fair trial, which is protected by the *Charter*. There may be situations where both of those cannot be reconciled and it then becomes a question of whether the prosecution of the individual or the protection of the information is more important in a particular situation'

22 Ibid, para. 68: 'When it enacted s. 38 of the CEA, Parliament was aware that limiting the trial judge's power to order disclosure may lead to the imposition of a more drastic remedy than might otherwise be justified. In s. 38.14, Parliament chose to live with that possibility by explicitly contemplating in such circumstances a stay of proceedings'

23 Ibid, para. 80

24 *Ribic v. Canada (Attorney General)* [2005] 1 F.C.R. 33 [hereinafter "*Ribic*"]. This case has been applied in a number of cases in which Federal Court judges decide whether to make an order pursuant to section 38.06 of the *CEA*, including *Khadr SC*

office has to special information and expertise'.[25] At first glance, this viewpoint appears to be indicative of the institutional competence claim, but Mosley makes clear that he does not owe the government substantial deference when he notes that 'mere assertions of injury' will be insufficient, and states that 'The judge must be satisfied that executive opinions as to potential injury have a factual basis which has been established by evidence'.[26]

While acknowledging the Attorney General's specific expertise in determining injury that could result from disclosure, Mosley also noted that several questions arise during this exercise, including: 'How much deference is appropriate? How does deference apply in a practical sense to a particular item of information? Does the nature of the underlying proceedings make a difference?'[27] These questions are indicative of Dyzenhaus's culture of justification, whereby Mosley expects the government to earn his deference by providing reasoned answers to questions of importance. It is clear that Mosley was not simply satisfied by the Attorney General's claims, as he noted that unnecessarily broad claims advanced at the beginning of the process were evidenced by the fact that the Attorney General lifted or removed redactions in 92 documents.[28] In conclusion, Mosley stated that although he believed the Attorney General had taken his task seriously, 'The process takes far too long, resulting in the frustrations expressed by the respondents and by the courts and public inquiries that must deal with these questions'.[29] As such, he ordered the production of a number of the documents, a full summary of which is available in Annex A of his decision. Minutes after the decision, the government appealed to the Federal Court of Appeal, which disagreed with Mosley's judgment, arguing that he had improperly weighed the potential injury that could result from disclosure of the information.

In *Almalki FCA,* the Federal Court of Appeal (FCA) allowed the government's appeal with regard to the disclosed material. In a very short judgment, the Federal Court of Appeal found that Mosley 'discounted the evidence of injury or did not give it the weight that it deserved' and, in doing so, 'committed palpable and overriding errors'.[30] Interestingly, despite the deferential judgment given towards

25 *Almalki,* para. 70
26 Ibid
27 Ibid, para. 90
28 Ibid, para. 108
29 Ibid, para. 111
30 *Almalki FCA*, para. 37. The entire judgment was only 38 paragraphs long, and only the last two pertained to Mosley's disclosure decisions: [37] 'We are satisfied that the Judge in his application of the *Ribic* test either discounted the evidence of injury or did not give it the weight that it deserved. It could also be that at the same time he gave undue weight to the respondent's claim of prejudice. This led him in the balancing test to give undue weight to the public interest in disclosure of the information. In turn, this is reflected in some of the summaries of the information where injury is not minimized as mandated by the Act. In so doing, he committed palpable and overriding errors.' [38] 'For these reasons, I would allow the appeal, set aside the Judge's disclosure order and Annex "A" relating to the impugned documents and issue a confidential order implementing the changes necessary to these documents to prevent and minimize injury to international relations, national security and national defence'

the disclosure decision, the Federal Court of Appeal dismissed the government's argument that Mosley had made an error by not applying an informer privilege to Canadian Security and Intelligence Service (CSIS) human sources, stating that 'to accede to the Crown's demand that the informer privilege be extended to CSIS human sources would run counter to section 38 of the Act and the express will of Parliament'.[31] According to the Court:

> The creation of a new privilege entails legal, political, social and economic impacts. I have been involved in law reform long enough to know that policies of the kind, precisely because of their serious diverse impacts, require extensive consultations and public debate. They need to be enacted by persons accountable to the people who will have to live with such policies. Not only is this Court ill-equipped to assess the appropriateness of extending to CSIS human sources the informer privilege, I think it would be usurping Parliament's function if it were to do so and defeat Parliament's intent expressed in section 38 of the Act that there be a balancing of the interests regarding the information, including that relating to the identity of the source.[32]

The Court's reasoning here is very similar to that of the Supreme Court in *Al Rawi*,[33] where the Court was extremely cautious about ordering a process without informed debate and consultation in Parliament. Again, Hunt's concept of due deference is applicable here, as the Federal Court of Appeal is not surrendering part of its responsibility but is referring an important policy decision back to the realm in which it considers it is most appropriate for it to be debated. That said, the Court of Appeal's decision on the disclosure illustrates that the highest court in Canada to rule on the matter was willing to adopt a substantially deferential stance, with very little indication in their reasons as to why. Almalki's civil suit continues, but without the benefit of recourse to an appeal for additional disclosure.[34]

5.1.3 The Khadr *cases*

Mr Khadr was a Canadian who had been detained at Guantanamo Bay since 2002 facing murder and terrorism-related charges after being taken prisoner when he was 15 years old. While there, Canadian officials, including CSIS agents, interviewed him in the absence of his counsel and shared the product of the

31 Ibid, para. 30
32 Ibid
33 Discussed along with other UK case law in the wider national security realm in the next section
34 The Supreme Court refused leave to hear Almalki's appeal from the Federal Court decision, without giving any reasons. This is not unusual practice in Canada, as there is a Convention whereby the Court never explains why it grants or refuses leave to appeal in any particular case. It is generally thought that the Court will not hear appeals from cases in which there was a unanimous judgment, or in cases that do not pertain to a significant point of law

interviews with US authorities. Once formal charges were laid against him in the US, Khadr sought disclosure of all documents relevant to his charges, including the interviews, and was granted the disclosure of unredacted copies of all relevant documents by the Federal Court of Appeal under section 38 of the *CEA*.[35] This is in stark contrast to *Almalki FCA* above, where the Federal Court of Appeal was deferential to the government's non-disclosure claims, but is perhaps somewhat analogous to the *Binyam Mohamed* case discussed further below. Like Binyam Mohamed, Khadr was facing serious charges in the US that could lead to terms of life imprisonment and severe restrictions on his liberty. It was also clear that Canadian officials had violated his section 7 *Charter* rights by interrogating him absent counsel, which raised a justiciable *Charter* issue.[36] The Federal Court of Appeal found that Khadr had made a case showing a substantial risk of not being able to present a full answer and defence to the charges he faced in the US if he were denied access to the relevant information.[37] As such, it appears as though Khadr's FCA case and *Binyam Mohamed* can be distinguished from *Almalki* and even *Tariq* in the sense that less deference was shown to the government's claims in respect of the former men because of the serious restrictions of liberty they were to face if convicted, the rights abuses they had suffered and the further impediments to their right to a fair trial that would be suffered in the event of non-disclosure.

After the Supreme Court of Canada upheld the disclosure decision of the Federal Court of Appeal,[38] the Canadian Government disclosed to Khadr the transcripts of interviews he had given to CSIS and the Department of Foreign Affairs and International Trade (DFAIT). After Khadr repeatedly requested that the Canadian Government seek his repatriation, and after the Prime Minister announced his decision not to do so, Khadr applied for judicial review and the case was heard by the Supreme Court. In *Khadr SC*, the key issue was whether the previously established breach of section 7 entitled him to the remedy of an order that Canada request his return from the US. The Supreme Court of Canada ultimately decided that it was 'not consistent with the separation of powers and the well-grounded reluctance of courts to intervene in matters of foreign relations' to grant this remedy.[39] In arriving at this decision, the Supreme Court made a number of highly deferential statements that were in stark contrast to the disclosure ruling of the Federal Court of Appeal that they had upheld.[40] The Court did state

35 *Khadr v. Canada (Minister of Justice)* [2007] FCA 182 [hereainafter "*Khadr FCA*"]

36 *Khadr FCA*, para. 1

37 Ibid, para. 3

38 *Canada (Justice) v. Khadr* [2008] SCC 28

39 *Khadr SC*, para. 2

40 Ibid, para. 37: 'The limited power of the courts to review exercises of the prerogative power for constitutionality reflects the fact that in a constitutional democracy, all government power must be exercised in accordance with the Constitution. This said, judicial review of the exercise of the prerogative power for constitutionality remains sensitive to the fact that the executive branch of government is responsible for decisions under this power, and that the executive is better placed to make such decisions'

that 'In some situations, courts may give specific directions to the executive branch of the government on matters touching foreign policy', noting that in *Burns,* the Court held that 'it would offend s. 7 to extradite a fugitive from Canada without seeking and obtaining assurances from the requesting state that the death penalty would not be imposed'.[41] However, the Court in *Khadr SC* ultimately decided that 'the evidentiary uncertainties, *the limitations of the Court's institutional competence*, and the need to respect prerogative powers of the executive, leads us to conclude that the proper remedy is declaratory relief'.[42] Shortly after the Supreme Court's decision, Mr Khadr accepted a plea deal with US authorities. He was repatriated to Canada on 29 September 2012, and became eligible for parole in 2013.[43]

5.1.4 The Abdelrazik *case*

The *Abdelrazik* case can be rightfully considered as the Federal Court pushing back against the listing process established by Resolution 1267 and the executive nature of this process. The facts of *Abdelrazik* are discussed in Chapter 2.2.9. It is important to reiterate here that the Federal Court found Mr Abdelrazik's right to enter Canada had been breached and that the Canadian Government should take steps to facilitate his immediate return to Canada largely because of issues with the 1267 listing process and the tension between Canada's international and national obligations.[44] In doing so, the judge in the case likened the 1267 Committee Regime to 'a situation for a listed person not unlike that of Josef K. in Kafka's *The Trial,* who awakens one morning and, for reasons never revealed to him or the reader, is arrested and prosecuted for an unspecified crime'.[45] He also noted that listing by the 1267 Committee carries severe sanctions, including subjecting the listed person to a global asset freeze and a global travel ban,[46] and characterized the process as a 'denial of basic legal remedies' that was 'untenable under the principles of international human rights'.[47] The Federal Court's decision

41 Ibid, para. 41. The Court distinguishes *Khadr* from *Burns* at paras. 42–3, noting that in Burns the fugitives were under the control of Canadian authorities, whereas this was obviously not the case in *Khadr.* The Court also noted at para. 44 its concern that it was unaware of the diplomatic conversations being engaged in between the US and Canada as another reason for its hesitance.

42 Ibid, para. 46 (emphasis added)

43 Khadr remains in federal prison after an unsuccessful attempt to be transferred to a provincial facility. The Conservative government maintains that it 'will continue to vigorously defend against any attempt to lessen his punishment': Michelle Shephard, 'Omar Khadr Must Stay in Federal Prison, Judge Rules' *The Toronto Star* (18 October 2013) available at: https://www.thestar.com/news/canada/2013/10/18/judge_decides_today_on_whether_to_move_omar_khadr_from_federal_prison.html [accessed 18 October 2013]

44 Ibid, para. 2

45 Ibid, para. 58

46 Ibid, para. 26

47 Ibid, para. 51

in *Abdelrazik* is a strong example of what Forcese and Roach have called the 'dualist' resistance to the listing regime set out by Resolution 1267, through which domestic courts have imposed due process expectations on what is an inherently political and executive exercise.[48] The Federal Court here is not alone in its dualist defence, as a similar decision in the *Ahmed* case in the UK also pushed back against the government's implementation of the 1267 listing process.[49] It has been argued that the *Abdelrazik* decision is an example of a strong rejection of the Canadian Government's 'the Security Council made us do it' argument.[50] It is fair to argue that this decision is indicative of the culture of justification envisioned by Dyzenhaus.

5.1.5 Summary analysis

It is difficult to provide a clear answer to the first question, How, and to what extent, do the judiciaries of Canada and the UK express deference to the executive in national security cases?, because analysis of the case law here provides a mixed picture of the Canadian judiciary's view of its role and its relationship with Parliament and the executive. In *Ahmad,* the Supreme Court engaged in a lengthy historical analysis to uphold the jurisdiction of the Federal Court in assessing disclosure claims, and also upheld the bifurcated system under section 38 of the *CEA*, whilst suggesting that Parliament should consider the wisdom of this scheme. The Supreme Court in *Ahmad* recognized that it is limited to ruling on the overall fairness of the proceedings, but it has also not refrained from suggesting proper consideration in Parliament about the wisdom of the *CEA* scheme. The difference in levels of deference between the Federal Court and Federal Court of Appeal in *Almalki* was also quite significant, with the latter more willing to defer than was Mosley J in the former.[51] By contrast, the Federal Court of Appeal and Supreme Court were less willing to defer to the government's non-disclosure claims in relation to Mr Khadr, perhaps because of the severe rights infringements that he had endured and the liberty interests that were at stake, similar to those

48 Craig Forcese and Kent Roach, 'Limping Into the Future: the U.N. 1267 Terrorism Listing Process at the Crossroads' (2011) 42 *George Washington International Law Review* 217 [hereinafter "*Forcese and Roach*"]

49 The *Ahmed* case was first discussed in Chapter 2.4.8 and will be discussed further below

50 *Forcese and Roach*, 243

51 As was noted in Chapters 1 and 2, a comprehensive judicial inquiry was released pertaining to Mr Almalki and the other respondents in his case. Although Mosley J. in *Almalki* discusses the inquiry at length, he notes that his Court, or any court for that matter, would not be able to rely on its findings to make determinations of fact. That being said, it may be possible that the Federal Court of Appeal in *Almalki FCA* took such a deferential view because it was aware that the Inquiry had released some information pertaining to the mistreatment of Almalki and the other respondents and would release further unredacted information in the coming months. As such, it may have felt that its non- disclosure decision would be mitigated by the 'compensation' this would provide

in *Abdelrazik*. In the latter case, it is again likely that the severe rights infringements associated with listing (and the due process concerns associated with the secret and unchallengable evidence that listing is based upon) played a part in the Federal Court arriving at what might be the least deferential decisions of all the cases canvassed. As such, it seems as though *Khadr FCA* and *Abdelrazik* can be distinguished from *Almalki* in the sense that less deference was shown to the government's claims in respect of the former men because of the rights infringements they had and may continue to endure. That being said, the Supreme Court in *Khadr SC* still deferred substantially to the government on the question of the appropriate remedy for the *Charter* abuses Khadr sustained, arguing that they could not require the Canadian Government to repatriate him as a result of limitations in their institutional competence, and their need to respect the prerogative powers of the executive in areas of foreign relations.

With regard to the second question, To what extent can judicial decisions in national security cases be argued to be indicative of a human rights culture in the two jurisdictions?, analysis of security certificates has shown that Canadian Courts have not refrained from challenging the government and striking down provisions of legislation, or reading down offending legislation to bring it into accordance with the rights enshrined in the *Charter*.[52] That said, analysis of the case law in the wider security realm has shown Canadian judicial reasoning pertaining to the judiciary's role in protecting the *Charter* and their relationship with Parliament and the executive to be quite mixed. Judgments made by the judiciary in Canada have given weight to Hunt's concept of due deference and Dyzenhaus's concept of a culture of justification, whilst at the same time being typical of the substantial deference described by Kavanagh, most especially in *Almalki FCA* and in the *Khadr SC* appropriate remedy decision. As such, taken in consideration with the reasoning expressed by the judiciary in the security certificate cases, it can be said that the legal culture in Canada is such that Courts have not refrained from protecting fundamental rights under the *Charter* in national security cases, particularly when severe liberty infringements are at stake, but they have not always found it appropriate to scrutinize the government and Parliament's decisions fully in the wider national security realm.

52 As was noted in Chapter 3, the Supreme Court in *Charkaoui* struck down down section 78(g) of the *IRPA* and declared it to be of no force or effect because it allowed for the use of evidence that is never disclosed to the named person without adequate measures to compensate for the non-disclosure and the constitutional problems it causes and also read foreign nationals into section 83 in order to ensure that foreign nationals received the same timely detention review as permanent residents. In *Charkoaui II*, the Supreme Court disagreed with the government and ordered the disclosure of a number of documents that CSIS thought it would never have to disclose. In *Almrei*, Mosley found that the involved Ministers and intelligence services had breached their duty of candour to the Court by providing information that was shown to be inconsistent and incomplete after the *Charkaoui II* ruling.

5.2 Judicial decisions pertaining to the wider use of secret evidence in the United Kingdom

The case law on the wider use of secret evidence in the UK is illustrative of two different kinds of judicial decision-making that will be analysed here. First, dicta from both majority and dissenting judicial opinions illustrate judicial reasoning pertaining to the appropriate role of the judiciary, and its relationship with Parliament and the executive within the constitutional separation of powers. Judicial reasoning on the this role and relationship are most clearly expressed in the decisions of *Al Rawi*,[53] *Binyam Mohamed*[54] and *Ahmed*,[55] cases that arise from the tension between national security confidentiality and the public interest in disclosure of potentially damaging information during the course of civil litigation or with regard to terrorist listing procedures. The political pertinence of the issues behind these cases, and the ongoing debate pertaining to the UK's system of Public Interest Immunity (PII) and the use of Closed Material Procedures (CMPs) in civil litigation will be further analysed in Chapter 6. Second, both majority and dissenting opinions in *Tariq*,[56] *Qatada*[57] and *Horncastle*[58] are analysed to illuminate judicial reasoning pertaining to UK courts' interpretation of the *HRA* and *ECHR*, and its relationship with the ECtHR. Like *Al Rawi* and *Binyam Mohamed*, these cases deal broadly with the tensions that can arise when courts are tasked with balancing the government's claims for national security confidentiality whilst ensuring open justice principles, most specifically the right to a fair trial and the right for an accused to know the case against them. That said, these three decisions are most specifically useful for analysing the judiciary's reasoning pertaining to their role of protecting rights under the common law, as well as under the *HRA* and *ECHR*.

53 *Al Rawi and Others v. the Security Service and Others* [2011] UKSC 34 [hereinafter "*Al Rawi*"]

54 *Mohamed, R (on the application of) v. Secretary of State for Foreign & Commonwealth Affairs* [2010] EWCA Civ 65 [hereinafter "*Binyam Mohamed*"]

55 *HM Treasury v. Ahmed* [2010] UKSC 2 [hereinafter "*Ahmed*"]

56 *Home Office v. Tariq* [2011] UKSC 35 [hereinafter "*Tariq*"]

57 *Abu Qatada v. SSHD* [2013] EWCA Civ 277 [hereinafter "*Qatada Court of Appeal*"]. Two previous judgments in the Qatada legal battle, including those most recently given by the Strasbourg Court and SIAC respectively, will also be discussed: *Othman (Abu Qatada) v. UK*, App No 8139/09 [2012] ECHR 56 [hereinafter "*Qatada ECtHR*"]; *Omar Othman (aka Abu Qatada) v. Secretary of State for the Home Department*, SC/15/2005, United Kingdom Special Immigration Appeals Commission, 26 February 2007 [hereinafter "*Qatada SIAC*"] Although the *Qatada* cases are not cases pertaining to secret evidence, they do deal with the important issue of deportation to torture and the prohibition on evidence obtained through torture. Moreover, they have been selected because they show evidence of the willingness of UK courts to protect fundamental justice principles even in the face of immense public and political pressure, which is further discussed in Chapter 6

58 *R v. Horncastle* [2009] UKSC 14 [hereinafter "*Horncastle*"]

5.2.1 *The* Al Rawi *case*

The main question for the Supreme Court in *Al Rawi*, whether it had the power to order a 'closed material procedure' for the whole or part of a trial of a civil claim for damages, arose in the context of claims for compensation brought by the respondents against the government for alleged complicity in their detention, rendition and mistreatment by foreign authorities in a number of locations, including Guantanamo Bay. Despite the fact that these claims were settled prior to reaching the Supreme Court, the appellants pursued their appeal and the Court decided to hear the matter in order to clarify the law. The government argued that they had security sensitive information that they wished to be considered in their defence but that it could not be disclosed to the respondents and, as such, they asked the Court to consider the sensitive material in closed hearings and judgments. This would essentially amount to a CMP, whereby closed material would be available to special advocates who would act on behalf of the excluded party, but would be unable to take instructions from the appellants or from the Court. While at first instance Silber J had found that it could be lawful for a court to order a CMP in a civil claim for damages,[59] the Court of Appeal disagreed that the Court had such a power.[60] In a majority opinion written by Lord Dyson, the Supreme Court dismissed the government's appeal, holding that the Court had no power at common law to replace the system of PII with a CMP. According to Ip, 'The decision therefore places a premium on legislative authorisation for CMPs and special advocates'.[61]

In coming to this decision, various statements were made by the members of the Supreme Court, most of whom reasoned that ordering a CMP without explicit statutory authorization from Parliament would be outside of their role as a Court. Lord Dyson noted the continually controversial nature of the use of CMPs and special advocates before stating that:

> It is not for the courts to extend such a controversial procedure beyond the boundaries which Parliament has chosen to draw for its use thus far. It is controversial precisely because it involves an invasion of the fundamental common law principles to which I have referred.[62]

The interesting thing about this line of reasoning and *Al Rawi* in general is how it turns the traditional 'institutional legitimacy' claim on its head. Whereas that

59 *Al Rawi and Others v. the Security Service and Others* [2009] EWHC 2959 (QB)

60 *Al Rawi and Others v. the Security Service and Others* [2010] EWCA Civ 482

61 John Ip, 'Al Rawi, Tariq, and the Future of Closed Material Procedures and Special Advocates' (2012) 75 *Modern Law Review* 606, 616

62 *Al Rawi*, para. 44. At para. 48, he also added: 'The common law principles to which I have referred are extremely important and should not be eroded unless there is a compelling case for doing so. If this is to be done at all, it is better done by Parliament after full consultation and proper consideration of the sensitive issues involved'

claim is normally used to refer to judges deferring to the executive because they lack legitimacy as a result of their unelected nature, here the Court chose not to adopt the CMP, as the government would have wished, reasoning its decision by not stepping into the realm of Parliament, whilst making important statements about the fundamental principles of open justice. As Lord Hope notes:

> The proposition that a closed material procedure should only be introduced in ordinary civil litigation if Parliament sees fit to do so should not be seen as surrendering to parliament something which lies within the area of the court's responsibility. Instead it is recognition that the basic question raises such fundamental issues as to where the balance lies between the principles of open justice and of fairness and the demands of national security that it is best left for determination through the democratic process conducted by Parliament, following a process of consultation and the gathering of evidence.[63]

This suggests support for Hunt's concept of due deference, as the Court here reasons that power in the Constitution is shared among the various actors within it, rather than parcelled out according to some inflexible notion of the separation of powers. As Lord Hope notes, the Court has not 'surrendered' part of its responsibility to Parliament, rather it is attempting to make a statement about the importance of these open justice principles by allowing them to be openly debated through a full and thorough parliamentary process.

5.2.2 The **Binyam Mohamed** *case*

In *Binyam Mohamed,* the Court of Appeal once again had the difficult task of reconciling national security and open justice. Binyam Mohamed was also detained at Guantanamo Bay, and subsequently applied to the High Court of England and Wales for an order to provide certain documents that would assist him in his defence against anticipated terrorist offence charges under US federal law, for which he could face the death penalty. Binyam Mohamed argued that the documents contained information about his torture or mistreatment that was material to the confessions that were being used as the basis for his charges.[64] The High Court ordered disclosure of the documents subject to the lodging of PII certificates by the Foreign Secretary. The Divisional Court, having examined these certificates, released a judgment with seven paragraphs that described the gist of the treatment to which Mohamed was subjected, and gave the Foreign Secretary the opportunity to view the document so that he could request its redaction, which he did.[65] As such, the case that came before the Court of Appeal was essentially concerned with whether the documents should be published in their

63 Ibid, para. 74
64 *Binyam Mohamed,* para. 60
65 Ibid, paras. 5–8

full, unredacted form, including the seven paragraphs that described Mohamed's treatment at the hands of the Central Intelligence Agency (CIA) and concluded that the US authorities and the UK secret services were aware of the treatment to which he had been subjected. Despite arguments by the Foreign Secretary that publishing the documents could damage the intelligence sharing relationships between the US and UK and, in turn, the country's national security, the Court of Appeal held that the paragraphs should be published.

In reaching their decision, Lord Judge, Lord Neuberger and Sir Anthony May all wrote judgments extensively detailing the importance of the open justice principle. Before analysing their judgments, it should also be noted that by the time their decision was to be made, the gist of the content of the paragraphs at issue had already been made available by a US judgment.[66] Murray has argued that a combination of the seriousness of the wrongdoing suffered by Mohamed facilitated by the UK in combination with a lack of risk to security cooperation because the material had been published in the US made the Court's decision much easier.[67] There is an interesting parallel here to the *Khadr FCA* and *Abdelrazik* judgments in Canada in that it seems courts are less willing to defer to the executive when substantial liberty infringements have occurred or could still occur. Regardless of whether the Court was impacted by the material having been released in the US, the case still required them to 'address fundamental questions about the relationship between the executive and the judiciary in the context of national security in an age of terrorism, and the interests of open justice in a democratic society'.[68] Lord Judge and Lord Neuberger both argue that the ultimate decision about the inclusion of the redacted paragraphs is a matter for judicial, rather than executive, determination.[69] In a statement that affirms the analysis provided above, Lord Neuberger opines that:

> Where the judgment is concerned with such a fundamental and topical an issue as the mistreatment of detainees, and where it reveals involvement – or worse – on the part of the UK Government in the mistreatment of a UK resident, there can be no doubt that the public interest is at the very top end of importance.[70]

66 C.G. Murray, 'Out of the Shadows: The Courts and the United Kingdom's Malfunctioning International Counter-Terrorism Partnerships' (2013) 18 *Journal of Conflict and Security Law* 193 [hereinafter "*Murray, Out of the Shadows*"] 225

67 Ibid

68 Ibid, para. 3

69 *Binyam Mohamed,* para. 132: 'Ever since the decision of the House of Lords in *Conway v. Rimmer* [1968] AC 910, it has been clear that the question whether a document should be exempted from disclosure in legal proceedings on the ground that disclosure would damage the public interest should ultimately be decided by the court. That is because it is ultimately for a judge, not a minister to decide whether a document must be disclosed, and whether it can be referred to, in open court'

70 Ibid, para. 184

It can be argued that these statements lend weight to Dyzenhaus's conception of the culture of justification, wherein the executive has to justify its position, especially in cases that raise such significant issues for human rights compatibility, rather than simply expect deference by virtue of some rigid conceptualization of the separation of powers. It should also be noted that the *Mohamed* 'protracted legal battle was easily cast as an effort by the UK government to protect national security agencies and their partners' and that 'this impression was reinforced by the Government's efforts to persuade Lord Neuberger to mitigate some of his more strenuous criticisms of security personnel'.[71]

In setting out his position, Sir Anthony May was clearly less comfortable with the role that the Court was taking, particularly with regard to its assessment of the damage that the disclosure could cause to the intelligence sharing relationship between the US and UK. The UK Government in the case used various statements made by members of the US security apparatus against full disclosure, though these were largely rebutted by the fact that the material was already in the public domain, and because the Obama administration had taken a very different attitude than its predecessor. Nonetheless, May expressed concern 'that the court is being invited to substitute its view for that of the Foreign Secretary',[72] and noted that it is not 'this court's function to speculate how likely it may be that foreign partners might react to a perception that the UK intelligence operation is potentially insecure'.[73] It is important to note May's concern in order to place it in the context of the institutional competence claim. Had the information in the paragraphs at issue not been released in the US court, the institutional competence claim may have carried more weight, as the Court may have been more ready to defer to the Foreign Secretary's judgement based on the fact that the information that was not in the public arena.[74] Nonetheless, *Al Rawi* and

71 *Murray, Out of the Shadows*, 225: Two weeks after the Court of Appeal's original judgment, Lord Neuberger restored these comments. See *Mohamed*, para. 168: 'As the evidence showed, some Security Services officials appear to have a dubious record relating to actual involvement, and frankness about any such involvement, with the mistreatment of Mr Mohamed when he was held at the behest of US officials. I have in mind in particular witness B, but the evidence in this case suggests that it is likely that there were others. The good faith of the Foreign Secretary is not in question, but he prepared the certificates partly, possibly largely, on the basis of information and advice provided by Security Services personnel. Regrettably, but inevitably, this must raise the question whether any statement in the certificates on an issue concerning the mistreatment of Mr Mohamed can be relied on, especially when the issue is whether contemporaneous communications to the Security Services about such mistreatment should be revealed publicly. Not only is there some reason for distrusting such a statement, given that it is based on Security Services' advice and information, because of previous, albeit general, assurances in 2005, but also the Security Services have an interest in the suppression of such information'

72 *Binyam Mohamed*, para. 286

73 Ibid, para. 289

74 May himself acknowledges this crucial difference at para. 295: 'In my view, the finding of the US District Court does make a difference because it changes what was an arguable case of

Binyam Mohamed illustrate that the UK legal culture is such that courts in recent years have rarely engaged in what Kavanagh called 'substantial deference',[75] and there is an expectation that deference has to be 'earned by the elected branches' in a manner similar to the justification in Dyzenhaus's conception. As Sir Anthony May notes,

> Relying on a bare principle in relation to material which now has no sensitive content is tantamount to saying that the Foreign Secretary's judgment should always determine the balance and that the court has no relevant balancing judgment of its own to make. That is not the law.[76]

5.2.3 The Ahmed *case*

The *Ahmed* case, similar to the Canadian decision in *Abdelrazik*, can be fairly characterized as an example of judicial pushback to the exercise of executive power. Chapter 2.4.8 gave an account of the facts in *Ahmed,* so it is only principally important here to reiterate the fact that the UK Supreme Court found the executive orders the UK Government implemented to give effect to the 1267 terrorist listing regime[77] to be *ultra vires.*[78] The Supreme Court argued that the UK Government's implementation of the terrorist listing regulations by way of executive order without any kind of parliamentary scrutiny raised 'fundamental questions about the relationship between Parliament and the executive and about judicial control over the power of the executive'.[79] The Supreme Court undoubtedly felt further compelled to arrive at this decision not just because of the improper exercise of executive power, but also because of the significant liberty implications that listing carries for an individual (these were clearly laid out and discussed in *Abdelrazik*) and because of the due process concerns associated with the 1267 listing process (including the use of secret evidence and difficulties associated with challenging a listing). Here again we see an instance where a court is willing to expect justifications from the executive (in line with Dyzenhaus's culture of justification) when serious liberty issues are at stake (as they also were in *Binyam Mohemed, Abdelkrazik* and *Khadr FCA*). As Forcese and Roach note that it is unlikely that radical reforms to the Security Council's 1267 process will occur,[80] it is likely that the UK Supreme Court will again be called upon to

torture into a case of torture which a US court has found to be true in proceedings in which the US Government had the opportunity to make a case that it was not true'

75 Aileen Kavanagh, *Constitutional Review Under the UK Human Rights Act* (Cambridge University Press, 2009) 182

76 *Binyam Mohamed,* para. 295

77 Terrorism (United Nations Measures) Order 2006 (S.I. 2006/2657); Al-Qaida and Taliban (United Nations Measures) Order 2006 (S.I. 2006/2952)

78 *Ahmed,* para. 5

79 Ibid

80 *Forcese and Roach,* 270

comment on the domestic implementation of international regulations aimed at combating terrorist finance. If the Court again responds as it did here in *Ahmed*, it will only further reinforce arguments about the potential existence of a Dyzenhaus-style culture of justification.

5.2.4 *The* Tariq *case*

There have also been cases in the wider national security realm where the UK judiciary has passed judgment on its role in upholding and developing the common law, as well as upholding the UK's human rights obligations under the *ECHR* and the *HRA*. In *Tariq*, the UK Supreme Court was once again called upon to decide on the compatibility of a CMP, this time in the context of an appeal originating from an employment tribunal. Mr Tariq was an immigration officer within the Home Office until he was suspended in 2006 while the withdrawal of his security clearance was considered. The decision to review his clearance and ultimately revoke it occurred shortly after his brother and cousin were arrested in relation to a counter-terrorism investigation. His cousin was eventually convicted in 2008 of conspiracy to commit murder, but his brother was released without charge and investigations found that Mr Tariq himself had not been involved. He subsequently commenced proceedings in the Employment Tribunal and complained that discrimination played a part in the revocation of his security clearance. The Employment Tribunal ordered a CMP and, although both the Employment Appeal Tribunal and the Court of Appeal dismissed Tariq's challenge to the order of a CMP, the Employment Appeal Tribunal declared that Article 6 of the *ECHR* required him to be provided with sufficient detail of the allegations against him so as to allow for effective challenge of these allegations. After the Court of Appeal upheld this declaration, the Supreme Court ruled by eight judges to one in favour of the Home Office, who had argued that the scrutiny of the secret material by the Employment Tribunal, and the appointment of a special advocate, was sufficient to overcome any disadvantage resulting from the CMP.

The balance between the principle of fair and open justice and the interests of national security was once again brought to the forefront in *Tariq*. Lord Hope stressed that 'The context will always be crucial to a resolution of questions as to where and how this balance is struck'[81] and, it was indeed clear that this context was a central distinguishing feature between *Tariq* and a number of the control order cases that were mentioned in the case.[82] While Tariq argued that he was entitled to the same level of procedural protection offered in *SSHD v. AF (No 3)*, the Supreme Court noted that those decisions were made in the context of the restrictions on the individual imposed by control orders which impinged 'directly

81 *Tariq*, para. 72

82 *A v. United Kingdom*, App No 3455/05 [2009] ECHR 301 (para. 25); *SSHD v. AF (No 3)* [2010] 2 AC 2 69 (paras. 26–7, 38, 42, 44); *SSHD v. MB* [2007] UKHL 46 (paras. 42, 44)

on personal freedom and liberty in a way to which Mr Tariq cannot said to be exposed'.[83] The Supreme Court relied on three decisions of the European Commission and Court of Human Rights to argue 'that the outcome of the balancing exercise may differ with the circumstances'.[84] In applying the *ECHR* case law here, the Supreme Court arrives at its decision in a different manner than when it begrudgingly decided 'it was bound to take into account' the ECtHR jurisprudence in *SSHD v. AF (No 3)*.

That said, it would be wrong to suggest that none of the judgments given in *Tariq* expressed concern pertaining to the *ECHR* and *HRA*. After noting that the balancing of an individual's Article 6 rights might occur differently outside of the security vetting context, Lord Dyson states that:

> It is said that this gives rise to undesirable uncertainty. But much of the content of the European Convention on Human Rights is about striking balances. This is sometimes very difficult and different opinions can reasonably be held. As a consequence, outcomes are sometimes difficult to predict. This is inevitable. But it is not a reason for striving to devise hard and fast rules and rigid classifications. It is, however, at least possible to say that, in principle, article 6 requires as much disclosure as possible.[85]

Whether or not this is an implicit criticism of the *ECHR*, it does raise an important issue discussed by the one dissenting judge in the case, Lord Kerr, who argued that even if the CMP was compatible with Article 6, the 'landmark' decision in the case was still 'a departure from the common law's long established commitment to this basic procedural right'.[86] In essence, Lord Kerr was arguing that the English common law should go further than the *ECHR*, repeating Lord Steyn's dictum that 'The Convention is not an exhaustive statement of fundamental rights under our system of law'.[87] To the same point, Lord Dyson in *Al Rawi* also made the argument that 'It is, therefore, open to our courts to provide greater protection through the common law than that which is guaranteed by the Convention'.[88]

83 *Tariq*, para. 27

84 *Leander v. Sweden*, App No 9248/81 [1987] ECHR 4, *Esbester v. United Kingdom*, App No 18601/91 [1993] ECHR 64 and *Kennedy v. United Kingdom* (Application No 26839/05) 18 May 2010. At para. 36 of *Tariq*, the Court says that 'These three cases – *Leander*, *Esbester* and *Kennedy* – establish that the demands of national security may necessitate and under European Convention law justify a system for handling and determining complaints under which an applicant is, for reasons of national security, unable to know the secret material by reference to which his or her complaint is determined. The critical questions under the Convention are whether the system is necessary and whether it contains sufficient safeguards'

85 *Tariq*, para. 161

86 Ibid, para. 108

87 Ibid, para. 109: Lord Steyn's comment came at para. 27 of *R (Anufrijeva) v. SSHD* [2003] UKHL 36

88 *Al Rawi*, paras. 67–8: in making the point, Dyson also quoted Lord Bingham in *R (Ullah) v. Special Adjudicator* [2004] UKHL 26, para. 20: 'It is of course open to member states to provide for rights more generous than those guaranteed by the Convention'

These statements provide evidence that certain members of the UK judiciary consider there are cases in which the common law can offer protections beyond those protections offered by the *ECHR*.

5.2.5 *The* Abu Qatada *cases*

The legal saga of Abu Qatada has been highly publicized and, while its extremely political nature will be further discussed in Chapter 6, it is also relevant here because of dicta pertaining to the *ECHR* and *HRA* in SIAC and the Court of Appeal's decisions following *Qatada ECtHR*. Following the decision by the ECtHR in that case, SIAC was called upon to decide whether there was 'a real risk of a flagrant denial of justice' contrary to Qatada's Article 6 rights should he be deported back to Jordan. This depended on whether there was a real risk that statements by his former co-accused, which it had been established were obtained by torture, would be admitted at his retrial.[89] After an extensive analysis of Jordanian law and criminal procedure, SIAC decided that this real risk still existed.[90] In *Qatada Court of Appeal*, the Home Secretary appealed the SIAC ruling on two grounds, namely: 1) that SIAC had erred in holding that there would be a flagrant denial of justice unless it could be established that the State Prosecutor would bear the burden of proving to a high standard that the statements would not be admitted in evidence; and, 2) that SIAC had failed to consider the question of whether there was a real risk of a flagrant denial of justice 'in the round'.[91] In disposing of the first ground, the Court of Appeal dismissed

89 *Qatada SIAC*, para. 1: SIAC set out two critical questions which would determine whether there is a real risk that the impugned statements would be admitted probatively; para. 54: 'i) Irrespective of the means by which they were obtained, are the impugned statements now admissible at all under Article 148.2 of the Code of Criminal Practice? ii) If they are, is there a real risk that they will be admitted even though there is a "real risk" that they have been obtained by torture?'

90 Ibid, para. 78: 'The Secretary of State has not satisfied us that, on a retrial, there is no real risk that the impugned statements of Abu Hawsher and Al-Hamasher would be admitted probatively against the appellant. Until and unless a change is made to the Code of Criminal Procedure and/or authoritative rulings are made by the Court of Cassation or Constitutional Court which establish that statements made to a public prosecutor by accomplices who are no longer subject to proceedings cannot be admitted probatively against a returning fugitive and/or that it is for the prosecutor to prove to a high standard that the statement was not procured by torture, that real risk will remain'

91 *Qatada Court of Appeal*, paras. 38–9: the second ground of appeal is broken into three elements. First, SIAC was wrong to give separate consideration to: i) the risk that the statements had been obtained by torture; and ii) the risk that the statements would be admitted at the retrial. Secondly, when assessing the risk that the statements would be admitted in evidence, SIAC was wrong to give separate consideration to the two 'critical' questions of Jordanian law to which we have referred in paras. 28–33 above. These questions should have been considered cumulatively: the existence of *two* potential obstacles to the admission of the statements reduced the risk that they would be admitted. Thirdly, in assessing the risk that the statements would be admitted, SIAC focused exclusively on the two critical

objections to SIAC's evaluation of facts rather than its application of the law and nonetheless still found that SIAC took into account the independence and impartiality of the Jordanian court.[92] In dismissing the second ground, the Court of Appeal noted SIAC's reiteration of the Strasbourg judgment, in which the ECtHR had found there was compelling evidence that the impugned statements had been obtained by torture. It did so in order to argue that SIAC had rightly focused on the admissibility of the statements and the flagrant denial of justice issue.[93] Accordingly, the Court of Appeal dismissed the government's appeal.

The decisions of SIAC and the Court of Appeal in the *Qatada* cases are particularly relevant because of their explicit affirmation of the ECtHR's decision, particularly in light of the fact that 'Mr Othman is considered to be a dangerous and controversial person. That is why this case has attracted so much media attention'.[94] It may have been tempting for the UK courts to decide against the reasoning of the ECtHR here, particularly given the politicized nature of the Abu Qatada case, and the public distaste towards him and the human rights protections that many believed were keeping a dangerous suspected terrorist within their country's borders. However, the Court of Appeal noted that SIAC resisted these pressures and conducted a 'detailed examination' of what it called a 'careful and comprehensive judgment' given by the ECtHR.[95] Moreover, the Court of Appeal noted that the ECtHR has not found an expulsion in violation of Aarticle 6 in 22 years,[96] and that the flagrant denial of justice test is a stringent test of unfairness whereby 'Strasbourg has rightly set the bar very high'.[97] Here the Court of Appeal seems to be both simultaneously affirming the ECtHR judgment, and using it to legitimate SIAC's reliance on the test set out in that judgment, a far cry from the dicta expressed by some judges in *SSHD v. AF (No 3)* who were unhappy that they were obliged to take into account the ECtHR's ruling.[98] The fact that the universal abhorrence of torture figured prominently in each of the *Qatada* cases

questions and failed to consider other possibilities that might have affected the assessment of that risk

92 Ibid, paras. 40–46

93 Ibid, paras. 47–55. The Court explicitly says in para. 49: 'We accept that, if SIAC had considered that the risk that the statements had been obtained by torture was remote, then it would have been necessary to take that fact into account, together with its assessment of the seriousness of the risk of the evidence being admitted, when it made its overall judgment as to whether there was a real risk of a flagrant denial of justice. But the ECtHR made strong findings as to the compelling nature of the evidence that the statements had in fact been obtained by torture. That is why the focus of the enquiry before SIAC was on whether there was a real risk that these statements would be admitted as evidence against Mr Othman at his retrial'

94 Ibid, para. 56

95 Ibid, para. 60

96 Ibid, para. 12

97 Ibid, para. 57

98 Recall Lord Hoffmann's dissent in para. 70: Hoffman refers to the decision in *A v UK* as 'wrong' and laments the fact that the Lordships 'have no choice but to submit' to it, because

discussed undoubtedly made it easier for the UK courts to reach the decision they did in the face of serious public and political pressure. That said, in doing so and upholding core legal principles despite the UK Government's best attempts to deport Qatada, they have lent support to the argument that there indeed exists a culture of justification in the UK within the national security realm or, at the very least, that the UK courts have been less willing to engage in substantial deference in recent years.

5.2.6 Summary analysis

This analysis of the UK case law pertaining to the wider use of secret evidence in the national security realm has helped to illustrate some judicial reasoning pertaining to the human rights instruments they uphold, but a note of caution should be raised. Outside of the national security realm, there do exist rare occasions where the UK Supreme Court has expressed concerns as to whether a decision of the Strasbourg Court sufficiently appreciates or accommodates particular aspects of UK domestic process. In such circumstances, it is open to this court to decline to follow the Strasbourg decision, giving reasons for adopting this course.[99] Although *Horncastle* is a judgment on hearsay evidence, it illustrates that UK courts will be willing not to take a decision of the ECtHR into account, if they consider that it doesn't properly accommodate their domestic process and is not clear and authoritative.[100] Even within the national security realm, it has been noted that Lord Kerr in *Tariq* argued that the English common law should go further than the *ECHR*, Lord Dyson argued the same in *Al Rawi* and a number of judges in *SSHD v. AF (No 3)*, most notably Lord Hoffman, argued that their domestic solutions to the fair trial issues raised by control orders more appropriately accommodated the UK legal context than did the Strasbourg decision that they were 'bound to take into account'.

With that said, the decisions in *Al Rawi, Binyam Mohamed, Ahmed* and *Qatada* illustrate that the UK judiciary is committed to protecting the open justice principle and the right to a fair trial even in the face of immense political and public pressure. These decisions, taken into consideration with the decisions in the detention without trial and control order decisions analysed in Chapter 3, can

to 'reject such a decision would almost certainly put this country in breach of the international obligation which it accepted when it acceded to the Convention'

99 *Horncastle*, para. 11

100 Ibid, paras. 119–20: 'Not merely was the Strasbourg ruling in A clear and authoritative but, whatever view individual members of the Committee may have taken about it (and it is evident that, whilst many agreed with it, others did not), it expressed an entirely coherent view. The contrasts with the present situation are striking. In the first place, we are faced here not with a Grand Chamber decision but rather with the possible need for one. Moreover, not merely is the Court's ruling in Al-Khawaja not as authoritative as a Grand Chamber decision, but it is altogether less clear than was the decision in A'

be taken up to argue that recent judicial decisions in the national security realm in the UK are indicative of a human rights culture. Martin and Scott Bray would agree with this assessment, as they have argued that although some traces of the long tradition of deference to the executive in national security still remains, there is a sharp contrast between recent decisions and those that were arrived at in the earliest national security cases.[101] As a result of the decisions analysed here, it seems fair to argue that the legal culture currently present in the UK appears to be illustrative of the 'rights culture' that Dyzenhaus argued was developing well before the *HRA*, even if it was given additional concrete institutional expression by that rights instrument. All of the UK decisions analysed (with the exception of *Tariq*, which may be distinguished because of the less serious liberty issues at stake) in this section have evidenced the willingness of the UK judiciary to protect the open justice principle and human rights more broadly, along the lines of Dyzenhaus's conception of a culture of justification.

5.3 Conclusion

The analyses of both the UK and Canadian case law in the wider national security realm, in combination with the analyses of the case law in Chapter 3, suggest that the courts in both countries are committed to protecting fundamental open justice principles, albeit to varying degrees under different circumstances. As such, the answer to the first question of how, and to what extent, the judiciaries of Canada and the UK express deference to the executive in national security cases is mixed. In *Ahmad*, the Supreme Court engaged in a lengthy historical analysis to uphold the jurisdiction of the Federal Court in assessing disclosure claims, and also upheld the bifurcated system under section 38 *CEA*, whilst suggesting that Parliament should consider the wisdom of this scheme. Like the UK Supreme Court in *Al Rawi*, the Supreme Court in *Ahmad* recognized that it is limited to ruling on the overall fairness of the proceedings, but has also not refrained from suggesting proper consideration in Parliament about the wisdom of the *CEA* scheme. The difference in levels of deference between the Federal Court and Federal Court of Appeal in *Almalki* was also quite significant, with the latter more willing to defer than was Mosley J in the former. By contrast, the Federal Court of Appeal and Supreme Court were less willing to defer to the government's non-disclosure claims in relation to Mr Khadr, perhaps because of the severe rights infringements that he had endured and the liberty interests that were at stake, similar to those present in *Binyam Mohamed*. As such, it appears as though *Khadr FCA* and *Binyam Mohamed* can be distinguished from *Almalki* and even *Tariq* in

101 Greg Martin and Rebecca Scott Bray, 'Discolouring Democracy? Policing, Sensitive Evidence, and Contentious Deaths in the United Kingdom' (2013) 40 *Journal of Law and Society* 624

the sense that less deference was shown to the government's claims in respect of the former men because of the rights infringements they had and may continue to endure. That said, the Supreme Court in *Khadr SC* still deferred substantially to the government on the question of the appropriate remedy for the *Charter* abuses Khadr sustained, arguing that they could not require the Canadian Government to repatriate him as a result of limitations in their institutional competence, and their need to respect the prerogative powers of the executive in areas of foreign relations. Despite these mixed results, *Ahmed* and *Abdelrazik* both provide excellent examples of both Canadian and UK courts holding the executive accountable for its decisions pertaining to implementation of international instruments allowing for terrorist listing, a welcome development given the severity of the liberty and due process infringements raised by terrorist listing.

Moreover, with regard to the second question, the case law reviewed here has illustrated that the UK judiciary has been less willing in recent years to engage in what Kavanagh calls substantial deference to Parliament and the executive. Though caution should again be expressed in relation to the *Binyam Mohamed* judgment, which may have been significantly different had the US District Court not released some of the information pertinent to the redacted paragraphs at issue, it is still fair to argue that the judgment is indicative of Dyzenhaus's culture of justification, whereby Parliament and the executive are expected to earn deference from the courts by ensuring that legislation is human rights compatible. The court in *Al Rawi* showed extreme caution in extending the power of a CMP, noting that this would require the express will of Parliament. This turns the traditional institutional legitimacy claim on its head because the court is not, as Lord Hope put it, simply surrendering to Parliament something which lies within the area of the court's responsibility. Rather, it is recognizing that the decision on the appropriate balance between open justice and the demands of national security in this case is best left for determination through the democratic process conducted by Parliament, following a process of consultation. This viewpoint lends support to Hunt's concept of due deference, as the court in *Al Rawi* operated under the assumption that power in the Constitution is shared among the various actors within it, rather than parcelled out according to some inflexible notion of the separation of powers. Furthermore, analysis of the *Abu Qatada* cases illustrated that the UK judiciary was willing to protect fundamental rights in the face of immense political pressure. This leads to a final conclusion that the cases surveyed here allow for an argument that a culture of justification may be more clearly evident in the UK than it is in Canada. That said, as was noted by Feldman at the outset of this chapter, no one body can establish a rights culture in a country, and the judgments of the judiciaries of Canada and the UK analysed in this chapter and Chapter 3 provide only half of the story to enable an analysis of whether such a culture exists in either country. It is for this reason that focus now turns to Chapter 6's analysis of decisions and statements made about human rights instruments in the realm of counter-terrorism by politicians, the media and the public.

Bibliography

Abdelrazik v. Canada (Minister of Foreign Affairs) [2010] 1 F.C.R. 267

Abu Qatada v. SSHD [2013] EWCA Civ 277

Almrei (Re) [2011] 1 FCR 163; 2009 FC 1263

Al-Qaida and Taliban (United Nations Measures) Order 2006 (S.I. 2006/2952)

Al Rawi and Others v. the Security Service and Others [2009] EWHC 2959 (QB)

Al Rawi and Others v. the Security Service and Others [2010] EWCA Civ 482

Al Rawi and Others v. the Security Service and Others [2011] UKSC 34

Canada v. Almalki [2011] FCA 199

Canada v. Almalki [2010] FC 1106

Canada (Justice) v. Khadr [2008] SCC 28

Canada (Prime Minister) v. Khadr [2010] 1 S.C.R. 44

Charities Registration (Security Information) Act, S.C. 2001, c. 41, s. 113

Charkaoui v. Canada (Citizenship and Immigration) [2009] 2 S.C.R. 326

Charkaoui (Re) [2010] 4 F.C. R. 448; 2009 FC 1030

Dyzenhaus, D. *The Constitution of Law: Legality in a Time of Emergency* (Cambridge University Press, 2006)

Feldman, D. 'The Internationalization of Public Law and Its Impact on the United Kingdom' in Jowell, J. and Oliver, D. (eds), *The Changing Constitution* (6th edn, Oxford University Press, 2007)

Forcese, C. and Roach, K. 'Limping into the Future: The U.N. 1267 Terrorism Listing Process at the Crossroads' (2011) 42 *George Washington International Law Review* 217

HM Treasury v. Ahmed [2010] UKSC 2

Home Office v. Tariq [2011] UKSC 35

Hunt, M. 'Sovereignty's Blight: Why Contemporary Public Law Needs the Concept of "Due Deference"' in Bamforth, N. and Leyland, P. (eds), *Public Law in a Multi-Layered Constitution* (Hart Publishing, 2003)

Ip, J. 'Al Rawi, Tariq, and the Future of Closed Material Procedures and Special Advocates' (2012) 75 *Modern Law Review* 606

Justice and Security Act 2013 c. 18

Kavanagh, A. *Constitutional Review Under the UK Human Rights Act* (Cambridge University Press, 2009)

Kavanagh, A. 'Judging the Judges under the Human Rights Act: Deference, Disillusionment and the War on Terror' [2009] *PL* 287

Khadr v. Canada (Minister of Justice) [2007] FCA 182

King, J.A. 'Institutional Approaches to Judicial Restraint' (2008) 28 *Oxford Journal of Legal Studies* 409

Lazarus, L. *Contrasting Prisoner's Rights: A Comparative Examination of Germany and England* (Oxford University Press, 2004)

Martin, G. and Scott Bray, R. 'Discolouring Democracy? Policing, Sensitive Evidence, and Contentious Deaths in the United Kingdom' (2013) 40 *Journal of Law and Society* 624

Murray, C.R.G. 'Out of the Shadows: The Courts and the United Kingdom's Malfunctioning International Counter-Terrorism Partnerships' (2013) 18 *Journal of Conflict and Security Law* 193

Nelken, D. 'Using Legal Culture: Purposes and Problems' in Nelken, D. (ed), *Using Legal Culture* (Wildy, Simmons and Hill, 2012)

Proceeds of Crime (Money Laundering) and Terrorist Financing Act, S.C. 2000, c. 17

R v. Ahmad [2009] OJ No 6156

R v. Ahmad [2011] 1 S.C.R. 110

Shephard, M. 'Omar Khadr Must Stay in Federal Prison, Judge Rules' (18 October 2013) *Toronto Star* available at: https://www.thestar.com/news/canada/2013/10/18/judge_decides_today_on_whether_to_move_omar_khadr_from_federal_prison.html [accessed 18 October 2013]

Terrorism (United Nations Measures) Order 2006 (S.I. 2006/2657)

Zedner, L. 'Securing Liberty in the Face of Terror: Reflections from Criminal Justice' (2005) 32 *Journal of Law and Society* 507

6 Canada and the United Kingdom's domestic political culture

Feldman's argument that 'no one body can establish a human rights culture' has been reiterated in several parts of this book.[1] Respect for human rights and the rule of law in a society, or lack thereof, is not only made evident by judicial decisions, such as those analysed in Chapter 5, it can also be made evident by the decisions and statements made by politicians, the public, the media and interested civil society groups. As Eric Feldman notes, when actors within a society talk about rights, they reflect societal beliefs.[2] As such, analysing the decisions and statements these actors make can, in combination with the analysis in Chapter 5, provide a basis for examining whether, and to what extent, a 'rights culture' has developed in the two countries. Rhetoric about rights can take a different form in different cultures because 'the histories and traditions of the countries being analysed have produced different conceptions about the right and the role of fundamental rights'.[3] If political actors consider these histories and traditions, as well as 'surrounding attitudes, political climate, and political receptivity'[4] when they make counter-terrorism policy decisions, they know that some policies may have higher political costs than others, and act accordingly. The first objective of this chapter is to answer the following question: Is there a difference in societal attitudes towards human rights in the two jurisdictions and, together with the analysis of legal culture in Chapter 5, can it be argued that a human rights culture exists in the two jurisdictions?

The second of objective of this chapter will be to analyse Canada and the United Kingdom's relationship with the United States to answer the following research question: What impact has the relationship with the United States had

1 David Feldman, 'The Impact of Human Rights on the UK Legislative Process' (2004) 25 *Stat LR* 9 [hereinafter '*Feldman, Impact of Human Rights*] 114–15
2 Eric Feldman, 'Patients' Rights, Citizens' Movements and Japanese Legal Culture' in Nelken, D. (ed), *Comparing Legal Cultures* (Aldershot, 1997)
3 Liora Lazarus, *Contrasting Prisoner's Rights: A Comparative Examination of Germany and England* (Oxford University Press, 2004) [hereinafter "*Lazarus*"] 12
4 Zedner has argued that promotion of rights varies according to these factors. See Lucia Zedner, 'Securing Liberty in the Face of Terror: Reflections from Criminal Justice' (2005) 32 *Journal of Law and Society* 507 [hereinafter "*Zedner*"] 519

on the evolution of domestic counter-terrorism measures in the two jurisdictions? A number of recent events and new academic commentary provide the impetus for a closer analysis of how this relationship might affect counter-terrorism policy-making.[5] The sections on Canada and the UK begin with a short discussion of the historical evolution of *The Canadian Charter of Rights and Freedoms*,[6] and the Human Rights Act[7] and *ECHR*,[8] respectively. Analysis then turns to current societal attitudes towards these instruments in order to discern whether a rights culture exists in the two countries. Academic commentary regarding societal attitudes towards the *HRA* and *ECHR* has been sharply divided,[9] and it has been argued that there is a patriotic attachment in Canada to the *Charter* as a specifically Canadian achievement that has not been paralleled in the UK with respect to the *HRA*.[10] The role of the media and politicians in influencing and promulgating these societal attitudes cannot be ignored, and will be analysed specifically with regard to counter-terrorism policies and issues, such as Bill S-7 and the UK's attempts to deport Abu Qatada. Both sections then turn to discussions of the potential impact of relationships with the United States on counter-terrorism policy. In the UK section, analysis focuses on the Justice and Security Act[11] and

5 These events include, but are not limited to: the passage of the Justice and Security Act in the UK, which some see as a response to the decisions in *Al Rawi* and *Binyam Mohammed*; the passage of Bill S-7 in Canada; the Omar Khadr repatriation affair in Canada; and the UK's attempts to deport Abu Qatada. For recent academic commentary on these events, as well as on the US/Canada and US/UK relationship, see Kent Roach, 'Substitute Justice? Challenges to American Counter-Terrorism Activities in Non-American Courts' (2013) 82 *Mississippi Law Journal* 901 [hereinafter '*Roach, Substitute Justice*']; Kent Roach, 'Uneasy Neighbours: Comparative American and Canadian Counter-Terrorism' (2012) 38 *William Mitchell Law Review* 1701 [hereinafter '*Roach, Uneasy Neighbours*']; Kent Roach, 'Counter-Terrorism in and outside Canada and in and outside the Anti-Terrorism Act' (2012) 6 *Review of Constitutional Studies* 243; Kent Roach, 'Secret Evidence and Its Alternatives' in Masferrer, A. (ed), *Post- 9/11 and the State of Permanent Legal Emergency: Security and Human Rights in Countering Terrorism* (Springer, 2011) 179

6 Part I of the Constitution Act 1982, Being Schedule B to the Canada Act 1982 (UK), 1982, c. 11 [hereinafter "*Charter*"]

7 Human Rights Act 1998 c. 42 [hereinafter "*HRA*"]

8 Council of Europe, *European Convention for the Protection of Human Rights and Fundamental Freedoms, as amended by Protocols Nos. 11 and 14*, 4 November 1950, ETS 5 [hereinafter "*ECHR*"]

9 See Chapter 1.3.4: Lord Lester and Kate Beattie argue that there is a deeply worrying failure to respect the culture of human rights that underpins the *HRA* that stretches to the highest level of government; Fenwick et al. suggest that there is a lack of popular support for the *HRA*; Kavanagh argues that the *HRA*, albeit slowly, is contributing to a change in the way we characterize the appropriate relationship between Parliament and the courts and has led to the reassessment of the theoretical foundations of UK constitutional law

10 Helen Fenwick, Gavin Phillipson and Roger Masterman, 'The Human Rights Act in Contemporary Context' in Fenwick, H., Phillipson, G. and Masterman, R. (eds), *Judicial Reasoning Under the UK Human Rights Act* (Cambridge University Press, 2007) 3

11 Justice and Security Act 2013 c. 18 [hereinafter "*Justice and Security Act*"]

issues associated with intelligence sharing and disclosure of security-sensitive information raised by the *Binyam Mohamed* and *Al Rawi* cases.

6.1 Societal attitudes towards human rights in Canada

The *Charter*, which was brought forward by Prime Minister Pierre Trudeau's Liberal Government, became law on 17 April 1982 and forms the first part of the 1982 Constitution Act that codified Canada's constitution. Although that government commissioned a Special Joint Committee on the Constitution that it initially envisioned would last a few weeks, in the end the Committee's work lasted for nearly a year as hundreds of people submitted letters or came to Ottawa to present briefs.[12] In total, 323 non-governmental organizations (NGOs) and 639 individuals made submissions and 'at no other time in Canadian history had the state engaged in such an expansive consultation with ordinary Canadians about human rights'.[13] Woehrling notes that at the time:

> Many Canadian politicians and legal scholars still held by the British political and constitutional ideal and were thus reluctant to give the courts the power to censure the will of elected members of the legislature on the basis of a vague, abstract constitutional catalogue of rights and freedoms.[14]

As such, they chose an original compromise whereby the federal parliament and provincial legislatures could exclude application of most guaranteed rights and freedoms through the invocation of a 'notwithstanding clause'.[15] The enactment of the *Charter* was 'accompanied by much media hype and political fanfare by the federal government' and there is a 'widely shared opinion that in 1982 one of the primary objectives of the Canadian Charter of Rights and Freedoms was nation-building: the establishment of an institution that would help to consolidate Canadian identity and the legitimacy of the central government, and thus foster centralization of power'.[16]

12 Canadian Human Rights Commission, *The Evolution of Human Rights in Canada* (Cat. No. HR4-19, Minister of Public Works and Government Services, 2012) 28

13 Ibid

14 José Worheling. 'The Canadian Charter of Rights and Freedoms and Its Consequences for Political and Democratic Life and the Democratic System' in Gagnon, A.-G. (ed), *Contemporary Canadian Federalism: Foundations, Traditions, Institutions* (University of Toronto Press, 2009) [hereinafter "*Worheling*"] 225

15 Ibid. Janet Hiebert has referred to the clause as an 'important turning point in reconciling Wesminster-based parliamentary systems to the possibility of a bill of rights' and has noted that the clause was 'a late concession to provincial premiers who, for ideological and democratic reasons, opposed the idea of assigning courts new power to constrain parliament'. See Janet L. Hiebert, 'Constitutional Experimentation: Rethinking How a Bill of Rights Functions' in Ginsburg, T. and Dixon, R. (eds), *Comparative Constitutional Law* (Edward Elgar Publishing, 2011) [hereinafter "*Hiebert*"] 300

16 Ibid, 226 and 236

That said, it should be noted that the *Charter* increased divisions and antagonism between Quebec and the rest of Canada, as Quebec has its own Charter of Rights and 'the way that the Canadian Charter has been used has made it appear incompatible with Quebec's efforts to protect its language and culture'.[17] Moreover, Rosenberg argues that few lawyers initially expected the *Charter* to cause a dramatic shift in the practice and administration of law, as 'there were too many signs that the judiciary and, indeed, the public as a whole would be resistant'.[18] However, from an early stage the Supreme Court signalled to both the profession and the public that it was committed to its post-*Charter* role in *Therens*, a modest breathalyser case in which 'The Court employed the exclusionary rule as a means of demonstrating the importance of Charter rights that are closely tied to the administration of justice, such as the right to counsel'.[19] This signal that the Court was willing to interpret the *Charter*'s provisions broadly and creatively encouraged litigants to bring more such cases which, as Epp notes, is 'evidenced by a dramatic growth between 1985 and 1990 in the number of requests for judicial review'.[20]

Rosenberg argues that the *Charter* created a fundamental shift in public perceptions about human rights, opening society's eyes to the fact that many elements of criminal procedure prior to 1982 were unfair.[21] That said, he is clear that the *Charter* is not a perfect document, and he notes that more can be done by courts to educate the public about its virtues and importance in modern Canadian society.[22] Nonetheless, current societal attitudes towards the *Charter* could be described as illustrative 'of a political culture of legal compliance, in which governments regularly accept the authority of judicial rulings and rarely invoke the notwithstanding clause (the government has never used this power) or refuse to revise legislation to satisfy judicial objections'.[23] Hiebert argues that 'The degree to which a bill of rights alters or constrains legislation in Westminster-based parliamentary systems is influenced significantly by whether governments perceive there are substantial political and legal consequences for failing to comply with rights'.[24] She argues that Canada has the highest costs associated with passing inconsistent legislation, not only because courts can invalidate that legislation, but also because of the aforementioned political culture of legal compliance. The fact that the government has never invoked the notwithstanding clause in relation

17 Ibid, 237

18 Marc Rosenberg, 'Twenty-Five Years Later: The Impact of the Canadian Charter of Rights and Freedoms on The Criminal Law' (2009) *Supreme Court Law Review* [hereinafter "*Rosenberg*"] 2

19 Ibid, 3

20 Charles Epp, 'Do Bills of Rights Matter? The Canadian Charter of Rights and Freedoms' [1996] *American Political Science Review* 776

21 *Rosenberg*, 5

22 Ibid, 16

23 *Hiebert*, 303–4

24 Ibid, 309

to a decision on *Charter* compliance indeed speaks to the political costs associated with failing to comply with court directions on rights in Canada.

Given the viewpoints espoused above, Fenwick et. al's argument that there is patriotic attachment to the *Charter* as a specifically Canadian achievement appears to have merit. The extensive public consultation behind its inception, its role as part of the wider nation-building exercise behind the Constitution and its broad and creative interpretation by the Supreme Court in its early years may have helped endear it to Canadian society in a manner that will be contrasted with the reception of the *HRA* in the UK. Granted, it must be noted that the *Charter* represents a pragmatic compromise, and it should not be forgotten that certain segments of Canadian society may not claim to have the same attachment to it, most especially those in Quebec who may see it as incompatible with their efforts to protect their language and culture. Nonetheless, it is fair to suggest that the political culture of legal compliance it backstops means that actors in Canada's political institutions may assess and recognize the political costs of implementing and defending counter-terrorism legislation that may be found not to be *Charter*-compliant. Moreover, the fact that the notwithstanding clause has never been invoked, and the rarity of occasions on which governments have refused to revise counter-terrorism legislation in accordance with court rulings, suggests that Canada's political actors recognize the political costs associated with such actions when they choose to implement and defend counter-terrorism legislation that could violate the *Charter*.

Analysis thus turns to whether a rights culture can be said to exist in Canada. Chapter 5's legal culture analysis suggested a mixed picture of the Canadian judiciary's view of its role and its relationship with Parliament and the executive in the wider realm of national security. While Canadian courts have not refrained from striking or reading down provisions of counter-terrorism legislation,[25] analysis of the case law in the wider national security realm has shown judicial reasoning pertaining to the their role in protecting the *Charter*, and pertaining to their relationship with Parliament and the executive to be more deferential. That said, analysis in this chapter has suggested that there are a number of reasons why Canadian political actors must consider the political costs of the counter-terrorism legislation they implement and defend, such as a political culture of legal compliance that is backstopped by a patriotic attachment to the *Charter*, and the ability and willingness of Canadian courts to invalidate counter-terrorism legislation inconsistent with human rights. The possible impact of an inability to directly invalidate counter-terrorism legislation, and the lack of patriotic attachment to the *HRA*, will be provided for useful contrast when this chapter analyses UK societal attitudes towards human rights mechanisms. Nevertheless, it seems fair to suggest at this point that a human rights culture may be said to exist in Canada. Although analyses in Chapters 3 and 5 illustrated that the

25 As noted in both Chapters 3 and 5

performance of Canadian courts in the security certificate cases and the wider national security realm cases were quite mixed, it has been shown here that public attitudes towards the *Charter* and human rights more generally are very positive, a situation which is certainly not mirrored in the UK.

That said, in fully answering the first question, some additional consideration should be given to what political actors argue when they debate counter-terrorism measures. While it is preferable to analyse actual legislative outcomes towards this assessment (which will also be done below), if actors illuminate societal beliefs when they talk about rights, as Eric Feldman argues, then what they say during the course of debates on counter-terrorism measures should also be considered. The Conservative Government frequently makes statements to reinforce their primary role as protector of the security of Canadians, whilst noting that the threat from terrorism is ever present and will remain so for the foreseeable future.[26] While it would be wrong to suggest that only Conservative MPs have recently used the 'continuing threat of terrorism rhetoric' to support their policies,[27] recent debates on counter-terrorism provisions, such as those on the recently re-enacted Bill S-7, have nevertheless involved much of this rhetoric with very little substantive analysis of the possible impacts of the provisions on the rights of individuals.[28] More specifically, not 1 of the 18 amendments to Bill S-7 that were tabled as the Bill made its way through the legislative process were implemented, with much of the debate instead focusing on: criticisms of the NDP for being 'soft' on terrorism in opposing the measures;[29] criticisms of the Liberal Party for supporting the measures because they originally instituted them in 2001, and for going against their party's culture as 'the Party of the Charter';[30] and, most significantly, criticisms of the Conservatives for their timing of the bill, and their suppression

26 Mr Colin Carrier, CPC: 'Mr. Speaker, I think the member realizes that the first job of any government is to keep Canadians safe from those who wish to harm us. International terrorism is going to continue to be a threat in the foreseeable future. Bill S-7 would provide law enforcement and national security agencies with further means to anticipate and respond effectively to terrorism', Canadian House of Commons, *Hansard Debates*, 23 April 2013

27 Hon. Roméo Antonius Dallaire: 'When this legislation was drafted, the Minister of Justice stated in his department's press release that "terrorism will continue to be a threat for the foreseeable future." He is correct. The nature of conflict in our era has changed. Conventional conflict and warfare are things of the past. Terrorism will continue to play a role in conflict in the future', Canadian House of Commons, *Hansard Debates*, 1 March 2012

28 The Bill S-7 measures, which provide for preventive arrest and investigative hearings, were provisions of the Anti-Terrorism Act 2001 that sunsetted in 2007. On 24 April 2013, they were re-enacted without amendment despite several suggestions for their improvement over the course of the last decade, including two parliamentary reports discussed in Chapter 4

29 Ms Candice Bergen, CPC: 'It is too bad that the NDP does not seem to understand that terrorism is a threat. We have seen it over this last week. It is not just a notion. It is not just something for academics to talk about', Canadian House of Commons, *Hansard Debates*, 22 April 2013

30 Mr Charlie Angus, NDP: 'I would like to ask my honourable colleague why he thinks the Liberal Party, which has wrapped itself in the flag of the Charter of Rights and Freedoms, has refused to come forward with even a single amendment to at least clarify and basically protect

of political debate since winning a majority.[31] It is also worth noting that more recent legislation enacted by the Conservative Government in the aftermath of the October 2014 terrorist attacks was also debated in a similar manner, with most comments focusing less on substantive rights issues with the Bill and more on (perhaps fairly made) arguments about the Conservatives' timing of the legislation.[32]

If political actors recognize their local histories and traditions,[33] as well as 'surrounding attitudes, political climate, and political receptivity'[34] and 'political and legal consequences'[35] when they make counter-terrorism policy decisions, it is fair to argue that they might do so knowing that some policies may have higher political costs than others, and act accordingly. While the existence of a strong rights culture in Canada could raise these political costs and thus affect how Parliamentarians vote on counter-terrorism measures, analysis of this is further complicated by other factors, such as political climate, which can vary enormously, particularly in periods of heightened public fear. For example, Ramraj notes that often a response to public fear is to 'respond legislatively to popular opinion, enacting strict anti-terrorism measures'.[36] The extension of the Bill S-7 measures, remnants of the post-9/11 Anti-Terrorism Act of 2001, was voted against by the Liberals in 2007, but supported by the Liberals in their most recent reincarnation in 2013. Arguably, the Liberals may have foreseen the high political costs associated with voting against measures they originally instituted, especially given the political climate of the debate occurring in the aftermath of the Boston attacks and the foiled VIA rail bomb plot.[37] This argument definitely also holds true with regard to the most recent post-October 2014 attacks legislation. As was just noted, some

the rights of Canadian citizens. If that party believes in the Charter, why is it not standing up for it?' Canadian House of Commons, *Hansard Debates*, 23 April 2013

31 Ms Irene Mathyssen, NDP notes that 'The government has shut down debate a record 31 times and is actively limiting debate, not just in the House but also in committees . . . Sadly, the government is clearly not interested in hearing other ideas. The problem is that our job here is to work together and collectively look at legislation to ensure it is in the best interest of all Canadians', Canadian House of Commons, *Hansard Debates*, 22 April 2013

32 Specifically the Protection of Canada from Terrorists Act 2015 and the Anti-Terrorism Act 2015, discussed in Chapter 2.3.2. See Canadian House of Commons, *Hansard Debates*, 18 February 2015, NDP leader Thomas Mulcair on Bill C-51: 'The Conservatives have even admitted it. They see the recent events, as one of their officials put it, as a strategic opportunity for them, so Canadians are right to suspect that the Prime Minister's new anti-terrorism bill, Bill C-51, goes too far'

33 *Lazarus*

34 *Zedner*

35 *Hiebert*, 3–4

36 Victor Ramraj, 'Terrorism, Risk Perception and Judicial Review' in Ramraj, V., Roach, K. and Hor, M.Y.M. (eds), *Global Anti-Terrorism Law and Policy* (Cambridge University Press, 2005), 107

37 This was suggested by Mr Marc-André Morin, who said: 'Clearly, they are not in a position to be too critical because they came up with this in the first place. So much for the Charter', Canadian House of Commons, *Hansard Debates*, 23 April 2013

Conservative MPs were accused of conceptualizing the attacks as a 'strategic opportunity', and many Liberal MPs supported Bill C-51 while they were members of the opposition, likely because political costs associated with doing so were low in the political climate that existed directly after the October 2014 terrorist attacks (with the next general election not far away). The fact that the Liberal Party (now that it has comfortably won a majority government) is now actively discussing repeal of various aspects of Bill C-51[38] (a welcome development, to be fair) represents a change in policy that usefully evidences how the purported existence of a rights culture needs to be tempered to take into account very real political climate factors that exist in the aftermath of significant terrorist attacks.

Similarly, the decision to move debate on Bill S-7 to the Monday after the Boston terrorist attacks and the announcement of the foiled VIA rail bomb plot may have been a strategic choice by the Conservatives, based on an assessment of lower political and legal consequences in the prevailing political climate.[39] Many MPs accused the Conservative Government of using the post-Boston and VIA rail bomb plot climate to pass the measures swiftly in order to show that they 'were doing something to combat terrorism'.[40] The political climate in the aftermath of the Boston attacks and the foiled VIA rail bomb plot provided the Conservatives with an opportunity to pass long-dormant counter-terrorism legislation that they had been trying to reintroduce since 2007. With regard to this specific and recent counter-terrorism policy debate, the existence of a rights culture may have been tempered by the post-Boston and VIA rail political climate (similar to the case with the post-October 2014 attack legislation noted above), which the Conservatives likely felt gave them the opportunity to pass Bill S-7 with low political and legal consequences. As such, the political costs associated with supporting it were low for the Conservatives, whilst the costs for the Liberals for not supporting counter-terrorism measures they originally instituted were high.

38 Ian McLeod, 'Liberals Planning Swift Overhaul of Controversial Anti-Terrorism Act, or Bill C-51' (22 October 2015) *National Post*, available at: http://news.nationalpost.com/news/canada/canadian-politics/liberals-planning-swift-overhaul-of-controversial-anti-terrorism-act-or-bill-c-51 [accessed 24 October 2015]

39 Mr Mike Sullvan, NDP: 'The bill was reported back to the House of Commons on 12 December of last year and it was not until today, more than four months later that it suddenly appeared. The only notice was given last Friday, by the government House leader that the bill would be replacing an opposition day motion that dealt with Conservative backbenchers' rights to speak here in the House. Therefore, the timing of the bill is very deliberately political', Canadian House of Commons, *Hansard Debates*, 22 April 2013

40 Mr Dany Morin, NDP: 'What we have before us is a government that is using the terrible tragedy that took place in Boston for partisan purposes'. This sentiment was echoed by several other MPs, including Liberal Philip Toone: 'We have to wonder if the bill in front of us today is simply some elaborate political ploy to capitalize on terrorist attacks that have recently taken place instead of actually doing the work that needs to be done on the ground to build up our security apparatus, protect Canadians and ensure that the safety of Canadians is paramount and not a play thing for political gain', Canadian House of Commons, *Hansard Debates*, 23 April 2013

This is not to suggest that several Parliamentarians did not express rights concerns in debating against the Bill,[41] but the analysis above suggests that in two recent sets of debate on significant anti-terrorism legislation, the impact of a rights culture was nullified or obscured by political climate factors.

Analysis of the Bill S-7 and Bill C-51 policy process has illuminated how political climate factors, such as recent successful or foiled terrorist attacks, can lower the political and legal consequences associated with implementing and defending counter-terrorism legislation that may give rise to human rights concerns. When this occurs, substantive debate about the impact of the provisions on the human rights of citizens is often replaced by rhetoric and political platitudes. When counter-terrorism policy is debated and passed in this manner, there is often a lack of meaningful debate on possible amendments to the policy that seek to address human rights concerns, as was the case with Bill S-7 policy process. Given the analyses in this section, the answer to the first research question, Is there a difference in societal attitudes towards human rights in the two jurisdictions and, together with the analysis of legal culture in Chapter 5, can it be argued that a human rights culture exists in the two jurisdictions?, must be qualified. Given the warm reception of the *Charter* by the judiciary and the public, and the compliance of the government with judicial decisions (i.e. the notwithstanding clause having never been used), it may seem fair to argue that a human rights culture exists in Canada. However, once the quite mixed record of the judiciary in the security certificate and wider national security context case law analysis are also taken into consideration, this becomes a more difficult argument to make. Add in this section's analysis of the Bill S-7 and Bill C-51 policy process, which has suggested that the impact of a human rights culture on the evolution of counter-terrorism measures can be tempered by other political climate factors, such as recent successful or foiled terrorist attacks that can lower the political and legal consequences associated with implementing and supporting rights-infringing legislation, and the argument becomes even more difficult.

6.2 Canada's relationship with the United States

Canada differs significantly geopolitically from the UK because it has not had to go through the same extensive history of terrorist attacks on its own soil and it has no permanent seat on the UN Security Council. Nonetheless, Roach has noted that Canada was affected by erroneous claims shortly after 9/11 that terrorists had entered the US through Canada, and notes that it is no coincidence

41 Hon. Irwin Cotler, Liberal, said that he hoped that, if the measures were enacted, 'parliamentary committees will be given the opportunity and resources necessary to undertake full review of the provisions in question during the next trial period and well in advance of any debate to extend it once again', Canadian House of Commons, *Hansard Debates*, 23 April 2013

that the US Patriot Act is entitled 'Protecting the Northern Border'.[42] Moreover, recent terrorist attacks that have occurred in the US (such as the Boston Marathon bombings), and foiled attacks such as the VIA rail plot to bomb a train originating in Toronto and destined for New York City, remind Canadians and their decision-makers that they are not immune to the threat of terrorism.[43] Such is the close symbolic and political relationship between the two countries that terrorist attacks in one jurisdiction are cited and discussed by political leaders in the other. In fact, earlier analysis in this chapter suggested that the Canadian Government may have used the political climate in the aftermath of the Boston bombings and the foiled VIA rail bomb plot to pass what had previously been perhaps more politically costly legislation in the form of Bill S-7. Moreover, Canada and the US are also parties to a number of counter-terrorism and national security-oriented border agreements, including the Canada–US Smart Border Declaration,[44] the more recent 2011 Safe Third Country Agreement[45] and a number of other border or transportation related agreements that are designed to strengthen the border's resilience to terrorism whilst minimally affecting commerce between the countries.

While the number of cooperation agreements between Canada and the US pertaining to counter-terrorism and border security underscores the close relationship between the two countries, there have also been a number of other events in the national security realm that have caused tension between the two countries. These include the extraordinary rendition of Maher Arar, the torture and imprisonment Abdullah Almalki in Syria[46] and, most recently, the Omar Khadr repatriation saga,[47] all of which became the subject of intense political attention in Canada after it was revealed that the joint activities of Canadian and American officials had resulted in serious rights violations. Roach has referred to the experiences of these men, and the political controversies they resulted in, as 'major irritants that underline the differences between American and Canadian counter-terrorism

42 *Roach, Uneasy Neighbours*, 1702

43 Hon. Irwin Cotler: 'The threat of transnational terrorism is real and Canada is not unaffected by it, as the recent events, whether they be in Boston or the aborted terrorist attack now in Canada, indicated', Canadian House of Commons, *Hansard Debates*, 23 April 2013

44 Foreign Affairs and International Trade Canada, *Canada–US Smart Border Declaration: Building a Smart Border for the 21st Century on the Foundation of a North American Zone of Confidence* (2001)

45 Citizenship and Immigration Canada, *U.S-Canada Safe Third Country Agreement* (2002); United States Government, *United States–Canada Beyond the Border: A Shared Vision for Perimeter Security and Economic Competitiveness* (2011). Roach extensively details a number of these agreements and their implications for Canadian and US cooperation on border security and counter-terrorism cooperation on border security and counter-terrorism efforts. See *Roach, Uneasy Neighbours*

46 For the full report, see The Honourable Frank Iacobucci QC LLD, *Internal Inquiry into the Actions of Canadian Officials in Relation to Abdullah Almalki, Ahmad Abou-Elmaati and Muayyed Nureddin* (Ottawa, 2008)

47 The Omar Khadr repatriation saga was most recently discussed in Chapter 5

and have made Canada and the United States uneasy neighbours'.[48] In his reflections on the experience of Maher Arar and the resultant political controversy, Roach has argued that the fact that the Arar Commission's recommendations with regard to enhancing and coordinating review of information sharing have not been implemented by the Canadian Government speaks to the government's concern with damaging its intelligence-sharing relations with the US.[49] The fact that the Canadian Government has failed to adopt these recommendations, which were made by a highly publicized, domestic public inquiry they set up and invested millions of dollars in, speaks to the complex nature of the cooperation arrangements between the US and Canada and the impact of the US on Canadian policy-making in the national security realm.

Similarly, the Canadian Government's refusal to repatriate Omar Khadr for several years, which finally took place in early 2013, despite immense domestic political pressure and even compulsion from their own Supreme Court (as noted in Chapter 5), also speaks to the impact that Canada's 'uneasy neighbours' to the south have had on Canadian counter-terrorism and national security policy. Although Khadr is now back in Canada, the Canadian Government did not request his repatriation until it did so as part of an agreement with the US.[50] Despite the aforementioned analysis that seems to suggest the presence of a rights culture in Canada, the impact of the US on Canadian foreign and counter-terrorism policy must be acknowledged as a significant political climate factor that impacts decision-making.[51] Canadian political actors are likely assess and recognize the political and legal costs associated with counter-terrorism policies that may strain what is a crucial, mutually cooperative, symbolic, financial and geographic relationship with the US.

This section has analysed two aspects of Canada's political culture, its societal attitudes towards human rights and its close relationship with the US. The inception of the *Charter* was a nation-building exercise, and its robust interpretation by the courts has led to a fundamental shift in public attitudes towards the criminal justice system. While it increased divisions and antagonism between Quebec and the rest of Canada, and needs to be seen as a product of compromise and pragmatism, it has led to a political culture of legal compliance insofar as the notwithstanding clause has never been invoked and governments have rarely refused to revise legislation to satisfy judicial objections. That said, while a rights culture is *arguably* present in Canada, assessing linkages between this culture and counter-terrorism policy is much more difficult. Actors in political institutions may recognize occasions when fear and insecurity are present in their

48 *Roach, Uneasy Neighbours*, 1703. Roach also has portions of this article specifically dedicated to in-depth discussion of the Maher Arar saga (1729–49) and the Omar Khadr saga (1749–87).

49 Ibid, 1748

50 Ibid, 1787

51 Ibid, 1789

political climate, and they sometimes seize the opportunity to adopt counter-terrorism policies that would normally carry high political costs as a result of their rights concerns.

Insofar as analysis of one set of the most recent counter-terrorism provisions can be seen as illustrative of how decision-makers may seize on political opportunities presented by fear and insecurity, proper and full consideration of substantial, rights-oriented amendments to the S-7 measures did not occur as a result of their swift passage in the aftermath of the Boston bombings and failed VIA rail bomb plot. A similar process has been observed with regard to the swift passage of the legislation that followed the October 2014 terrorist attacks. The consequences of a lack of meaningful debate on these measures and any future measures is exacerbated in Canada because of the lack of parliamentary review mechanisms noted in Chapter 4. Finally, while Canada is not necessarily seen as a leader on the geopolitical stage, the idea that it is immune to terrorism has recently been challenged, and national security and counter-terrorism have been put back on the Canadian public agenda by a number of high-profile events, including the October 2014 attacks and public inquiries concerning treatment of Canadians by Canadian and American officials. That said, analysis pertaining to the relationship between the US and Canada in the fields of counter-terrorism and national security suggests that this relationship has an impact on political actors when they assess the political and legal consequences associated with implementing and defending counter-terrorism and national security policy that places strains on Canada's relationship with the US.

6.3 Societal attitudes towards human rights in the United Kingdom

This section begins with a short discussion of the historical evolution of the *HRA* and *ECHR*. Focus then turns to analysis of current societal attitudes towards these instruments in order to discern whether a rights culture exists in the country. The role of the media and politicians in influencing and promulgating these societal attitudes will be analysed particularly with regard to the UK's attempts to deport Abu Qatada. In attempting to discern the linkages between counter-terrorism legislation and a rights culture, analysis will focus on the Justice and Security Act 2013[52] and the Counter-Terrorism and Security Act 2015,[53] two recent and significant pieces of UK counter-terrorism legislation that have been discussed at several points in this book. The section then turns to discussion of the UK's geopolitical position and relationship with the US, in order to analyse its possible impact on UK counter-terrorism policy. The UK/US analysis focuses particularly

52 C. 18 [hereinafter "*JSA*"]

53 C. 6 [hereinafter "*CTSA*"]

on recent issues raised by the *Binyam Mohamed*[54] and *Al Rawi*[55] cases, including those associated with the intelligence sharing arrangements between the two countries, and disclosure of security-sensitive information in US and UK courts.

According to the recent UK Bill of Rights Commission (BoRC):

> The term 'human rights' began to come into common usage in Britain and in Europe in the second half of the 20th century as the survivors of the appalling abuses of World War II sought to create instruments to prevent such abuses from ever taking place again. But the concept of 'rights' in the United Kingdom goes back almost to the very beginning of government as we now know it, to Magna Carta in 1215, the Petition of Right of 1628, the Bill of Rights in 1689 in England and the Claim of Right of 1689 in Scotland.[56]

That said, it was not until 1966 that the UK allowed individuals to take cases under the *ECHR* to the European Court of Human Rights (ECtHR).[57] While UK courts showed themselves increasingly willing to regard the Convention and its case law as a source of legal principle,[58] individuals could not seek specific redress for rights infringements in the UK courts until what Hiebert calls 'the time of the next rights revolution, the United Kingdom's introduction of the Human Rights Act, which came into effect in 2000'.[59] It should be noted that the history of rights in the UK and discussions pertaining to a UK Bill of Rights long predates discussion, and eventual passage, of the *HRA*. Lord Lloyd offered his view that a Bill of Rights was not necessary because the UK already possessed a 'better method, tried and tested over generations, for establishing, delimiting and enforcing human rights, than the proposed substitute of a pre-determined Bill of Rights under judicial control'.[60] Milne argued that the UK 'should not have a Bill of Rights, at least not so long as we retain our present system of parliamentary

54 *Mohamed, R (on the application of) v. Secretary of State for Foreign & Commonwealth Affairs* [2010] EWCA Civ 65

55 *Al Rawi and Others v. The Security Service and Others* [2011] UKSC 34 [hereinafter "*Al Rawi*"]

56 UK Bill of Rights Commission, *A UK Bill of Rights? The Choice before Us* (December 2012, Vol 1) [hereinafter "*BoRC*"] para. 6

57 Ibid, para. 14

58 Ibid, para. 18

59 *Hiebert*, 302. She also notes that 'Political reluctance to formally relinquish the principle of parliamentary supremacy had long represented a serious sticking point for those in the United Kingdom proposing a bill of rights . . . A 1993 Labour policy contemplated use of a notwithstanding mechanism based on Canada's notwithstanding power. But as discussion about a bill of rights evolved, this proposal subsequently disappeared. The political architects of the *HRA* became increasingly aware of how political attitudes to the notwithstanding clause were evolving in Canada, and concern set in that if the Canadian approach were emulated, reluctance to use the notwithstanding clause would contradict the spirit of constrained judicial power'

60 Lord Lloyd, 'Do We Need a Bill of Rights?' (1976) 39 *Modern Law Review* 121, 125

sovereignty'.[61] Further, along these lines, Griffith suggested that 'law is not and cannot be a substitute for politics'.[62] These and other debates[63] illustrate how the Diceyan concept of the separation of powers was often taken up against the idea of codifying rights, but also illustrate that the importance of individual liberty within the common law has always been a feature of these debates.[64]

Nonetheless, the *BoRC* notes that, in the aftermath of the passage of the *HRA*, there was a lull in the discussion of whether it should be seen as 'sufficient legislative underpinning of human rights' or if the UK should take a further step by introducing a UK Bill of Rights.[65] Following his election in 2006, David Cameron advocated replacing the *HRA* with a 'modern British Bill of Rights' that would define 'core British values'.[66] There were also subsequent calls for reform in the forms of 2007 and 2009 government Green Papers for a Bill of Rights that represented a 'fuller articulation of British values'.[67] In May 2010, the new Coalition Government announced as part of its coalition programme that it would establish a commission to investigate the creation of a British Bill of Rights and, as such, the *BoRC* was established in March 2011. Some commentators believe that this was the result of Cameron and other senior Conservatives trying to 'allay anger within the party, and among some voters, directed at decisions made under the Human Rights Act'.[68] Fenwick notes that the Commission's membership reflects an uneasy compromise between the coalition parties in setting it up, as does the fragmented nature of the report itself.[69]

61 A.J.M. Milne, 'Should We Have a Bill of Rights?' (1977) 40 *Modern Law Review* 389

62 J.A.G. Griffith, 'The Political Constitutions' (1979) 42 *Modern Law Review* 1, 16

63 Lord Scarman, *English Law – The New Direction* (Stevens, 1974); Report of the House of Lords European Communities Select Committee (1980–81 H.L. 362); Lester, A., 'Fundamental Rights: The UK Isolated?' (1984) *Public Law* 46; Zander, M., *A Bill of Rights?* (4th edn, Sweet & Maxwell 1997)

64 The Diceyan constitutional viewpoint was previously discussed in Chapter 1

65 *BoRC*, para. 18

66 Ibid, para. 19

67 This process has not been without its complications. See *BoRC*, para. 19: 'The Liberal Democrats reiterated their support for a written constitution which would include a Bill of Rights that continues to incorporate Convention Rights into UK law'. In the 2007 paper, the Labour government proposed a 'British statement of values and a British Bill of Rights and Duties' and, in its subsequent 2009 Green Paper, said that while the *HRA* 'had been an important first step . . . a fuller articulation of values, while still incorporating Convention rights into UK law, would promote a stronger commitment to fundamental freedoms'

68 Helen Fenwick, 'The Report of the Bill of Rights Commission: Disappointing Expectations or Fulfilling Them?' (21 March 2013) *The UK Constitutional Law Association*, available at: https://ukconstitutionallaw.org/2013/03/21/helen-fenwick-the-report-of-the-bill-of-rights-commission-disappointing-conservative-expectations-or-fulfilling-them/ [accessed 24 April 2013] [hereinafter "*Fenwick BoRC*"] 1: The Commission was announced at Prime Minister's Questions as a reaction to criticism of a Supreme Court decision pertaining to the Sex Offender Registry

69 Ibid, 2: the report contains eight separate papers by Commission members or groups of members, dwarfing sections of the report that the majority managed to agree on.

With this in mind, there are aspects of the *BoRC*'s report that are illuminating for this chapter's purposes, particularly those that deal with current societal attitudes towards the *HRA* and *ECHR*. Particularly relevant is the Commission's finding that there was, and is, a lack of public education and 'ownership' of the *HRA*, which is a constant theme that runs through the report. For instance, paragraphs 32–33 note that more could have been done 'before, during or after the Act's enactment to explain its effect to the British public', and paragraph 35 further notes that the current rights framework is 'widely regarded by the public as foreign or European and therefore lacks both popular support and legitimacy'. While the Commission notes that many of its respondents argued that the *HRA* was, and is, 'a carefully drafted piece of legislation which has now been in place for approaching 15 years and which has had the capacity to engage with different legal systems',[70] it nonetheless notes that those who advocate for a UK Bill of Rights claim that such an instrument could better 'reflect the domestic heritage and legal culture of the UK which . . . would help both with public perceptions and feelings of ownership'.[71]

This lack of ownership is in stark contrast to the societal attitudes expressed towards the *Charter* in Canada, and political actors in the UK may recognize these attitudes when they act and speak in the public and political domain. Recent statements by politicians have led some commentators to argue that they do, and that they may even be propagating anti-*HRA* and *ECHR* views, along with the mainstream media.[72] While these attacks on the *HRA* are nothing new, 'the idea – part of the media campaign against the *HRA* – that human rights concerns stand in the way of Britain's ability to combat terrorism, has found a particular focus in relation to Abu Qatada'.[73] David Cameron, referencing the UK's past difficulties in deporting Qatada, told the Council of Europe in January 2012 that it was 'not surprising that some people start asking questions about whether the current arrangements are really sensible'.[74] After subsequent failed attempts to deport him, Qatada had become the subject of numerous media reports and speeches by politicians.[75] The past failures to deport Qatada, and the handling of the situation

70 Ibid, para. 68

71 Ibid, para. 36

72 See Justice Secretary Chris Grayling's comments to the *Sunday Telegraph*: 'I cannot conceive of a situation where we could put forward a serious reform without scrapping Labour's Human Rights Act and starting again. We cannot go on with a situation where people who are a threat to our national security, or who come to Britain and commit serious crimes, are able to cite their human rights when they are clearly wholly unconcerned for the human rights of others. We need a dramatically curtailed role for the European Court of Human Rights in the UK': Peter Hennessy, 'Tory Attack Dog Chris Grayling Comes Off the Leash' (6 April 2013) *Telegraph*

73 *Fenwick BoRC*, 5. The Qatada legal saga has been extensively detailed in Chapter 5 of this book

74 David Cameron, Council of Europe Speech, 25 January 2012

75 On 9 March 2013, Theresa May told the Conservative Victory 2015 Conference: 'When Strasbourg constantly moves the goalposts and prevents the deportation of dangerous men

by involved politicians, had further fuelled the media's interest in the case. News reports described Cameron as 'boiling over the Abu Qatada case' and alluded to 'having all options, including leaving altogether' on the table with regard to *ECHR* withdrawal.[76] The media attention surrounding Qatada and such comments by politicians have only further fuelled anti-*HRA* sentiment, leading the *BoRC* to worry out loud whether a new UK Bill of Rights might be similarly attacked as a rebadged *HRA*.[77] This anti-*HRA* and *ECHR* sentiment, which stands in stark contrast to the patriotic attachment to the *Charter* in Canada, illustrates the role media can play in shaping societal attitudes, and lends weight to Lazarus's claim that 'the histories and traditions of the countries being analysed have produced different conceptions about the right and the role of fundamental rights'.[78]

Analyses here suggest that there is a difference in societal attitudes towards human rights in the two jurisdictions, particularly with regard to the treatment of the *HRA* by the UK public and politicians when contrasted with the Canadian attitudes towards the *Charter*. The analyses in this chapter support Fenwick et al.'s contention that the *Charter* has enjoyed a 'patriotic attachment' among the public and politicians in Canada, who view it as a home-grown, specifically Canadian achievement.[79] While the importance of individual liberty in common law has always had a place in the UK, the *HRA* (and the *ECHR* that it gives effect to) has not been able to capture this same attachment, as it is too often attacked by the media and politicians as 'foreign' or externally imposed. As such, it becomes difficult to answer the second part of the research question, which asks if it can be argued that a positive human rights culture exists in the UK. Analysis of the decisions in *Al Rawi*, *Binyam Mohamed* and *Qatada* (and decisions on detention without trial and control orders analysed in Chapter 3) illustrated that the UK judiciary is committed to protecting the open justice principle and the right to a fair trial even in the face of immense political and public pressure. That said, if the establishment of a human rights culture demands an interaction of systems and institutions to achieve and maintain the equilibrium between interests and values

like Abu Qatada, we have to ask ourselves, to what end are we signatories to the Convention?' Moreover, Dominic Raab has been quoted as saying that 'This case shows we urgently need to overhaul the law on deportation, scrap the Human Rights Act and start standing up for British democracy rather than kowtowing to the European Court in Strasbourg': Nicholas Watt and Alan Travis, 'UK May Withdraw from European Rights Convention over Abu Qatada' (24 April 2013) *Guardian*

76 Alan Travis, 'Abu Qatada will not be Deported for Many Months, Admits Theresa May' (24 April 2013) *Guardian*

77 *BoRC*, para. 80: 'The majority of members find it hard to persuade themselves that public perceptions are likely to change in any substantial way as a result, particularly given the highly polemical way in which these issues tend to be presented by both some commentators and some sections of the media'

78 *Lazarus*, 16

79 Helen Fenwick, Gavin Phillipson and Roger Masterman, 'The Human Rights Act in Contemporary Context' in Fenwick, H., Phillipson, G. and Masterman, R. (eds), *Judicial Reasoning under the UK Human Rights Act* (Cambridge University Press, 2007) 2

on which human respect for human rights depends, as Feldman suggests,[80] then the current UK political climate (the societal attitudes towards human rights held by politicians, the media and general public noted above) makes it difficult to argue that such a culture is truly present in the UK.

The UK courts, like the Canadian courts, have not refrained from declaring counter-terrorism legislation to be incompatible with human rights in recent years.[81] Nonetheless, the analysis above suggests that the political costs associated with implementing or defending counter-terrorism policies potentially offensive to human rights may not be as high in the UK as they are in Canada, where a political culture of legal compliance backstopped by a patriotic attachment to the *Charter* exists, and where the ability and willingness of courts to strike down counter-terrorism legislation inconsistent with human rights is present. A recent example of this is the policy process behind the *JSA* and the *CTSA*. The existence of a strong rights culture may have made the political costs associated with passing the *JSA* without many of the human rights safeguards suggested by the Joint Select Committee on Human Rights (JCHR) (discussed extensively in Chapter 4) too high. The result is a final version of the Bill that does not take into account many of the amendments suggested by the House of Lords. Similarly, the passage of the *CTSA* through a semi-fast track procedure with limited parliamentary consideration of its human rights implications also raises the question of whether a strong rights culture exists. That said, there are once again complex political climate factors at play here with regard to both pieces of legislation. The political costs associated with fast-tracking the *CTSA* might not have been as high as they might have been as a result of the terrorist attacks that had occurred at the Paris offices of *Charlie Hebdo*. Moreover, the passage of the *JSA* was intricately linked to the decisions in *Al Rawi* and *Binyam Mohamed* and, more broadly, concerns about maintaining the UK's intelligence sharing relationships with the US and the disclosure of security sensitive information in UK or US courts.[82] Focus now turns to analysis of the impact of the UK's geopolitical position and relationships on counter-terrorism and national security policy, including analysis of the relationships it shares with the US.

6.4 The United Kingdom's 'special relationship' with the United States

The UK's relationship with the US is the last element of its political culture to be analysed in this section. The nature of this relationship has been significantly

80 *Feldman, Impact of Human Rights*

81 As was noted in both Chapters 3 and 5

82 Roach has argued that the Justice and Security Act represents a 'vigorous response' by the UK Government to the 'Binyam Mohamed case and threats by American officials to share less intelligence with them'. See *Roach, Substitute Justice*, 63. Both *Binyam Mohammed* and *Al Rawi* are further discussed below

affected in recent years by the *Al Rawi* and *Binyam Mohamed* cases[83] which, according to Roach, serve as 'a reminder that non-American courts and legislatures cannot ignore the impact of American laws and processes with respect to their attempts to obtain substitute justice. American practices of secrecy and extra-legalism cast a large shadow over the world'.[84] The UK/US relationship is a political climate factor that had a significant impact on the UK Government's development, and passage, of the *JSA*. As was noted extensively in Chapter 5, the need to protect and maintain the intelligence sharing relationships between the two countries featured prominently in the UK Government's claims for non-disclosure of security sensitive information in both *Al Rawi* and *Binyam Mohamed*. As Roach notes, American extra-legalism casts a large shadow over the world, but the special nature of the UK/US relationship was so significant that the UK Government decided to settle lawsuits in order to avoid further disclosure, and went so far as to implement new, unprecedented and controversial legislation in order to allow the use of secret evidence in civil litigation (likely to assuage concerns that activities of American officials and security officials may again one day be released in UK courts).[85]

Much has been written about how the *Binyam Mohamed* and *Al Rawi* legal affairs and the subsequent passage of the *JSA* have revealed the close relationship between the US and the UK, particularly in the realms of intelligence information sharing and cooperation. Otty has argued that the cases have exposed how after the 9/11 attacks cooperating with the US became an absolute priority that trumped all over factors, including a bypassing or watering down of ordinary rules pertaining to intelligence cooperation.[86] Murray notes that the *Binyam Mohamed* and *Al Rawi* cases

> have sparked concern among partner agencies, particularly in the USA. As a result, the UK Government has often settled with the claimants rather than fight litigation, ostensibly to protect information received in confidence from partner intelligence services from disclosure in the course of civil proceedings.[87]

Murray further argues in relation to the *JSA* that 'It is questionable whether this legislation is not more concerned with preventing any repetition of the acute embarrassment caused to the UK's Security and Secret Intelligence Services as a

83 For complete analysis of the decisions in *Al-Rawi* and *Binyam Mohammed*, see Chapter 5

84 *Roach, Substitute Justice*, 63

85 Ibid, 61–2

86 Tim Otty, 'The Slow Creep of Complacency and the Soul of Justice' (2012) *European Human Rights Law Review* 267, 274

87 C.R.G. Murray, 'Out of the Shadows: The Courts and the United Kingdom's Malfunctioning International Counter-Terrorism Partnerships' (2013) 18 *Journal of Conflict and Security Law* 193, 195

result of the revelations resultant from these cases'.[88] That the UK was willing to enact such a piece of legislation speaks volumes about the impact of its special relationship with the US.

In response to the question about the impact of the US on UK counter-terrorism measures, the *Binyam Mohamed* and *Al-Rawi* legal affairs and the process behind the development and passage of the *JSA* by the UK Government all speak to the unique nature of the UK/US relationship and the impact that the US has had on UK counter-terrorism and national security policy. Analysis here suggests the reach of American influence on UK counter-terrorism policy-making, albeit with regard to one specific piece of legislation. Nonetheless, the passage of the Justice and Security Act could have serious implications for the rights of those who seek disclosure of security sensitive information to aid in their civil litigation, and perhaps even wider reputational damage for the UK, a country that carries a significant amount of soft power globally as a defender of open justice, the rule of law and human rights. The fact that the UK Government was willing both to face the political costs of this legislation and to pass the *CTSA* with limited political scrutiny and the analyses above that suggest a significantly different set of societal attitudes towards human rights in the UK make it very difficult to argue that a human rights culture exists in the UK, irrespective of some admirable activism on the part of the UK judiciary.

6.5 Conclusion

The first objective of this chapter was to answer the question: Is there a difference in societal attitudes towards human rights in the two jurisdictions and, together with the analysis of legal culture in Chapter 5, can it be argued that a human rights culture exists in the two jurisdictions? As was noted at the outset, respect for human rights and the rule of law in a society, or lack thereof, is not only made evident by judicial decisions, such as those analysed in Chapters 3 and 5, but can also be seen in the decisions and statements made by politicians, the public, the media and interested civil society groups. As such, analysing the decisions and statements these actors have made provided a basis for examining whether, and to what extent, a rights culture has developed in the two countries. While Canadian courts have not refrained from striking or reading down provisions of counter-terrorism legislation, analysis of the case law in the wider national security realm has shown judicial reasoning concerning their role in protecting the *Charter* and their relationship with Parliament and the executive to be more deferential. That said, this chapter has suggested that there are a number of reasons why Canadian political actors must consider the political costs of the counter-terrorism legislation they implement and support, because of the existence of a patriotic attachment to the *Charter* and the ability and willingness of Canadian courts to invalidate

88 Ibid

counter-terrorism legislation inconsistent with human rights. However, analysis of the Bill S-7 and Bill C-51 policy process has shown how political climate factors, such as recent successful or foiled terrorist attacks, can lower the political and legal consequences associated with implementing and defending counter-terrorism legislation that may give rise to human rights concerns. When this occurs, substantive debate about the impact of the provisions on the human rights of citizens is often replaced by rhetoric and political platitudes. When counter-terrorism policy is debated and passed in this manner, there is often a lack of meaningful debate on possible amendments to the policy that seek to address human rights concerns and, when this occurs, it is difficult to argue that a human rights culture exists in a jurisdiction. As such, despite strong patriotic attachment and societal support of the *Charter* in Canada, it is suggested here that the existence of a human rights culture throughout all of Canada's legal and political institutions is arguable at best.

Based on the analysis in this chapter, and that undertaken in Chapter 5, it appears difficult to argue that a human rights culture currently exists in the UK. Granted, Chapter 5 found that the decisions in *Al-Rawi, Binyam Mohamed* and *Qatada* show that the UK judiciary is committed to protecting human rights even in the face of immense political and public pressure. That said, if the establishment of a human rights culture demands interaction between institutions to achieve and maintain the equilibrium between interests and values on which human respect for human rights depends, then the current UK political climate (the societal attitudes towards the *HRA* held by politicians, the media and general public noted above) makes it difficult to argue that such a culture is truly present in the UK. This is indeed the key difference in societal attitudes towards human rights in the two jurisdictions. Whereas it has been argued that the Canadian *Charter* came about as a nation-building exercise and has garnered a sense of patriotic attachment, the *HRA* suffers from a lack of public feelings of ownership and there is considerable public hostility to the Strasbourg Court. Furthermore, political actors in the UK may even be contributing to the lack of ownership and negative attitudes towards the *HRA* and *ECHR*. Recent statements by politicians and the mainstream media have done this particularly in relation to Abu Qatada. The past failed attempts to deport Qatada, as well as the numerous associated statements by politicians with regard to withdrawal from the *ECHR*, have only fuelled anti-*HRA* sentiment. While it might be fair to argue that the judicial decisions in the cases canvassed in Chapters 3 and 5 suggest that there is strong support amongst the UK judiciary for individual liberty at common law, societal attitudes towards the *HRA* voiced by politicians, the public and the media make it difficult to argue that a human rights culture exists through the jurisdiction in both legal and political spheres. This finding is further reinforced by analyses of the passage of the *CTSA* (with very limited political scrutiny) and the *JSA*, the latter of which is also crucially important to answering the second question of this chapter.

The second objective of this chapter was to answer the question: What impact has the relationship with the US had on the evolution of counter-terrorism measures in the two jurisdictions? Analyses in this chapter suggest that the UK's special and complex relationship with the US might have such an impact that the *JSA* was passed despite serious concerns raised by the JCHR, legal professionals and academic commentators that it would cause reputational damage to the UK and have deleterious effects on the right of the individual to open justice. The process behind its development and passage by the UK Government all speak to the unique nature of the UK/US relationship and the impact that the US can have on UK counter-terrorism and national security policy. Analysis in the Canadian section illuminated the impact of the US on Canadian counter-terrorism policy, particularly with regard to the legal cases of Omar Khadr and Maher Arar. These experiences illustrate the Canadian Government will go to great lengths to ensure that its relationship with the US, particularly its intelligence sharing arrangements, are not strained. Moreover, instruments such as the Canada-US Smart Border Declaration, the more recent 2011 Safe Third Country Agreement and a number of other border or transportation related agreements that are designed to strengthen the border's resilience to terrorism whilst minimally affecting commerce between the countries speak to the extremely close economic, geographic and symbolic relationship shared between the two nations.

Bibliography

Al Rawi and Others v. The Security Service and Others [2011] UKSC

Cameron, D., Council of Europe Speech, 25 January 2012

Canadian House of Commons, *Hansard Debates*, 1 March 2012

Canadian House of Commons, *Hansard Debates*, 22 April 2013

Canadian House of Commons, *Hansard Debates*, 23 April 2013

Canadian Human Rights Commission. *The Evolution of Human Rights in Canada* (Cat. No. HR4-19, Minister of Public Works and Government Services, 2012)

Citizenship and Immigration Canada. *U.S–Canada Safe Third Country Agreement* (2002)

Council of Europe, *European Convention for the Protection of Human Rights and Fundamental Freedoms, as amended by Protocols Nos. 11 and 14*, 4 November 1950, ETS 5

Counter-Terrorism and Security Act 2015 c. 217

Epp, C. 'Do Bills of Rights Matter? The Canadian Charter of Rights and Freedoms' (1996) *American Political Science Review* 765

Feldman, D. 'The Impact of Human Rights on the UK Legislative Process' (2004) 25 *Stat LR* 9

Feldman, E. 'Patients' Rights, Citizens' Movements and Japanese Legal Culture' in Nelken, D. (ed), *Comparing Legal Cultures* (Aldershot, 1997)

Fenwick, H. 'The Report of the Bill of Rights Commission: Disappointing Expectations or Fulfilling Them?' (21 March 2013) *The UK Constitutional Law Association*, available at: https://ukconstitutionallaw.org/2013/03/21/helen-fenwick-the-report-of-the-bill-of-rights-commission-disappointing-conservative-expectations-or-fulfilling-them/ [accessed 24 April 2013]

Fenwick, H., Phillipson, G. and Masterman, R. 'The Human Rights Act in Contemporary Context' in Fenwick, H., Phillipson, G. and Masterman, R. (eds), *Judicial Reasoning Under the UK Human Rights Act* (Cambridge University Press, 2007)

Foreign Affairs and International Trade Canada. *Canada–US Smart Border Declaration: Building a Smart Border for the 21st Century on the Foundation of a North American Zone of Confidence* (2001)

Griffith, J.A.G. 'The Political Constitutions' (1979) 42 *Modern Law Review* 1

Hennessy, P. 'Tory Attack Dog Chris Grayling Comes Off the Leash' (6 April 2013) *Telegraph*, available at: http://www.telegraph.co.uk/news/politics/conservative/9976549/Tory-attack-dog-Chris-Grayling-comes-off-the-leash.html [accessed 10 April 2013]

Hiebert, J.L. 'Constitutional Experimentation: Rethinking How a Bill of Rights Functions' in Ginsburg, T. and Dixon, R. (eds), *Comparative Constitutional Law* (Edward Elgar Publishing, 2011)

Human Rights Act 1998 c. 42

Justice and Security Act 2013 c. 18

Lazarus, L. *Contrasting Prisoner's Rights: A Comparative Examination of Germany and England* (Oxford University Press, 2004)

Lester, A. 'Fundamental Rights: The UK Isolated?' [1984] *Public Law* 46

Lord Lloyd, 'Do We Need a Bill of Rights?' (1976) 39 *Modern Law Review* 121

Lord Scarman. *English Law – The New Direction* (Stevens, 1974)

McLeod, I. 'Liberals Planning Swift Overhaul of Controversial Anti-terrorism Act, or Bill C-51' (22 October 2015) *National Post*, available at: http://news.nationalpost.com/news/canada/canadian-politics/liberals-planning-swift-overhaul-of-controversial-anti-terrorism-act-or-bill-c-51 [accessed 24 October 2015]

Milne, A.J.M. 'Should We Have a Bill of Rights?' (1977) 40 *Modern Law Review* 389

Mohamed, R (on the application of) v. Secretary of State for Foreign & Commonwealth Affairs [2010] EWCA Civ 65

Murray, C.R.G. 'Out of the Shadows: The Courts and the United Kingdom's Malfunctioning International Counter-Terrorism Partnerships' (2013) 18 *Journal of Conflict and Security Law* 193

Otty, T. 'The Slow Creep of Complacency and the Soul of Justice' (2012) *European Human Rights Law Review* 267

Ramraj, V. 'Terrorism, Risk Perception and Judicial Review' in Ramraj, V., Roach, K. and Hor, M. (eds), *Global Anti-Terrorism Law and Policy* (Cambridge University Press, 2005)

Report of the House of Lords European Communities Select Committee (1980–1 H.L. 362)

Roach, K. 'Secret Evidence and Its Alternatives' in Masferrer, A. (ed), *Post-9/11 and the State of Permanent Legal Emergency: Security and Human Rights in Countering Terrorism* (Springer, 2011) 179

___. 'Counter-Terrorism in and outside Canada and in and outside the Anti-Terrorism Act' (2012) 6 *Review of Constitutional Studies* 243

___. 'Uneasy Neighbours: Comparative American and Canadian Counter-Terrorism' (2012) 38 *William Mitchell Law Review* 1701

___. 'Substitute Justice? Challenges to American Counter-Terrorism Activities in Non-American Courts' (2013) 82 *Mississippi Law Journal* 907

Rosenberg, M. 'Twenty-five Years Later: The Impact of the Canadian Charter of Rights and Freedoms on the Criminal Law' (2009) *Supreme Court Law Review* 1

The Constitution Act, 1982, Schedule B to the Canada Act 1982 (UK), 1982, c. 11, Part I

The Honourable Frank Iacobucci QC LLD. *Internal Inquiry into the Actions of Canadian Officials in Relation to Abdullah Almalki, Ahmad Abou-Elmaati and Muayyed Nureddin* (Ottawa: 2008)

Travis, A. 'Abu Qatada will not be Deported for Many Months, Admits Theresa May' (24 April 2013) *Guardian*

UK Bill of Rights Commission, *A UK Bill of Rights? The Choice before Us* (December 2012, Vol 1)

United States Government. *United States-Canada Beyond the Border: A Shared Vision for Perimeter Security and Economic Competitiveness* (2011)

Watt, N. and Travis, A. 'UK May Withdraw from European Rights Convention over Abu Qatada' (24 April 2013) *Guardian*

Worheling, J. 'The Canadian Charter of Rights and Freedoms and Its Consequences for Political and Democratic Life and the Democratic System' in Gagnon, A.-G. (ed), *Contemporary Canadian Federalism: Foundations, Traditions, Institutions* (University of Toronto Press, 2009)

Zander, M. *A Bill of Rights?* (4th edn, Sweet & Maxwell, 1997)

Zedner, L. 'Securing Liberty in the Face of Terror: Reflections from Criminal Justice' (2005) 32 *Journal of Law and Society* 519

7 Conclusions

This book has acknowledged the force of international legal instruments, specifically UN Security Council Resolution 1373,[1] but has nonetheless argued that the evolution of counter-terrorism polices in different jurisdictions is best analysed and understood as a product of the institutional structures and cultures present in those jurisdictions. Put simply, it has forwarded the argument that while Resolution 1373 undoubtedly had an impact on how and when the Anti-Terrorism Act (*ATA*)[2] and Anti-Terrorism, Crime and Security Act (*ATCSA*)[3] were implemented, it is the domestic structures and cultures[4] in the two jurisdictions that have had the greatest impact on how counter-terrorism measures have since evolved. This has been accomplished by answering several analytical questions in each chapter designed to assess the impact of domestic structures and cultures on the evolution of counter-terrorism measures. Holistic answers to these questions, based on the analyses undertaken in Chapters 3–6, are discussed below. The subsequent section seeks to situate the most recent counter-terrorism legislation in both jurisdictions in light of these analyses, arguing that lessons that should and could have been learned from almost 15 years of post-9/11 experience have been largely ignored, particularly with regard to the continued enactment of rushed legislation in the aftermath of significant terrorist events, the continued use of secret evidence and measures outside of the ordinary criminal law and the continued ignorance of the need for in-depth parliamentary scrutiny of counter-terrorism legislation.

1 Discussed at length at Chapter 1.1.3 and 2.1: UN Security Council, *Security Council resolution 1373 (2001) [on threats to international peace and security caused by terrorist acts]*, 28 September 2001, S/RES/1373 (2001) [hereinafter "*Resolution 1373*"]

2 Anti-Terrorism Act, S.C. 2001, c. 41 [hereinafter "*ATA*"]

3 Anti-Terrorism, Crime and Security Act 2001 c. 24 [hereinafter "*ATCSA*"]

4 Conceptualized in Chapter 1.3 and discussed throughout this book

7.1 The impact of domestic legal and political structures and cultures on the evolution of counter-terrorism measures

Evidence for the argument that the evolution of counter-terrorism policies in different jurisdictions is best analysed and understood as a product of the institutional structures and cultures present in those jurisdictions was evident throughout this book, as legal and political structures were shown to impact counter-terrorism measures in analyses throughout Chapters 3–6. That said, the evident willingness of courts in both jurisdictions to look to other jurisdictions for guidance in their decision-making, and evidence as to the impact of the US on decision-making in both jurisdictions did suggest some limitations of this argument. Nonetheless, based on the holistic answers to questions asked throughout this book and discussed further below, it is fair to argue that while Resolution 1373 undoubtedly had an impact on how and when the *ATA* and *ATCSA* were implemented, it was the domestic structures and cultures in the two jurisdictions that have had the greatest impact on how counter-terrorism measures have since evolved.

Chapter 3 was principally concerned with the differences in the legal structure of the two jurisdictions. To explore the impact of these differences on the evolution of counter-terrorism measures two questions were investigated: 1) How, and to what extent, are domestic legal decisions on counter-terrorism influenced by the structure of the rights adjudication systems in each jurisdiction?; and 2) How, and to what extent, do domestic legal structures allow for international legal instruments to impact domestic legal decisions on counter-terrorism? Case law pertaining to security certificates in Canada and detention without trial and control order provisions in the UK was analysed. This analysis focused on how national courts operate within their respective legal structures and how, and to what extent, these structures influence how judges reason and reach their decisions. It was noted that several authors agree that the terrain of international law has shifted and greater attention must be paid to the operation of domestic institutions, but that they all have different conceptions of how national courts are interacting with one another, and with the international legal order. The extent to which each of these conceptions applied in the case law analyses was used to help answer the second research question.

In the *Suresh*[5] analysis, the Supreme Court of Canada argued that it was an element of its own legal structure, namely, the fundamental justice balance under section 7 of the *Charter*[6] that precluded deportation to torture, rather than relevant international instruments. Conversely, the Court used an international instrument to fill a void in Canada's legal structure by adopting the definition

5 *Suresh v. Canada (Minister of Citizenship and Immigration)* [2002] 1 S.C.R. 3 [hereinafter "*Suresh*"]

6 *The Canadian Charter of Rights and Freedoms*, Part I of the Constitution Act 1982, Being Schedule B to the Canada Act 1982 (UK), 1982, c. 11 [hereinafter "*Charter*"]

of terrorism found within the International Convention for the Suppression of Financing of Terrorism.[7] The same void was not present in *Belmarsh*[8] and, as such, the UK House of Lords proceeded in its analysis on the basis of its own domestic definition of terrorism. Conversely, the discrimination argument that had been successfully raised against differential treatment of non-citizens in *Belmarsh* did not succeed in *Charkaoui*[9] because the structure of the Canadian legal system, namely section 6 of the *Charter*, legally provides for this differential treatment. The Special Immigration Appeals Commission (SIAC) was created as a result of a gap in the UK's legal structure that was recognized by *Chahal*,[10] a case that turned on the existence of a similar system in Canada. Furthermore, while some of the judges noted a preference towards issuing a declaration of incompatibility, the majority in *MB*[11] decided that they were essentially mandated by an element of their legal structure, section 3(1) of the Human Rights Act[12] (*HRA*), to read down the legislation. Similarly, the majority in *SSHD v. AF (No 3)*[13] spoke clearly about how they were essentially bound to take into account *A v. UK*[14] by their legal constraints under the *ECHR*[15] and the *HRA*. Finally, the *Harkat*[16] case evidenced a willingness on the part of the Supreme Court of Canada to uphold the constitutionality of the security certificate scheme, largely on the basis of the role that Federal Court judges play within that scheme. Two elements of the existing legal structure – the ability of Federal Court judges to authorize special advocate communication under section 85.4(2) and the ability to issue a stay of proceedings under section 24(1) based on an assessment of the overall fairness of the proceedings – had a large impact on the Supreme Court's reasoning. These analyses illustrate how, and to what extent, domestic legal decisions on counter-terrorism are influenced by the structure of domestic rights adjudication systems.

Moreover, the question of how, and to what extent, domestic legal structures allow international legal instruments to impact on domestic legal decisions on counter-terrorism was answered in several different ways by the analyses in Chapter 3. The argument that international legal instruments are often invoked

7 UN General Assembly, *International Convention for the Suppression of the Financing of Terrorism*, 9 December 1999, No. 38349 [hereinafter "*1999 Convention*"]
8 *A v. Secretary of State for the Home Department* [2004] UKHL 56 [hereinafter "*Belmarsh*"]
9 *Charkaoui v. Canada (Citizenship and Immigration)* [2007] 1 S.C.R. 350 [hereinafter "*Charkaoui*"]
10 *Chahal v. UK*, App No 22414/93 [1996] ECHR 54 [hereinafter "*Chahal*"]
11 *Secretary of State for the Home Department v. MB* [2007] UKHL 46 [hereinafter "*MB*"]
12 C. 42 [hereinafter "*HRA*"]
13 *Secretary of the State for the Home Department v. AF (No 3)* [2009] UKHL 28 [hereinafter "*SSHD v AF (No 3)*"]
14 *A v. United Kingdom*, App No 3455/05 [2009] ECHR 301 [hereinafter "*A v. UK*"]
15 Convention for the Protection of Human Rights and Fundamental Freedoms (European Convention on Human Rights, as Amended) [hereinafter "*ECHR*"]
16 *Canada (Citizenship and Immigration) v. Harkat* [2014] 2 S.C.R. 33 [hereinafter "*Harkat*"]

to add rhetorical force to a decision was most forceful in the *Suresh* analysis, when the Supreme Court used both the Canadian and the international experience to engage in its section 7 analysis but made it clear that it was the fundamental justice balance under the *Charter* that precludes deportation to torture, and not the constraining force of the Convention Against Torture. This argument was also useful in the *Belmarsh* analysis, where it seems reasonable to argue that the Court's consideration of international sources provided largely rhetorical backing for a decision that was already strongly based on the domestic definition of terrorism and a long-standing English common law tradition. The argument that courts are open to looking to solutions in other jurisdictions to fill in gaps in their own legal structure was also very relevant, most especially in the *Charkaoui* analysis, where the Supreme Court of Canada placed strong emphasis on the case law pertaining to control orders and system of special advocates present in the UK.

Chapter 4 analysed the differences between the political structures present in the two jurisdictions. It noted that Canada and the UK have both had experience of minority (or coalition) governments since 9/11, albeit at different times. As such, the following research question was posed: Has the existence of minority (or coalition) governments had an impact on domestic counter-terrorism legislation? In response to this question, it was argued that the instability of Canada's minority government resulted in the stalling of anti-terrorism reviews, the lack of a much needed domestic national security scrutiny mechanism and, at least partially, the rushed consideration of amendments to the security certificate regime. It was argued that the current security certificate regime may have looked very different if none of these things had taken place. This was contrasted with the rushed and ill-considered passage of significant pieces of legislation under majority governments in the form of the *ATA* and the legislation passed in the aftermath of the October 2014 terrorist attacks (i.e. the *ATA 2015*[17] and the *PCTA*[18]). Similarly, it was argued that the process behind the drafting, tabling and passing of the *TPIMs Act*[19] could have been different in a majority government that did not require the kind of compromise insisted upon by the Liberal Democrat minority coalition partners. The passage of the *ATCSA* and the *CTSA*[20] were noted to serve as examples of pieces of significant legislation that were subject to limited parliamentary scrutiny before their passage.

After noting that the jurisdictions differed significantly in the levels of parliamentary oversight and review that existed within their political structure, the following question became necessary: How, and to what extent, have systems for parliamentary review and oversight of counter-terrorism measures had an impact on domestic counter-terrorism legislation? It was subsequently argued that systems for parliamentary review and oversight of counter-terrorism measures

17 Anti-Terrorism Act, S.C. 2015, c. 20 [hereinafter "*ATA 2015*"]

18 Protection of Canada from Terrorists Act, S.C. 2015, c. 9 [hereinafter "*PCTA*"]

19 Terrorism Prevention and Investigation Measures Act 2011 c. 23 [hereinafter "*TPIMs Act*"]

20 Counter-Terrorism and Security Act 2015 c. 6 [hereinafter "*CTSA*"]

often reinforced the recommendations of other domestic committees or inquiries, made the case for additional domestic scrutiny mechanisms and make targeted recommendations for amendments that were taken up in public Bill committee debates. Nonetheless, analysis of domestic scrutiny mechanisms in Canada revealed that these mechanisms had very little influence on the evolution of security certificates, likely because the few mechanisms that exist have no regular mandate, and because the previous government type precluded their proper consideration of amendments to security certificates. By way of contrast, although the UK has a wealth of parliamentary scrutiny mechanisms, the views of the Independent Reviewer of Terrorism Legislation seemed to carry more weight than those of the Joint Committee on Human Rights. As a result, it was argued that the debates surrounding annual renewal of sunset clauses, and the subsequent vote which was extremely close, might have been different had the Independent Reviewer not been a part of the country's domestic political structure. Similarly, it was argued that several other debates on amendments recommended to the *TPIMs Act* by the Joint Select Committee on Human Rights (JCHR) were swayed by the views of the Independent Reviewer. As such, analysing the oversight mechanisms of both countries usefully demonstrated that the presence of these mechanisms within a country's domestic political structure (namely, the presence of an Independent Reviewer whose views are influential in debates on the substance of bills) could in theory play an important role in the evolution of counter-terrorism legislation. Nevertheless, it was difficult to assign a tangible impact between review and oversight mechanisms and legislative outcomes, particularly in Canada. due to the significant absence of any meaningful operation of such mechanisms. It is thus recommended as a matter of urgency that Canada work towards bolstering its system of parliamentary and independent review and oversight of counter-terrorism activities.

Chapter 5 analysed key decisions pertaining to the wider use of secret evidence in civil litigation, criminal prosecutions and terrorist listing in order to make observations about the differences in the legal culture in Canada and the UK in the wider national security realm. In doing so, it provided a useful basis of comparison for Chapter 6's analysis of political culture. The chapter noted at its outset that opinions vary widely about the role of the courts and the proper exercise of deference to the executive and, as such, sought to discern if, and to what extent, these concepts are evident in judicial decision-making with a view to answering the following research question: How, and to what extent, do the judiciaries of Canada and the UK express deference to the executive in national security cases? Moreover, through its analyses of judicial decisions in the wider national security realm, in combination with judicial decisions analysed in the previous chapters, the chapter sought to identify whether a 'rights culture' is part of the legal culture in the two countries. As such, the following question was asked: To what extent can judicial decisions in national security cases be argued to be indicative of a human rights culture in the two jurisdictions?

Chapter 5's analyses of both the UK and Canadian case law in the wider national security realm, in combination with the analyses of the case law in Chapter 3, suggested that the courts in both countries are committed to protecting fundamental principles of open justice, albeit to varying degrees under different circumstances. As such, the answer to the first research question of how, and to what extent, the judiciaries of Canada and the UK express deference to the executive in national security cases is mixed. In *Ahmad*,[21] the Supreme Court engaged in a lengthy historical analysis to uphold the jurisdiction of the Federal Court in assessing disclosure claims, and also upheld the bifurcated system under section 38 of the Canada Evidence Act[22] (*CEA*), whilst suggesting that Parliament should consider the wisdom of this scheme. Like the UK Supreme Court in *Al-Rawi*,[23] the Supreme Court in *Ahmad* recognized that it is limited to ruling on the overall fairness of the proceedings, but has also not refrained from suggesting proper consideration in Parliament about the wisdom of the *CEA* scheme. The difference in levels of deference between the Federal Court and the Federal Court of Appeal in *Almalki FCA* [24] was also quite significant, with the latter more willing to defer than was Mosley J in the former. By contrast, the Federal Court of Appeal and the Supreme Court were less willing to defer to the government's non-disclosure claims in relation to Mr Khadr, perhaps because of the severe rights infringements that he had endured and the liberty interests that were at stake, similar to those present in *Binyam Mohamed*.[25] As such, it seems the *Khadr FCA*[26] and *Binyam Mohamed* cases can be distinguished from the *Almalki FCA* case and even the *Tariq* case[27] in the sense that less deference was shown to the government's claims in respect of the former men because of the rights infringements they had and could continue to endure. That said, the Supreme Court in *Khadr SC*[28] still deferred substantially to the government on the question of the appropriate remedy for the *Charter* abuses Khadr sustained, arguing that they could not require the Canadian Government to repatriate him as a result of limitations in their institutional competence, and their need to respect the prerogative powers of the executive in areas of foreign relations. Despite these mixed results, *Ahmed*[29] and *Abdelrazik*[30] both provide excellent examples of both Canadian and UK courts holding the executive accountable for its decisions pertaining to the implementation of international

21 *R v. Ahmad* [2011] 1 S.C.R. 110 [hereinafter "*Ahmad*"]
22 R.S.C., 1985, C-5 [hereinafter "*CEA*"]
23 *Al Rawi and Others v. the Security Service and Others* [2011] UKSC 34 [hereinafter "*Al-Rawi*"]
24 *Canada v. Almalki* [2011] FCA 199 [hereinafter "*Almalki FCA*"]
25 *Mohamed, R (on the Application of) v. Secretary of State for Foreign & Commonwealth Affairs* [2010] EWCA Civ 65 [hereinafter "*Binyam Mohamed*"]
26 *Khadr v. Canada (Minister of Justice)* [2007] FCA 182 [hereinafter "*Khadr FCA*"]
27 *Home Office v. Tariq* [2011] UKSC 35 [hereinafter "*Tariq*"]
28 *Canada (Prime Minister) v. Khadr* [2010] 1 S.C.R. 44 [hereinafter "*Khadr SC*"]
29 *HM Treasury v. Ahmed* [2010] UKSC 2 [hereinafter "*Ahmed*"]
30 *Abdelrazik v. Canada (Minister of Foreign Affairs)* [2010] 1 F.C.R. 267 [hereinafter "*Abdelrazik*"]

instruments allowing terrorist listing, a welcome development given the severity of the liberty and due process infringements raised by terrorist listing.

Moreover, with regard to the second question, the case law reviewed in Chapter 5 illustrated that in recent years the UK judiciary has been less willing to engage in what Kavanagh calls substantial deference to Parliament and the executive. Though caution should again be expressed in relation to the *Binyam Mohamed* judgment, which may have been significantly different had the US District Court not released some of the information pertinent to the redacted paragraphs at issue, it is still fair to argue that the judgment is indicative of Dyzenhaus's culture of justification, whereby Parliament and the executive are expected to earn deference from the courts by ensuring that legislation is human rights compatible. The Court in *Al-Rawi* showed extreme caution in extending the power of a Closed Material Proceeding (CMP), noting that this would require the express will of Parliament. This turns the traditional institutional legitimacy claim on its head because the Court is not, as Lord Hope put it, simply surrendering to Parliament something which lies within the area of the Court's responsibility. Rather, it is recognizing that the decision on the appropriate balance between open justice and the demands of national security in this case is best left for determination through the democratic process conducted by Parliament, following a process of consultation. This viewpoint lends support to Hunt's concept of due deference, as the Court in *Al-Rawi* operated under the assumption that power in the Constitution is shared among the various actors within it, rather than parcelled out according to some inflexible notion of the separation of powers. Furthermore, analysis of the *Abu Qatada*[31] cases illustrated that the UK judiciary was willing to protect fundamental rights in the face of immense political pressure. This leads to a final conclusion that the cases surveyed here allow an argument that a culture of justification may be more clearly evident in the UK than it is in Canada. That said, as was noted by Feldman at the outset of Chapter 5, no one body can establish a rights culture in a country, and the judgments of the judiciaries of Canada and the UK that were analysed only give half of the story whether such a culture exists in either country. It is for this reason that the focus turned to Chapter 6's analysis of decisions and statements made about human rights instruments in the realm of counter-terrorism by politicians, the media and the public.

Chapter 6 was principally concerned with the differences in political culture in the two jurisdictions, namely, societal attitudes towards human rights and the impact of relationships with the US. The first objective of this chapter was to build on the analysis from Chapter 5 to answer the following research question: Is there a difference in societal attitudes towards human rights in the two jurisdictions and, together with the analysis of legal culture in Chapter 5, can it be argued that a human rights culture exists in the two jurisdictions? The Canadian analysis noted

31 *Abu Qatada v. SSHD* [2013] EWCA Civ 277 [hereinafter "*Abu Qatada*"]

that the decisions of Canadian courts in Chapters 3 and 5 provided a mixed picture of a human rights culture amongst the judiciary. That said, it was suggested that there are a number of reasons why Canadian political actors must consider the political costs of the counter-terrorism legislation they implement and defend because of the existence of a patriotic attachment to the *Charter*, and the ability and willingness of Canadian courts to invalidate counter-terrorism legislation inconsistent with human rights. However, analysis of the Bill S-7 and Bill C-51 policy process illustrated how political climate factors, such as the recent successful or foiled terrorist attacks, can lower the political and legal consequences associated with implementing and defending counter-terrorism legislation that may give rise to human rights concerns. It was argued that when counter-terrorism policy is debated and passed in this manner, there is often a lack of meaningful debate on possible amendments to the policy that seek to address human rights concerns and when this occurs it is difficult to argue that a human rights culture exists in a jurisdiction. As such, despite the strong patriotic attachment to and societal support of the *Charter* in Canada, it was suggested that the existence of a human rights culture throughout all of Canada's legal and political institutions is arguable at best.

Similarly, it appears difficult to argue that a human rights culture currently exists in the UK. While the decisions in *Al-Rawi*, *Binyam Mohamed* and the *Qatada* cases all evidence the judiciary's willingness to protect human rights in the face of immense political and public pressure, the current political climate (particular societal attitudes towards the *HRA* that were shown to be held by politicians, the media and general public) make it difficult to argue that such a culture is truly present in the UK. The *HRA* suffers from a lack of public feeling of ownership and there is considerable public hostility to the *ECHR*, in direct contrast with public views of the *Charter*. Furthermore, political actors in the UK may even be contributing to the lack of ownership and negative attitudes towards the *HRA* and *ECHR*. Recent statements by politicians and the mainstream media have done this particularly in relation to Abu Qatada. The past failed attempts to deport Qatada, as well as the numerous associated statements by politicians with regard to withdrawal from the *ECHR*, have only fuelled anti-*HRA* sentiment. The finding that it is difficult to argue that a human rights culture exists in the UK was further reinforced by analyses of the passage of the *CTSA* (with very limited political scrutiny) and the *JSA*,[32] both pieces of legislation that should have carried significant political costs and would have been consequentially amended if such a culture truly existed.

The second of objective of Chapter 6 was to analyse Canada and the UK's relationship with the US to answer the following research question: What impact has the relationship with the US had on the evolution of domestic counter-terrorism measures in the two jurisdictions? It was argued that the UK's special

32 Justice and Security Act 2013 c. 18 [hereinafter "*JSA*"]

and complex relationship with the US might have such impact that the *JSA* was passed despite serious concerns raised by the JCHR, legal professionals and academic commentators that it would cause reputational damage to the UK and have deleterious effects on the right of the individual to open justice. The process behind its development and passage by the UK Government all speak to the unique nature of the UK/US relationship and the impact that the US can have on UK counter-terrorism and national security policy. Analysis in the Canadian section illuminated the impact of the US on Canadian counter-terrorism policy, particularly with regard to the legal cases of Omar Khadr and Maher Arar. These experiences illustrate that the Canadian Government will go to great lengths to ensure that its relationship with the US, particularly its intelligence sharing arrangements, are not strained. Moreover, instruments such as the Canada-US Smart Border Declaration, the more recent 2011 Safe Third Country Agreement and a number of other border or transportation related agreements that are designed to strengthen the border's resilience to terrorism whilst minimally affecting commerce between the countries speak to the extremely close economic, geographic and symbolic relationship shared between the two nations.

Considered as a whole, the analyses in Chapters 3–6 go a long way towards completing the cultural comparativist exercise by going beyond rule-comparison and considering the social, political and cultural dynamics that shape laws differently in different jurisdictions. The findings in this book pertaining to the impact of legal and political structures and cultures are important in and of themselves (and for the deeper understanding of the evolution of counter-terrorism policies that they provide), but they are also important because of the way they contribute to the overall literature on comparative criminal justice and the purposes of comparison. This book situates itself within this methodological tradition and proudly adds itself to the works of Lazarus, Legrand, Nelken[33] and many others in the field who may consider themselves cultural comparativists through their dedication to conceptualizing and understanding the law as something much more than a form of universal, scientific principles. More specifically, this book has shown the value of a cultural comparativist methodology for those who study complex societal issues such as terrorism, which cut across disciplinary borders and benefit from (if not require) a nuanced understanding of the interplay between various domestic legal and political institutions.

7.2 Conclusion: future challenges and lessons to be learned

This book's analyses have allowed a retrospective look at several important flashpoints and landmark moments in the post-9/11 evolution of counter-terrorism measures in the 15 years since the attacks of 11 September 2001. The nature of terrorism has changed exponentially in each of these years, and there is

33 Discussed extensively in Chapter 1.2, as well as in subsequent chapters

no reason to believe that this will not continue to be the case going forward into the future. Acceptance of this fact is not an exercise in defeatism, nor does it entail giving up on continuing to engage in extensive discussion and debate pertaining to the most fair and effective ways to combat terrorism in the future. Nonetheless, to proceed into the future without having learned lessons from the past is both illogical and irresponsible. Unfortunately, as has been noted at several points throughout this book, recent pieces of terrorism legislation in both Canada and the UK (particularly the *ATA 2015* and *PCTA* in Canada and the *JSA* and *CTSA* in the UK) repeat the mistakes of the past and do not appear to have sufficiently learned lessons from the experiences of the past 15 years. This book's analyses of the evolution of terrorism measures since 9/11 provide at least three important broad lessons to take forward into the future: 1) counter-terrorism measures that are enacted in the direct aftermath of terrorist attacks and are subject to limited pre-legislative scrutiny will always prove to be problematic; 2) counter-terrorism mechanisms that operate outside the normal criminal justice process, particularly immigration law measures and other mechanisms that utilize secret evidence, will continue to provide both logistical and philosophical challenges to the protection of fundamental due process and human rights, imposing a huge burden on the courts and those subjected to these measures; and 3) political instability or uncertainty should not preclude the appropriate and comprehensive consideration of legislation once it has been enacted.

Our earliest warning of the dangers of enacting counter-terrorism legislation in the aftermath of significant terrorist attacks came in the form of the *ATA* in Canada and the *ATSCA* in the UK.[34] This book has detailed how these pieces of legislation were born out of a post-9/11 climate and a very real compulsion from UN Security Council Resolution 1373.[35] This was despite the fact that the UK in particular had just enacted detailed, comprehensive and thoughtfully considered legislation in the form of the *Terrorism Act*.[36] Nonetheless, this book spent several chapters detailing how the passage of the *ATA* and *ATCSA* has lead to domestic and international legal challenges and serious human rights implications for those subject to aspects of it. Even after 15 years' worth of court decisions, legislative amendments, public inquiries into scandals of a vast scale and expansive civil society criticism, these pieces of legislation remain on the statute books. The implication should be clear: political climates fuelled by fear and rhetoric lead to exceptional measures that never undergo the appropriate amount of pre-legislative scrutiny and, over time, become normalized measures. Canada's post-October 2014 attack legislation, the *PCTA* and *ATA 2015* in particular, continues this trend and should be viewed as a missed opportunity at best and a significant cause for concern at worst. The same can be said of the *JSA* and the *CTSA*. These pieces of legislation expand the use of secret evidence in both jurisdictions to a number

34 See Chapters 2.2.2 and 2.4.2, respectively

35 See Chapter 2.1

36 Terrorism Act 2000 c. 11 [hereinafter "*Terrorism Act*"]

of new legal contexts, with no guarantee that the legal principles arduously developed over the last decade will apply. They create new, dangerous and unnecessary provisions that fundamentally alter the nature of intelligence agencies and raise questions about the meaning of citizenship. It is wholly unacceptable that this legislation was passed in the aftermath of terrorist attacks without full and proper consideration of its implications, and the governments of both countries should move to amend and/or repeal the most problematic aspects of this legislation, and refrain from repeating this mistake again in the future.

Historical precursors to Canada and the UK's use of 'exceptional' measures outside the ordinary criminal law, including the use of secret evidence, pre-dated the 9/11 terrorists attacks.[37] Canada and the UK's post-9/11 focus on the use of measures outside the ordinary criminal law, particularly its reliance on immigration law and secret evidence, ignores lessons from its past historical experiences with proscription, the invocation of the *War Measures Act*[38] and the enactment of a number of temporary provisions pertaining to the Irish Republican Army (IRA).[39] As noted above, the *PCTA, ATA 2015, JSA* and *CTSA* all contain new measures that will significantly expand the use of secret evidence in a variety of legal contexts, with no guarantee that the human rights and due process principles that have been developed over the course of 15 years will apply. The special advocate system as it currently stands after challenges to security certificates and control orders may not pass constitutional muster when more significant violations of human rights are in play, and there is some confusion (or at least a lack of legislative guidance) about how and when the special advocate system will be utilized with regard to the new measures. While arguing for a significant repeal, the amendment or scaling back of the use of measures that utilize secret evidence almost seems idealistic and unrealistic at this stage, given the apparent attachment to these measures in both jurisdictions, the governments of both countries should at least take a proactive approach to clarifying how and when the special advocate will apply in secret proceedings that occur in these new contexts. The burden for this work should not (although it very likely will) fall on the shoulders of the courts in the two jurisdictions, with those subject to the measures bearing the costs of rushed and improperly considered expansions of measures outside the ordinary criminal justice process that utilize secret evidence. Relatedly, the governments of both countries should consider the wisdom of allowing regulations pertaining to the 1267 Resolution[40] listing process to continue, unless they would rather have

37 See Chapters 2.2.1 and 2.4.1, respectively

38 War Measures Act, R.S.C. 1970, c. W-2 [hereinafter "*War Measures Act*"]

39 Prevention of Terrorism (Temporary Provisions) Act 1974 s. 1(7); Prevention of Terrorism (Temporary Provisions) Act 1989 c. 4; Nothern Ireland (Emergency Provisions) Act 1996 c. 22

40 UN Security Council, *Security Council resolution 1267 (1999) [Afghanistan]*, 15 October 1999, S/RES/1267 (1999)

courts continue to mitigate the extremely invasive aspects of this process whilst likening it to Kafka's *The Trial*.[41]

Lastly, if there is any hope of the *ATA 2015*, *PCTA*, *JSA* and *CTSA* evolving in a more democratically productive and legally sound manner than its historical post-9/11 precursors, then political instability or uncertainty should not preclude the appropriate and comprehensive consideration of this legislation as it evolves. The uncertainty associated with Canadian minority governments throughout most of the 2000s is already responsible for the death of a National Security Committee of Parliamentarians[42] that it still severely lacks and needs now more than ever. Furthermore, the current Liberal Government should consider whether establishing such a committee (without some supplementary form of expert precursor review similar to the role of the Independent Reviewer in the UK) in and of itself will suffice to even match up with the plethora of UK oversight and review mechanisms tasked with studying the implications raised by recent counter-terrorism legislation. Analyses of the UK's mechanisms for parliamentary and independent review and oversight of counter-terrorism activities[43] illustrated a clear deficiency in Canada's political structure that needs to be rectified as a matter of urgent priority. Despite analyses that suggested the Independent Reviewer of Terrorism in the UK had a greater impact, the JCHR should (and it surely will) continue the impressive and energetic scrutiny of counter-terrorism legislation for human rights compliance that it has engaged in since its inception.

Bibliography

A v. Secretary of State for the Home Department [2004] UKHL 56
A v. United Kingdom, App No 3455/05 [2009] ECHR 301
Abdelrazik v. Canada (Minister of Foreign Affairs) [2010] 1 F.C.R. 267
Abu Qatada v. SSHD [2013] EWCA Civ 277
Al Rawi and Others v. the Security Service and Others [2011] UKSC 34
Anti-Terrorism Act, S.C. 2001, c. 41
Anti-Terrorism Act, S.C. 2015, c. 20
Anti-Terrorism, Crime and Security Act 2001 c. 24
Canada (Citizenship and Immigration) v. Harkat [2014] 2 S.C.R. 33
Canada (Prime Minister) v. Khadr [2010] 1 S.C.R. 44
Canada Evidence Act, R.S.C., 1985, C-5
Canada v. Almalki [2011] FCA 199
Chahal v. UK, App No 22414/93 [1996] ECHR 54
Charkaoui v. Canada (Citizenship and Immigration) [2007] 1 S.C.R. 350
Convention for the Protection of Human Rights and Fundamental Freedoms (European Convention on Human Counter-Terrorism and Security Act 2015 c. 217 Rights, as Amended)

41 As a Canadian Federal Court Judge famously did in *Abdelrazik*, see para. 53
42 See Chapters 4.1–4.3
43 See Chapters 4.5–4.6

HM Treasury v. Ahmed [2010] UKSC 2
Home Office v. Tariq [2011] UKSC 35
Human Rights Act 1998 c. 42
Justice and Security Act 2013 c.18
Khadr v. Canada (Minister of Justice) [2007] FCA 182
Mohamed, R (on the Application of) v. Secretary of State for Foreign & Commonwealth Affairs [2010] EWCA Civ 65
Nothern Ireland (Emergency Provisions) Act 1996 c. 22
Prevention of Terrorism (Temporary Provisions) Act 1974 s. 1(7)
Prevention of Terrorism (Temporary Provisions) Act 1989 c. 4
Protection of Canada from Terrorists Act, S.C. 2015, c. 9
R v. Ahmad [2011] 1 S.C.R. 110
Secretary of State for the Home Department v. MB [2007] UKHL 46
Secretary of the State for the Home Department v. AF (No 3) [2009] UKHL 28
Suresh v. Canada (Minister of Citizenship and Immigration) [2002] 1 S.C.R. 3
Terrorism Prevention and Investigation Measures Act 2011 c. 23
The Canadian Charter of Rights and Freedoms, Part I of the Constitution Act 1982, Being Schedule B to the Canada Act 1982 (UK), 1982, c. 11
UN General Assembly, *International Convention for the Suppression of the Financing of Terrorism*, 9 December 1999, No. 38349
UN Security Council, *Security Council resolution 1267 (1999) [Afghanistan]*, 15 October 1999, S/RES/1267 (1999)
UN Security Council, *Security Council resolution 1373 (2001) [on threats to international peace and security caused by terrorist acts]*, 28 September 2001, S/RES/1373 (2001)
War Measures Act, R.S.C. 1970, c. W-2

Index

7/7 London bombings 64

Abdelrazik, Abousfian 52, 68, 137–139
Abou-Elmaati, Amhad 133
Abu Qatada 6, 166, 148–150, 169–70, 174, 185
advanced passenger and crew information 72
Air India Flight 182 bombing 24n138, 41–3
airline carriers 72
Ajouaoum, Djamel 60
Almalki, Abdullah 133, 164
Almrei, Hassan 53–4, 88
Anderson, David 119
Arar, Maher 164, 165, 175, 186
arbitrariness 80
asset freezing 6; and listing process 39, 52–53, 68; global 52, 137

bail with recognizance 6, 43, 45–51
Bin Laden Network 54
Bingham, Lord 63, 65, 95–7, 99
Birmingham pub bombings 58
boarding refusal 72
border controls 37; security-related agreements 164
Boston bombings 52, 161, 162, 164
Brown, Lord 99, 100

Cameron, David 72, 168–70
Canada: 'danger to the security of' 82, 84; evolution of post-9/11 measures 41–58; impact of minority government 106–10; October 2014 attacks 56–8; pre-9/11 experiences with terrorism 41–3; relationship with the United States 163–6, 186; role of parliamentary committees 110–14; societal attitudes towards human rights 157–63; use of secret evidence 131–40; *see also* Supreme Court (Canada)
Canada–US Smart Border Declaration 164, 186
Canadian Muslim Lawyers Association 113
Canadian Network for Research on Terrorism, Security and Society (TSAS) 41
Canadian Security and Intelligence Service (CSIS) 42; disclosure of intelligence 87–8; disruption powers 57; extraterritorial surveillance 56–7; informer privilege 135
Carlile, Lord 24, 64, 116–20, 123–6
Carswell, Lord 99, 100
Central Intelligence Agency (CIA) 143
certificates of inadmissibility 46
charities, and financing terrorism 44, 46
Charkaoui, Adil 53–4
Charlie Hebdo magazine 71, 171
CIA *see* Central Intelligence Agency
civil society organizations 28
Closed Material Proceedings (CMPs) 71, 120, 140–2, 146–7, 184
closed materials: and control orders 67–8, 100; and right to fair trial 65–7, 98; and special advocate procedure 67, 71; as justification for detention 66; *see also* Closed Material Proceedings (CMPs)
coalition governments 4, 20, 21, 106, 116–18
Committee of Ministers of the Council of Europe 96
comparative law: cultural comparativist view 9, 11–15; methodology 9–15; universalist view 9–12
confidential information 48, 113

Conley, Richard 20, 21, 117
control orders 6, 23, 47, 49, 64; and Counter-Terrorism Act 2008 65–6; and curfews 65, 69, 98; and deprivation of liberty 65, 98; and detention for deportation 64; and special advocate procedure 65–6; and TPIMs 116; and use of closed materials 67–8, 100; annual renewal 121, 125; case law 94–101; derogating 63; disclosure obligations 101; human rights validity of 17; non-derogating 63, 65; procedural protection 65–6; repeal of 69–70
Counter-Terrorism Committee (CTC) 1, 8, 37–9
courts: domestic 16–17; judgments on incursions into rights 26; national 79, 82–6, 90, 97, 101, 179; powers of 3; relationship with the Parliament 28
Criminal Code (Canada) 43–4, 49, 51, 57, 83, 109
criminal law 1, 39, 61
criminal proceedings 7, 37, 59
Cross, James 42
cross-cultural research 14
cross-examination 19–20
cruel and unusual punishment 80, 83
CSIS *see* Canadian Security and Intelligence Service
CTC *see* Counter-Terrorism Committee
cultural comparativism 9, 11–15
culture: and judicial decisions 10, 14, 24; insider-outsider view 13; of domestic legal institutions 24–7; of domestic political institutions; of rights 25, 27; of justification 26–7, 130, 134, 144, 151, 184; *see also* cultural comparativism; rights culture
curfews 65, 69, 98

death penalty 137, 142
declaration of incompatibility 18, 63, 87, 94, 99, 101, 180
deference 3, 16, 93, 134–9, 144, 151–2, 182–4; 'due deference' approach 26, 135, 139, 142, 152, 184; substantial 26, 132, 134, 139, 145, 150, 152, 184; *see also* judicial deference
Department of Foreign Affairs and International Trade (DFAIT) 136
deportation: and danger to life or security 82; detention for 64; differential treatment of citizens and non-citizens 86, 89–90; potential consequences of 85; to torture 39, 46, 82–4, 89–91, 94, 148–50; under security certificates 45
deradicalization 72
derogation order 60, 97
detention: as the last resort 60; for deportation 64; grounds for 44; indefinite 47, 62, 66; indeterminate 39; legality of 19; maximum period 64; of foreign nationals 39, 80, 96; preventive 23; review 48, 86, 87; under security certificates 45; without trial 6, 47, 59–64, 94–101
determination 92
DFAIT *see* Department of Foreign Affairs and International Trade
Diceyan constitutionalism 27–8
differential treatment 86, 89–90, 93, 101, 180
Director of Public Prosecutions (DPP) 69, 122
discrimination 86, 89, 92–3, 96, 101, 146, 180
domestic courts 16–17
domestic legal culture 130–52
domestic legal institutions: culture 24–7, 179–86; structure 15–20, 179–86
domestic legal structure 78–102
domestic political culture 3, 5, 155–75
domestic political institutions: culture 27–8; structure 20–4, 106–27
DPP *see* Director of Public Prosecutions
Dubs, Lord 125
due deference approach 26, 130, 135, 139, 142, 152, 184
due process 7, 31, 38–9, 46, 119–21, 138, 145, 152; and listing process 68–9
Dyson, Lord 141, 146, 150

ECtHR *see* European Court of Human Rights
effective remedy, right to 94, 95
elections 21
Eminent Jurist Panel on Counter-terrorism and Human Rights 120
Equality and Human Rights Commission 120
European Commission against Racism and Intolerance 96

European Commissioner for Human Rights 96
European Court of Human Rights (ECtHR) 66–7, 78, 92–5, 100–1, 147–50, 167
European Union (EU) 8–9
evidence: hearsay 17; *in camera* 19; merged with intelligence 70; non-disclosure of 47, 86; obtained by torture 97–8, 148–9; sensitive 67; *see also* secret evidence
expediency requirement 92
expertise 26
extradition 60, 81
extraterritorial surveillance 56–7

fair hearing 98
fair process 55, 88–9
fair trial: and national security 132; and *Resolution 1373* 39; and use of closed materials 65–7, 98; right to 7, 19, 20, 92, 98
Feldman, David 20, 22, 27, 63, 130, 171
Feldman, Eric 25, 155, 160
FLQ *see* Front de Libération du Quebec
financing terrorism 6–7; and charities 44, 46; and *Resolution 1373* 37, 38, 39; and secret evidence 44, 46; international instruments suppressing 68
foreign nationals: detention 60, 63, 66, 87, 96; security certificates 46–7; *see also* non-citizens
free speech 72
Front de Libération du Quebec (FLQ) 42
functionalism 10
fundamental justice: and deportation to torture 83–5, 89; principles of 79–81
fundamental rights 62, 67, 129, 139, 147, 152, 155

Gearty, Connor 59
global asset freeze 52, 137
global travel ban 53, 137
governments: coalition 4, 20, 21, 106, 116–18; majority 4, 20, 21, 106; minority 4, 20, 21, 29, 106–10; scrutiny of 22; types 4, 20–1
gross disproportionality 80
Guantanamo Bay 135, 141, 142

Hale, Baroness 99
Harkat, Mohammad 53–4
Harper, Stephen 51, 106, 109, 110
hearsay evidence 17
Henley, Lord 125
Hoffman, Lord 67–8, 100, 150
Home Affairs Committee 22, 59–60
Home Office 58, 146
Home Secretary 60–2, 69, 117, 148
Hope, Lord 142, 146, 184
House Final Report 48
House Interim Report 45, 48
House of Lords 17, 62, 95–101; judgments on control orders 65–7, 98
Howard, Lord 117, 118
human rights: abuses in Canada 42; and control orders 17; and *Resolution 1373* 38–9; attitudes to 3, 15, 16, 29, 156–63, 166–71; derogation from 62, 93, 95; fundamental 39; history 167; implications 7; legislation 3–4; systematic engagement with 20; *see also* rights culture
human source privilege 57, 135
Hunt, Lord 116

immigration law 3, 6, 18–20, 40–1, 58; use of security certificates 6
incompatibility, declaration of 18, 63, 87, 94, 99, 101, 180
indefinite detention 47, 62, 66
Independent Reviewer 64, 119, 123–7, 182, 189
Independent Review of Terrorism Legislation 70
indeterminate detention 39
information: advanced passenger and crew 72; confidential 48, 113; disclosure of 19–20, 57, 133–5, 142–5
institutional competence 25, 26
institutional legitimacy 25, 141–2
intelligence: disclosure of 87–8; merged with evidence 70; review of 57; *see also* intelligence-led model
intelligence-led model 70
interdisciplinary research 13
interlocutory hearings 55
International Civil Liberties Monitoring Group 111
international law 83–6, 90, 97, 101, 179
internet bans 69
investigative hearings 6, 23, 43, 45–7

Irish Republican Army (IRA) 58

JCHR *see* Joint Select Committee on Human Rights
Joint Committee on Statutory Instruments 22
Joint Select Committee on Human Rights (JCHR) 22–3, 61–2, 119–27, 171, 182, 186, 189
Judd, Lord 122–4
Judge, Lord 143
judges, decisions on national security 4–5, 25; *see also* judicial decisions; judicial deference
judicial decisions 4–5, 7, 10, 25, 29–30, 86, 129–30, 139–40, 173–4
judicial deference 5, 25–6, 129–30; *see also* deference
jurisdictions, selection of 2–6
jus cogens 82
JUSTICE 28
justification, culture of 26–7, 130, 134, 144, 151, 184

Kerr, Lord 147, 150
Khadr, Omar 5–6, 135–7, 151–2, 164, 165, 183

Laporte, Pierre 42
Lazarus, Liora 11–14, 25
legal culture 3, 4, 14, 24–5; *see also* domestic legal culture
legal structure 3; *see also* domestic legal structure
Legrand, Pierre 11–14
liberty: deprivation of 65, 91–2, 98; restrictions on 91; right to 63, 67, 91
listing: and asset freezing 52, 68, 137; and due process protection 68–9; and global travel ban 52, 137; Federal Court ruling on 52–3, 137–8; *ultra vires* 145
Lloyd, Lord 167
Lords Delegated Powers and Regulatory Reform Committee 22

Macdonald, Lord 69–70, 116, 120, 121, 124
Maher Arar Commission 85, 112, 165
majority governments 4, 20, 21, 106
margin of appreciation 16, 67, 94
May, Sir Anthony 143, 144
Members of Parliament (MPs) 25
Memoranda of Understanding 64
Merryman, John 11
Mia, Ziyaad 113
minimal impairment standard 81, 85–6, 90
Minister of Citizenship and Immigration 18–19, 46
Minister of Public Safety and Emergency 46
minority governments 4, 20, 21, 29, 106–10
Mohamed, Binyam 142–3
Mosley J 53–4, 88, 133–5, 138, 151, 183

national authorities 16, 66
national courts 79, 82–6, 90, 97, 101, 179
national security: and disclosure of information 19–20, 133; and fair trial 132; judiciary's role 4–5, 25; parliamentary review 23–4
National Security Committee of Parliamentarians 45, 114, 189
Nelken, David 9, 11–14
Neuberger, Lord 143, 144
Neville-Jones, Baroness 121
Newton Committee 95, 96
Newton Report 61, 62
NGOs *see* non-governmental organizations
Noel J 54, 87
non-citizens, differential treatment 86, 89–90, 101; *see also* foreign nationals
non-governmental organizations (NGOs) 157
Nurredin, Muayyed 133

Oakes test 81, 85
O'Connor J 111, 112
October Crisis 42
open justice principle 142–3, 146, 150–2, 170, 175, 183
Ottawa 41, 56

Pannick, Lord 123, 124
Parliament: 'Diceyan' viewpoint 27–8; relationship with courts 28
parliamentary committee reviews 20–3; Canada 110–15; UK 119–27
personal liberty 43, 96, 147
Phillips, Lord 17, 100
PII *see* Public Interest Immunity

policy-making 16, 165, 173; and international norm 23; criminal justice 21
political bias 10, 14
political culture *see* domestic political culture
political instability 24, 31,109
political systems 20–1
powers, separation of 28, 130, 136, 168
PREVENT strategy 72
preventive arrest 47–9, 51
preventive detention 23
prisoner's dilemma 21
Privy Councillors 24
Privy Counsellor Review Committee 61
procedural protection 65–6, 82, 85, 146
procedural rights 20, 80, 91
Proscribed Organization Appeals Commission 59
proscription 58–9
prosecution, priority of 123–4
public emergency 60, 62–3, 66, 93, 95, 99
public inquiries 23, 24n138, 187
public interest 19, 131, 133, 140, 143; *see also* Public Interest Immunity (PII)
Public Interest Immunity (PII) 140, 141
public opinion 28

Quebec 42, 158, 159, 165

racial profiling 43
RCMP *see* Royal Canadian Mounted Police
reasonable belief 44, 69, 122, 125; as grounds for detention 44
reasonable suspicion 44, 122, 125
refugee status: applications 18; abuse of 37, 39
relocation 69, 125
remedial orders 22
Review of Security and Counter-Terrorism Powers 69
Ribic analysis 133
Rideh, Abu 60
rights: compatibility 22; culture of 25, 27; fundamental 25, 156; legal basis for limitation 81; rhetoric 25; to effective remedy 94, 95; to fair trial 7, 19, 20, 92, 98; to liberty 63, 67, 91, 96; violation of 81; *see also* human rights; rights adjudication systems; rights culture
rights adjudication systems 15–18, 29, 66–7; Canada 79–82; UK 90–4
rights culture 5, 130, 139, 151, 159, 170–1, 182, 185
rights-infringing legislation 18
Rouleau, Martin 56
Royal Canadian Mounted Police (RCMP) 42, 57
rule of law 19, 20, 26, 37, 62

Safe Third Country Agreement 164, 186
Scheinin, Martin 119
secret evidence 7, 28, 56, 58, 67, 70–1, 182; Abdelrazik case 137–8; Abu Qatada cases 148–50; Ahmad case 131–3; Ahmed case 145–6; Almalki cases 133–5; Al-Ravi case 141–2; and financing terrorism 44, 46; Binyam Mohamed case 142–5; future challenges 188; in Canada 131–40; in the UK 140–51; Khadr cases 135–7, 151–2; Tariq case 146
security: 'governing through' 44; *see also* security certificates; security clearance
security certificates 6, 18–19, 46–50, 181–2; and foreign nationals 46–7; case law analysis 82–90; concerns about 111; constitutionality 29, 54–6, 79, 81–82, 85, 88; impact of minority governments 106–9; legal challenges 53–6; reasonable limits clause 81; renunciation of torture 46; reviews of 110–15
security clearance 146
security-cleared lawyers 48
Security Intelligence Review Committee (SIRC) 48
Security of Freedom, The 44
self-reflection 14
sensitive evidence 67
separatism terrorism 42
SIAC *see* Special Immigration Appeals Commission
Silber J 141
SIRC *see* Security Intelligence Review Committee
Slynn, Lord 84
special advocates 19–20, 48, 114; and control orders 65–6; and use of closed materials 67, 71; authorizing

communication 124, 180; enhancing procedural justice 98; future challenges 188; restrictions on communication 55, 89
Special Immigration Appeals Commission (SIAC) 19–20, 61, 94, 95, 100, 148–9, 180
Special Senate Committee Main Report 45
Standing Committee on Justice, Human Rights, Public Safety and Emergency Preparedness 45
Standing Committee on Public Safety and National Security 52, 113
statutory interpretations 18
Steyn, Lord 147
Strasbourg Court 16–17, 99, 149, 150
Strasbourg jurisprudence 78, 94, 100
Sullivan J 65
sunset clause 43–5, 47, 50–2, 65, 119, 182
Supreme Court (Canada) 3, 17, 78; secret evidence 131–3, 136; security certificates 46, 54–6, 85, 88; deportation 79, 82–3
Supreme Court (UK) 17; fair process 55, 88–9; listing regulations 68
surveillance 70; extraterritorial 56–7

tagging 69
telephone bans 69
temporary exclusion orders (TEOs) 72
TEOs *see* temporary exclusion orders
terrorism: advocating or promoting offences 57; definition 84, 95, 101; glorification 64; separatist 42; support abroad 84; war on 39; *see also* financing terrorism
Terrorism Prevention and Investigation Measures (TPIMs) 6, 59, 69–70, 182; and control orders 116; impact of coalition government 116–18; parliamentary committee review 119–27
Toronto 52
torture 23; and security certificates 46; as fundamentally unjust 83; claims of 133; deportation to 39, 46, 82–4, 89–91, 94, 148–50; disclosure of information about 142–5; evidence obtained by 97–8, 148–9; prohibition of 90
TPIMs *see* Terrorism Prevention and Investigation Measures
travel bans 53, 72, 137
Tremblay-Lamer J 53
Trudeau, Justin 57
Trudeau, Pierre 157
TSAS *see* Canadian Network for Research on Terrorism, Security and Society

UNHRC *see* United Nations Human Rights Committee (UNHRC)
United Kingdom: evolution of post-9/11 measures 58–73; impact of coalition government 116–19; pre-9/11 experience with terrorism 58–9; relationship with the United States 171–3, 185–6; rights adjudication systems 90–4; role of parliamentary committees 119–27; societal attitudes towards human rights 166–71; *see also* Supreme Court (UK)
United Kingdom Joint Committee on Human Rights 18
United Nations (UN) 7–8
United Nations Committee against Torture 111, 120
United Nations Human Rights Committee (UNHRC) 96, 111
United Nations Security Council 7–8, 52, 96, 138, 145, ; *Resolution 1373* 1–2, 6–9, 36–41, 178
United Nations Special Rapporteur on the Protection of Human Rights and Fundamental Freedoms 119
United Nations Working Group on Arbitrary Detention 111
United States: intelligence sharing 143, 144; relationship with Canada 30, 163–6, 186; relationship with the UK 30, 171–3, 185–6

VIA rail bomb plot 52, 161, 162, 164

war on terrorism 39
witnesses 19–20
Woolf, Lord, CJ 61, 98

Zehaf-Bibeau, Michael 56

For Product Safety Concerns and Information please contact our EU representative GPSR@taylorandfrancis.com
Taylor & Francis Verlag GmbH, Kaufingerstraße 24, 80331 München, Germany

www.ingramcontent.com/pod-product-compliance
Ingram Content Group UK Ltd.
Pitfield, Milton Keynes, MK11 3LW, UK
UKHW011009180926
475701UK00004B/651
* 9 7 8 0 3 6 7 2 6 6 4 6 2 *